The Courts

Fulcrum of the Justice System

The Courts

Fulcrum of the Justice System

H. Ted Rubin
Institute for Court Management

Goodyear Publishing Company, Inc.
Pacific Palisades, California

Library of Congress Cataloging in Publication Data

Rubin, H. Ted, 1926–
The courts: fulcrum of the justice system.

Includes index.
1. Courts—United States. I. Title.
KF8700.R8 347'.73'1 75-30450
ISBN 0-87620-898-7

Pacific Palisades, California

Current printing (last digit):
10 9 8 7 6 5 4 3 2 1

ISBN: 0-87620-898-7
Y-8987-3

Interior design: Jackie Somogyi

Printed in the United States of America

To Bunny and our courtship,
and to Marjorie, Steve, and Jefferson

Contents

Foreword

It is only in the last fifteen years that judges in this country have begun going back to school in earnest. To attract them to the training programs offered by the National Council of Juvenile Court Judges, it was my duty during 1965–68 to recruit faculty. The most effective teacher of fellow judges that could be found anywhere was then the creative juvenile court judge in Denver, Ted Rubin. He became our core faculty member, and with this book his insights on our courts are now available to all of us.

I intend to make wide use of it. I'll be referring it to prelaw and law students, to criminal justice planners and other court-related personnel, and to students of government who want a solid profile of its judicial branch. For the press corps who cover our courts, for community leaders who seek to upgrade them, and for all citizens who are concerned about our system of justice, this is the book to own.

The courts themselves will be the principal beneficiary of Ted Rubin's text. Misunderstanding of their processes and purposes causes many current problems and, more than any other factor, fosters cynicism and mistrust. Sometimes referred to as the "invisible" third branch of government, the courts come through in sharp focus in these pages with all their strengths and weaknesses—and will emerge far stronger for it. Those of us who work in the justice system should applaud.

John F. X. Irving
Dean, School of Law
Seton Hall University

Introduction

The concept of justice permeates society. It is a principle that governs the relationships within an individual family, and must equally govern relationships within the family of nations. We need to be treated fairly, to obtain our "fair share," to have an equal opportunity to make our mark.

We have created an institution, the courts, to embody principles of fairness and impartiality in arbitrating allegations of violations of fairness codes, the right not to be injured by another. Courts also function to protect children from abuse, to check governmental agencies from acting unfairly, to regulate legal relationships so as to avoid unjust dealings, to provide just compensation to injured parties, and more.

Justice is the hallmark of the courts. Views of justice differ, however, and the courts function in a wider justice system which spans the range from police through corrections, and, in the civil sphere, may touch all citizens. The courts are the fulcrum of this system. Despite their serious imperfections, it is frightening to contemplate a nation without courts, a complex society without a formal institution to enforce the rules set forth by that society.

We need to strengthen this third branch of government. The role of the courts continues to evolve, with constant changes as to what should be the courts' business. Court officials recognize, increasingly, that they need citizen assistance to achieve their great objectives. One starting point is citizen knowledge of the courts.

Another is for the courts to reach out to invite citizen consultation on the shortcomings of the justice system.

This book is an attempt to describe contemporary courts, their progress, problems, and processes. Its basic focus is the state and local court system. Its emphasis is a wide search for policies and strategies to enhance the administration of justice. It describes, criticizes, prescribes.

This work is directed to university students, at undergraduate and graduate levels, but should also meet the concerns of others who seek a fundamental comprehension of contemporary courts. It can serve as a basic or as a supplementary text in fields such as criminal justice, public administration, political science, law, and judicial administration. It can assist in fulfilling the needs of present and future professionals whose positions will be more or less directly related to the courts. Its contents cover the criminal and juvenile courts far more broadly than do the proliferating texts on criminal justice. The civil and appellate courts receive attention as well, forums for which it is difficult to find analysis in present works. Prosecution and defense counsel, vital legs of the tripod of justice, are accorded extensive consideration. Court administrators, newcomers to the courts, also receive coverage. Hopefully, this work will encourage university development of a self-contained course on the courts.

My perspective draws broadly on my past experiences: in rehabilitation, in law, as a legislator, judge, and teacher, and now as a court consultant. Countless people and a myriad of interactions forged my views, concerns, and prejudices. My bias is that of effective justice. My yearning is for social justice. My concern is to strengthen the brace of justice on which must depend the equilibrium of a democratic government in a free society.

1 The Courts and the Public

Contemporary society has separated the citizen from the courts. This has happened with the other branches of government as well—but it is more than rhetoric to say that the courts belong to the people. Judges occupy the public's bench of justice. They implement the public's sense of justice. They interpret and enforce laws which have been enacted by popularly elected representatives. The officials who fund the courts' operations are also citizen representatives. The title to the courthouse vests in a governmental entity which derives its powers from the people.

But the people do not or should not "own" the judges who are the pivot of the justice system. It is obviously inappropriate for judges to conduct public opinion polls prior to deciding cases at law. While such a search for public opinion would be more appropriate to elected legislators, lawmakers more typically cast their votes on the basis of their own value systems—on the special economic, ethnic, religious, or environmental characteristics of their jurisdiction, or on the pressures of a relatively small but vocal group of constituents. They do listen more closely than judges to the voices of their electors. Yet judges, particularly trial court judges, are quite aware of what is happening in their communities, and understand community power structures quite well, although in general they are less acute in perceiving the powerless and the social changes coursing through our society.

Judges owe their allegiance to the law: to the constitutions, federal and state; to legislative enactments which proclaim law and govern relationships between people, and between people and their governments; and to the case rulings by federal and state appellate courts which bind trial court decisions unless distinctions can be drawn between the present issues and the prior decisions. This is as it should be. It is not to say, however, that judges and juries, police officials and trial attorneys, exercise absolutely objective standards in fulfilling their roles.

The court system in the United States, of course, derives from the English. The English court system, though today very different from ours, stems from the "common law." And the common law—that is, nonlegislative law—derived from the English people. As English courts were formed early in this millennium, the king and the magistrates he appointed to hear cases on his behalf based their legal judgments on what they believed most Englishmen considered was either right or wrong. They sought to extract the customs and beliefs of the people, and to apply them to the disputes or the reported violations brought to their attention. They recorded these decisions. Other judges became aware of them, and as more judges accepted these interpretations, the decisions became law. Judge-made law would change, however, as customs and beliefs changed.

Legislative developments in this country have superimposed legislative law over the common law. Yet there is a continuing relationship between the citizen and the law. Legislators, as representatives of the people, enact statutes which in varying degrees express the views of their constituents.

In certain ways the old English common law continues to apply right up to the present. The chief judge of a metropolitan trial court recounted to this author, in 1974, a case where a sixteen-year-old girl had asked him to declare her emancipation from her parents, who were planning to bring an action against her in juvenile court for "runaway and incorrigibility." The girl, who was pregnant and had earlier delivered another child, was living with a young man in a common-law marriage. They held themselves out as husband and wife, although in that state she was too young to receive a marriage license unless her parents consented, which they did not, or unless a judge ordered the issuance of a marriage license, which had not occurred. At common law, a sixteen-year-old could enter into a valid common-law marriage. The judge, despite his moral concern, followed the common-law precedent, and declared her emancipated, thereby voiding the pending juvenile court action. In that state, contemporary marriage laws had not repealed the unwritten common law of marriage.

Purpose of the Courts

If we try to describe the purpose of courts, someone will usually suggest that their purpose is to "do justice." This is true, but whether justice is done depends typically upon the interests or viewpoints of the affected or interested parties. We are confident that some guilty people have been found innocent in our courts, and that innocent persons have been found guilty. These trials may have been conducted fairly, but was justice done? An injured party wins a claim against a negligent driver to compensate for the loss of an arm in an auto accident. The claimant may consider the money award sufficient; the insurance company which insured the negligent driver, may consider this same award excessive. Was justice done? A divorced father is ordered to increase the monthly support of his children who are in the custody of their mother. Despite a lengthy hearing, he feels wronged, since inflation has gouged away the money left to him after paying taxes and basic living costs. His former wife also complains that the increase is grossly insufficient in the face of the higher costs of child care associated with maturing youngsters. Was justice done?

In light of these and other examples, we need to add that another purpose of the courts is "to *appear* to do justice." The court's responsibility is to provide a fair hearing with rights accorded to all parties to speak or not to speak, to have the assistance of counsel, to cross-examine the other side, to produce witnesses in their own behalf, to produce relevant documents, and to argue their viewpoint. The judge or the jury must weigh the evidence and render a judgment or verdict based on this evidence and the law. This process, the due process of law, must appear to do justice.

A purpose of the courts is also to provide a forum where disputes between people can be resolved "justly." When a dispute arises within a framework which the law encompasses within the jurisdiction of a court, the parties may "have their day in court." A judge or jury's decision or verdict resolving the dispute is seen as a more civilized approach to conflict-resolution than a party's invading the other's house or store to grab back his original property or money, or to the disputants punching each other in the nose. While neither side may be fully satisfied with the court's order, there has been an appearance of justice.

Courts also exist to censure wrongdoing—violations of the criminal law—and to remove or restrict the freedom of those who have been found to have violated community norms and public welfare concerns—as embodied in legislative enactments of the criminal law. The court is the forum where orderly legal procedures are provided to one charged with an offense as a preferable alternative to lynch mobs or unregulated citizen punishment of alleged offenders. Low public respect for the courts diminishes the cooperation required from the public in reporting criminal offenses and in testifying as witnesses. The appearance of justice must be undergirded by the substance of justice.

Some will add that the courts have the function of punishing offenders, of asserting community sanctions over law violators; others urge that courts have a rehabilitation responsibility for those who violate the criminal laws, including juvenile laws. The punishment-rehabilitation debate rages. Some punishment may be rehabilitative; other punishment may be counterproductive to the individual and to the community. Some rehabilitative strategies are quite punitive; others quite humane. Sentencing or disposition decisions by judges should seek to enhance the community's protective interest as well as the defendant's ability to refrain from future wrongdoing. That probation services were originally grafted onto the court's administrative responsibilities is reflective of a rehabilitative purpose for the courts. Today, in some states, probation still serves the courts, but has been shifted administratively to executive branch agencies. Under such sponsorship the courts should be no less concerned about fulfilling their goals of protection of the community and enhancement of the individual's conduct.

Many advocate that the courts have the function of deterring crime. That the courts and a criminal justice system exist is a natural deterrent to some. But the immense crime and delinquency problem in this nation must support the view that, at best, the courts have a limited deterrent role. Crime-prone individuals know the odds are in their favor. With many types of offenses they have a better than even chance the crime will not be reported. If reported, the odds favor their not being apprehended. Further, the case may not be proven, and if proven, the offender may well be sentenced to probation rather than incarceration. It is probably realistic to suggest that strong improvements throughout the courts and the criminal justice system will not substantially reduce the rate of law violations.

A further court function is the determination of a status. A marriage is dissolved or a divorce granted by a court; children are adopted by substitute parents who secure court approval; a judge approves the distribution of funds and properties of a deceased person in accordance with his will, or in accordance with a statute if there is no will.

A further purpose for the courts may be that of protecting the citizen against arbitrary governmental action. Government officials have failed to expend funds which have been lawfully appropriated; have denied public employment to persons because of their race or sex or age; have improperly applied statutory or administrative provisions; have brutalized citizens; have prohibited the exercise of First Amendment rights; have illegally invaded citizens' privacy; have perpetrated countless violations upon the public based on both good and bad intentions. The citizen requires a recourse for considered review of alleged abuses by the government and its agents.

In seeking to fulfill their purposes the courts have become a delicate and cumbersome instrument. While courts can improve their efficiency without any sacrifice of justice, efficiency and justice are not synonymous. In criminal law, for example, we can move cases more quickly, but we must not do this summarily. We have interposed the right to defense counsel, and to free defense counsel for indigents, not only because we aim at equalized justice for the poor and the rich, but also because we have learned that in the absence of defense counsel, police interrogation more frequently abuses the constitution; prosecutors fail to introduce mitigating evidence; judge and jury bias may not be appropriately neutralized; press sensationalism may make a fair trial impossible.

Court reformers talk increasingly of improving the courts through improving citizen relationships to and interest in the courts. Such recommendations generally accompany concerns regarding any system or institution which suffers serious problems. We accept that the citizen knows little about the courts, and that greater knowledge and closer acquaintance will be of value to him and to the court system.[1]

The Citizen's Relationship to the Courts

As Jurors

Countless citizens interact with the court system when they are called to participate on a jury. They serve more commonly on the petit juries which hear and deliberate civil causes as well as law violations. Smaller numbers participate on grand juries, particularly common to states east of the Mississippi River, which have historically and routinely reviewed a prosecutor's presentation of evidence and determined whether a felony indictment shall issue.

Juror selection methods have been under attack for many years now, and a number of decisions have revealed either an unconstitutional systematic exclusion of certain groups, or selection methods which have failed to provide a representative cross section of the community.[2] Too often the white middle-class property owner has been given priority in jury selection. The less propertied, the poor, women, blacks and Spanish-surnamed persons, and young adults, have in general been underrepresented. Jury verdicts may well be skewed by such imbalance. Underrepresented groups are less able to identify with the court system or to understand its complexities. This is changing under lawyer challenges, new legislation which has broadened the base for juror eligibility, and better juror management.

Further, studies increasingly show that many courts fail to effectively utilize those jurors who come to the courthouse,[3] provide them with rather substandard waiting rooms, and pay them very poorly.

In some communities petit jurors who are obliged to serve for two weeks may actually serve only two or three hours during that time. Scheduled jury trials do not take place when a party to an action, a key witness, or an attorney inadvertently or advertently fails to appear; when a judge is ill with no substitute; when too many jurors were called in the first place; when legal arguments on late-filed motions delay the beginning of the trial. Potential jurors read the morning newspaper and wait. They go to the coffee shop and wait. They go back to the waiting room and wait.

More courts now study how jurors are utilized, impanel more appropriate numbers, have an orientation program for new jurors, maintain attractive waiting rooms, air conditioned courtrooms, and jury deliberation rooms, and pay jurors a reasonable stipend. Jurors love to tell about their "days in court." It is wise court management to maximize juror satisfaction.

Citizens as Defendants, or as Clients of the Court

The traffic court is the major forum where citizens appear as court clients. The facilities of these courts—in urban, suburban, and rural settings—often are shabby, and lack dignity. In this court of heavy volume, judges have done much, but can do more to individualize justice. We are reducing excessive traffic in this court by permitting persons, ticketed for lesser traffic offenses, to mail in their fines instead of taking off work and coming to court. But we still have speed traps, judges who overly lecture defendants, and judges who are too chummy with the police or the prosecuting attorney. Many of these courts operate at a net profit each year, and judges may be tempted to collaborate with local officials who count on a traffic court profit to defray other public costs. The administration of trials, and the ordering of fines and occasional jail sentences, must be done fairly.

Vast numbers of citizens also enter the divorce courts, and many of these cases require ongoing hearings to consider revisions in child support or alimony, a change of custody from one parent to another, or to better regulate visitation programs. Here at least the appearance of justice must prevail in the face of heated and emotional litigation.

The lower criminal courts experience an enormous population flow, and as will be shown in a subsequent chapter, these are the courts probably most in need of reform and improvement.

The small claims courts; the upper civil courts with their unlimited money-claim potentials; the felony courts; the juvenile courts; and the probate courts, concerned with the administration of decedents' estates, and often with mental illness-retardation commitment procedures; all add up to a substantial volume of court-citizen interaction.

Citizens as Witnesses in Court Cases

Citizens, as complaining witnesses or as witnesses whose testimony may be valuable to the trial of an offense, are interviewed or interrogated by police officials, prosecutors, grand juries, defense counsel, attorneys in civil actions, and probation officers. And of course they testify at trials. Attention to witness convenience is sporadic. Some officials are solicitous of witnesses, others treat them in summary fashion, not infrequently failing to notify them when a case has been continued and their presence is not needed on a given day. Hopefully justice system officials will more carefully address their dealings with witnesses.

The Citizen as an Elector

In most jurisdictions judges are still subject to some form of election or voter retention system. In some states this is on a partisan basis; elsewhere it is nonpartisan. Some states have adopted the Missouri plan where, following initial appointment by a governor, usually from among several names suggested by a nominating commission, a judge is appointed but faces a retention election at a later date, when he runs not against an opponent but on his record of service. While the federal courts and states such as Massachusetts appoint a judge for life, this is not the dominant pattern. Voting on judges is difficult for citizens, since they have limited information on which to base intelligent judgments. Lawyers, who have the opportunity to assess judicial ability better than almost any other group, increasingly poll their members and advise voters as to their assessments.

The Citizen as the Taxpayer for the Courts

The costs of a court system represent only a fraction of overall state/local tax expenditures. Citizens are little aware of the funds involved in maintaining or upgrading the courts. Legislative bodies at state and local levels provide and determine judicial pay and the salaries of court personnel, appropriate monies for the maintenance of court facilities and other court expenses. There are splendid courthouses and there are also courthouses severely inadequate for today's judicial functions. Judicial pay scales vary widely, and judges in some states are paid little more than half of what judges in other states receive.[4] The funding sufficiency of court administrative operations varies widely as well. Good state and local courts are correlated with high caliber judges, strong judicial leadership, active community interest in the courts, and adequate funding. For many reasons, judges, court officials, and attorneys have done a mediocre job of providing relevant information to the public. The taxpayer is getting something for his money from the courts. But he does not know what he is getting, how much it costs, or the additional costs of a better justice system. It is clearly the responsibility of the courts to present their case better to the community.

Media Presentation of the Courts

Americans like to read the daily newspaper. Press coverage of courts more typically focuses on sensational trials, or on routine accounts of run-of-the-mill criminal sentences. United States Supreme Court and state high court decisions are often summarized; radio and television present vastly more news than analysis of the courts. Perhaps the public's broadest exposure to court processes comes from television, with the dramatized weekly series on the trials and tribulations of fictionalized trial attorneys. Despite the severe limitations of media presentation of the courts, and the certain inaccuracies, the overall effect of this public interpretation should be seen as a definite plus. The courts are the public's business. In general the public's business should be conducted in public view, or at least be observed by media representatives who in effect represent the public. In the interest of a fair trial, courts exclude television cameras and radio microphones from the trial itself, out of concern that witnesses, attorneys, and perhaps jurors and judges might be substantially distracted from the basic purpose and procedures of the trial by the opportunity to communicate with the media public.

Other Sources of Public Information on the Courts

School children learn about the three branches of government in their social studies curricula, and there have been gains in strengthened public school presentation of United States Supreme Court decisions and their relevance. Educational institutions at different levels have expanded course offerings in order to increase awareness of constitutional rights, and also to provide substantive knowledge of law: consumer law, contract law, landlord-tenant law, domestic relations law, juvenile law, and other branches of law.

Citizens learn of the courts through their contacts with private attorneys, legal aid services, and public defenders. But problems sometimes beget solutions, and public opinion surveys reflecting that the general public does not hold the court system in high esteem have brought a flurry of interest on the part of the bench and the bar to develop a variety of constructive approaches aimed at improving the relationship between the courts and the community.

The Organization and Structure of the Courts

The general public has a basic perception that each state has trial courts and at least one appellate court, that there is a federal court system and a United States Supreme Court. Within a state, courts are created by state constitutions, by legislative enactments, and by municipal and county-level legislation. In too many jurisdictions the proliferation of courts has left the citizen unsure of what court to go to for a particular cause of action, and for that matter attorneys are not always sure of where to file a particular suit. Some actions can be filed in two or three different courts, and appeals can be taken to several forums. For example, in 1962 Cook County (Chicago), Illinois, had 208 courts: the Circuit Court; the Superior Courts; the Family Court; Criminal Court; Probate Court; County Court; Municipal Court of Chicago; 23 city, village, town, and municipal courts; 75 justice of the peace courts; and 103 police magistrate courts. Problems of limited jurisdiction, and of overlapping original and appellate jurisdiction, were largely erased by the judicial amendment to the Illinois Constitution which took effect in January, 1964. These structural problems and their constitutional reorganization are graphically illustrated by Figure 1. Illinois' creation of a unified trial court structure, which combined lower, upper, and specialized or separate trial courts into one, is seen as a model of trial court unification and simplification.

Constitutional reorganization of the Florida court system in the early 1970s consolidated a variety of courts, while maintaining a lower (county) court in each county (lesser criminal, lesser civil, traffic actions), together with regional circuit courts (the highest courts of general trial jurisdiction). To provide better integration and communication between the county and circuit courts, the presiding judge of each circuit court was granted administrative responsibilities over the county court.

A dual trial court system characterizes New England states. Typically there is a single lower trial court, the district court, and a single upper court, the superior court. The approach to the administration of these courts differs, however, from Florida and Illinois, and from most other states, in that there is, generally, a chief justice for all of the district courts, a separate chief justice for all of the superior courts, and, in addition, a chief justice of the supreme court.

Colorado also should be cited. This state, like Illinois and Florida, has empowered its chief justice to act as the supervisory and administrative head of the entire state court system. With limited exceptions, all Colorado courts are now funded through state legislative appropriations to the state judicial system. This contrasts with the dominant American model of limited *state* funding and strong *local* funding for the courts. During fiscal year 1969 states, as opposed to local governments, funded 26 percent of total judicial expenditures. Three years later this ratio had increased slightly to 28 percent.[5] Colorado court employees, including all probation personnel, are employees of the state court system, and subject to its pay

Figure 1. Cook County (Chicago), Illinois, Court System

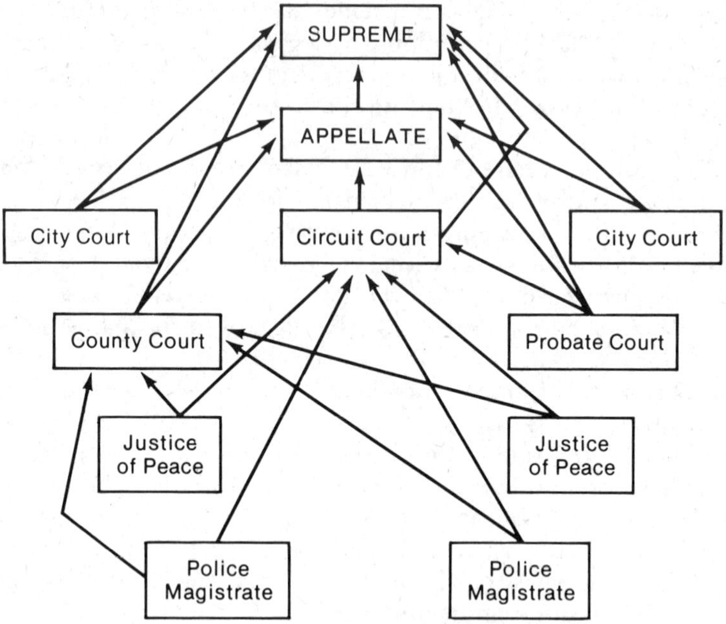

Channel of Appeals Prior to 1964

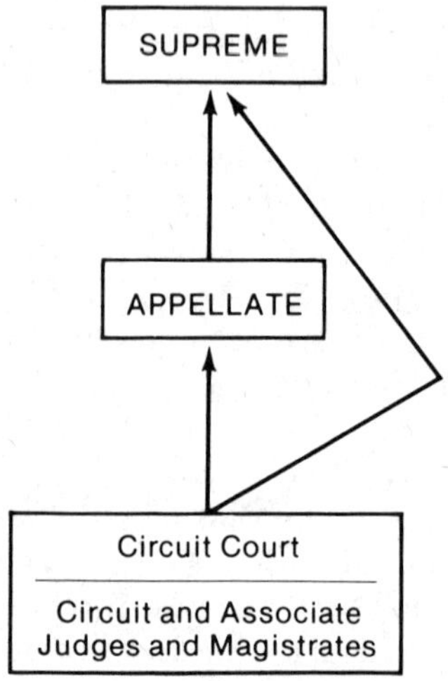

Channel of Appeals after January 1, 1964, the Date the Judicial Amendment to the Illinois Constitution Became Effective

SOURCE: Adapted from *A Short History of the Illinois Judicial System* (Springfield: Administrative Office of the Illinois Courts, 1971), pp. 19–20.

and personnel practices. The chief justice and the state court administrator make a single presentation to the state legislature in support of the proposed judicial system budget. Those state court systems which are largely state funded are not the more populous ones. In addition to Colorado, they include Alaska, Connecticut, Delaware, Hawaii, New Mexico, North Carolina, Rhode Island, Vermont, and South Dakota, and possibly a few others.

California stands in contrast to Colorado, both because the state legislature of California provides about 10 percent of the costs of the courts, and also because a judicial council, rather than the chief justice, provides administrative direction to the courts. The judicial council is composed of fifteen judges, two legislators, and four attorneys, and is served by a large professional staff. Due to the fact that California counties and communities provide the lion's share of court costs, there is less centralized direction and control over the courts in that state.

While far too many states still have court structures which represent responses to historical developments, to ad hoc considerations, and to political factors, many states have taken decisive action to restructure their courts, and this trend is accelerating in the face of growing public concern that the administration of justice be made both more effective and more efficient.

Public Awareness of Judicial Decision-Making

It used to be said that the role of the judge was to "find the law." In old common law courts, when an issue was presented to the judge, he performed legal research to ascertain whether this identical issue had earlier been determined. (The Latin term for this search for a legal precedent is *stare decisis,* "to stand by decided matters.") Although changing social conditions could result in overturning a prior holding, the new precedent required strong justification. Also, if the facts varied from previously determined cases, then a new precedent could be enunciated.

As statutory law became more widespread, judicial research would look to find whether legislative enactment governed the facts of the case; there would also be the search for the prior written judicial opinion. But legislative draftsmen often prepare imperfect legislation: language is ambiguous, one statutory reference is inconsistent with another, a provision is incompletely set forth, an enactment fails to cover a dispute which was not anticipated by the lawmakers, the passage of time makes an old statute appear ridiculous.

Overriding all of the law are the constitutions, federal and state. The United States Constitution is referred to as "the Supreme Law of the Land," and United States Supreme Court decisions prevail on issues involving federal citizenship and federal purview. But the federal constitution, including the constitutional amendments, does not apply to all issues which arise within a state, and in those circumstances a state constitution, as interpreted by the highest court of the state, is supreme. Conversely, state constitutional provisions have been held to be in violation of the federal constitution and have been voided, as in certain reapportionment cases.

The decision by one trial court judge is not binding upon other trial court judges. A decision by the highest appellate court does bind all trial court judges within the state, but not in other states.

While trials before a jury are not a universal alternative to a trial before a judge, where a jury trial right does exist and where it is exercised the jury acts basically as the fact finder, and enters its verdict after it has heard the evidence and received the instructions of law provided by the judge. In some states, following a jury verdict of "guilty," the jury exercises sentencing power and determines or recommends the type and length of sentence for the offender. Generally, jury sentencing is regarded as a poor procedure, but in all, or virtually all states which have maintained or reinstated capital punishment, the jury typically determines whether the sentence shall be that of death or life in prison.

The American Bar Association's Code of Judicial Conduct provides: "A judge should be faithful to the law and maintain professional competence in it. He should be unswayed by partisan interests, public clamor, or fear of criticism."[6] While there are proud examples of judicial independence and integrity, few judicial observers would suggest that judges are not unmindful of public opinion and public concern in reaching their decisions. Their decisions may be subject to critical press editorials. Judges tend to be products of a middle-class background, and absorb middle-class biases and stereotypes into their judicial decisions. In many jurisdictions judges have been elected to office in a partisan political election. Further, in most states judges seek reelection to the bench through an electoral process. In states where judicial continuation is dependent upon reappointment by a governor, a mayor, or city and county officials, the judge who is out of step with the average judge in his jurisdiction may well have difficulty gaining reappointment. Theoretically, judges appointed for life (as in federal and some New England courts) have great independence in their functioning and need not face the wrath of electors. Life tenure for judges has its severe critics who argue these judges are too independent, become too arrogant, and should be subjected to public vote in some form.

Judges do strive to be consistent with themselves, and to rule in the same way under the same facts. But sentencing consistency is more difficult. While most judges follow a sentencing middle ground, some judges are more consistently on the harsher end of the continuum, and others are on the more moderate end. Severe problems arise from disparate sentencing practices between judges. Defendants with similar prior records and similar present offenses may receive very different sentences from different judges in different parts of a state, or even within the same court. When these offenders enter the same prison and exchange notes, and learn that one received a five-to-ten-year sentence, while the other received a twenty-five-to-forty-year sentence, offender respect for the law becomes nonexistent.

The United States Supreme Court and the Public

Any study of the United States Supreme Court reflects that the interpretation of the federal constitution depends upon the political viewpoints and the social sensitivities of the nine men who, at any given time, sit as justices on that bench. The constitution represents broad brush strokes rather than detailed and clearly delineated provisions. Interpretation depends upon the interpreters, as well as the conditions of the times. Franklin D. Roosevelt understood this well. The Supreme Court which he inherited rejected certain of his social legislation as unconstitutional. He sought but failed to secure legislation which would have enlarged the number of justices, and would have granted him the opportunity to add appointments to the bench. However, the passage of time and his long tenure as president provided him the opportunity to appoint more liberal attorneys to this position, and to achieve decisions more to his liking.

Richard M. Nixon also understood this concept very well. He made clear his intentions to appoint more conservative jurists, and his appointees have largely upheld his confidence in them. Both Roosevelt and Nixon engendered severe criticism over their politicized approach to such appointments. Further, President Nixon precipitated serious public disrespect for the vital, independent role of this court when he forwarded for nomination four persons subsequently rejected for appointment for reasons of relative incompetency or particular prejudices. A president's nominations must receive the advice and consent of the United States Senate, and are also pre-screened through the American Bar Association, whose rejection of several Nixon nominees resulted in their withdrawal without submission to the Senate.

A further problem in recent years has been that the Supreme Court has been known as the Nixon court as much as it has been known as the Burger court (after Chief Justice Warren Burger), whereas the court from 1954 through 1968 was clearly known by the name of its chief justice, the Warren court. Earl Warren was appointed chief justice by President Dwight D. Eisenhower. His tenure, until his voluntary retirement in early 1969, carried through three presidents. It is known as the court which substantially widened the application of Bill of Rights protections to criminal defendants as they experienced police and court handling.[7] The majority of justices of the Warren court perceived that criminal defendants were not matched evenly against law enforcement agencies, and determined to redress citizens' rights in relation to police agents. That court's concerns over police practices related only to practices which could reasonably be interpreted as violating constitutional procedures and safeguards. The Warren court ruled that police practices in the states must attain a higher standard of fairness than they had shown before. It preferred to invalidate a police practice even though this might result in the freeing of an otherwise guilty offender, since it viewed adherence to a free society's constitutional precepts as more important than the punishing of an individual offense.[8] The means must not contradict the ends.

Public concern, in part incited by law enforcement officials, scored the court as "handcuffing the police," but this did not seem to dissuade the court from its pattern of pronouncements against police practices it found unconstitutional.[9] The court expanded the obstacles to more summary criminal processing in the states, and among many such opinions, interpreted the constitution as compelling the states to make available free counsel to indigent felony defendants.[10] It also compelled the right to free counsel for juveniles processed in juvenile courts.[11]

The Warren court both responded to and contributed to the civil rights movement of the 1950s and 1960s, as it extended First Amendment, due process, and equal protection coverage to the American poor, and to our racial and ethnic minorities.[12] It inveighed against governmental intrusion into the privacy of religious belief, banning prayer readings in the public school classroom,[13] and gave protection to the privacy of the bedroom by prohibiting restrictions on the distribution of contraceptive information and devices by a state.[14] The court also rejected the pre-eminent right of the states to decide how they shall apportion their legislative representation when such schemes failed to meet the requirements of the federal constitution. Its reapportionment decision, the one-man, one-vote doctrine, struck at rural-dominated legislatures and recognized urban-suburban population growth implications on the right to equal representation.[15]

The succeeding Burger court, as expected, has made substantial retreat from the advances of its predecessor as to the rights of criminal defendants, but it has forged ahead on some of the same track.[16] Even though Nixon appointees represented four of nine justices, the court unanimously extended the right to free counsel to apply to all lesser offenses which offered the possibility of any jail sentence for guilty defendants.[17] Further, it unanimously struck down former Attorney General John Mitchell's claim that he had the power, without approval of a court, to wiretap the conversations of persons he held threats to our domestic security.[18] Again, without dissent, this court declared unconstitutional a typical vagrancy law often used to jail persons held in low esteem by police officials.[19] Further, it held judicial practices which required convicted indigents to work off their fines in a jail or workhouse to be discriminatory against the poor.[20] This court also declared the death penalty unconstitutional, in a five to four decision, though all four dissents were from Nixon appointees.[21] The court applied due process to parole revocation hearings,[22] extended the right to a free transcript for appeal of a lower court decision on nonfelony cases,[23] and furthered nondiscriminatory requirements in jury selection.[24] It held restrictive abortion statutes unconstitutional,[25] and ruled that birth control devices could not be constitutionally withheld from unmarried persons,[26] that courts must waive filing fees for indigents who seek a divorce,[27] and that Amish youth who had completed the eighth grade in their own private school could not be forced by compulsory education law to continue their education until their sixteenth birthday.[28]

The Burger court's solicitude for socially disadvantaged groups and religious minorities has been applied less generously to persons accused of crimes. It narrowed the requirement of the right to counsel by prohibiting its application prior to the formal charging process;[29] it permitted a limited use of statements obtained illegally by police officials;[30] it weakened the standards determining whether a confession had been voluntarily offered;[31] it broadened police powers to search persons without a search warrant;[32] it eroded the jury system by upholding a guilty determination when nine of twelve jurors found guilt;[33] it also approved of a six-member jury for criminal cases.[34] Perhaps the court responded to public concerns of law and order, and, in addition, stimulated these concerns by its own holdings.

Other significant decisions proclaimed that a newsman had no constitutional privilege to deny information to a grand jury inquiry into alleged criminal misconduct;[35] permitted private shopping centers to prohibit distribution of handbills within the interior walls of the center;[36] and transferred the standard for obscenity to local rather than national measures.[37] Among other rulings, the court disturbed the status quo of several entrenched American institutions. It held that public school students had a statutory right to education and, facing short-term suspension, were entitled under the Fourteenth Amendment to notice and a hearing, preferably prior to removal from school.[38] The justices also held that local school board members were not immune from damages if they knew or reasonably should have known their actions violated students' constitutional rights, or if they acted with malice.[39] The court also decided that a state "cannot constitutionally confine, without more, a non-dangerous individual who is capable of surviving safely in freedom," and that state law which authorizes the confinement of "the harmless mentally ill does not itself establish a constitutionally adequate purpose for the confinement."[40]

One observer of the Burger court has suggested that the "strict construction" viewpoint forecast for it, has been applied only where the appellant-protagonists have lacked an organized political movement.[41] Thus, decisions narrowing the rights of criminal defendants may reflect this group's absence of extensive political power. Conversely, the existence of a widespread women's rights movement may have influenced the progressive holding on the abortion issue. A variety of decisions on prisoner rights may reflect both the explosive inmate response to substandard prison conditions, and also the inability of prisoners to mount full scale political movements paralleling those of racial and ethnic minorities and women. Among other decisions, the court struck down a California regulation which authorized censorship of inmate mail,[42] and ruled unconstitutional a New York statute denying voting rights to jailed persons who were awaiting trial.[43] On the other hand the court upheld a California statute prohibiting the voting franchise to felons who had completed their sentence and parole,[44] and affirmed the California Department of Corrections regulation denying press interviews with specific individual inmates.[45]

Supporters and detractors of the Burger court probably agree that its justices observed their finest hour in ruling on the dispute between the special Watergate prosecutor and President Nixon. To the question of "who decides," the court determined that it is for the judicial branch, not the executive, to decide when the public interest requires disclosure of presidential discussions.[46]

Evaluating the Courts

There are many ways to study the courts. Useful studies have been conducted by lay groups, joint citizen-professional committees, court administrative personnel, and independent consultants and researchers. Citizen organizations interested in the reform of bail practices have recorded bail-setting decisions by judges, interviewed judicial system personnel and defendants, and entered recommendations for procedures to reduce unnecessary pretrial detention. Organizations such as the National Council of Jewish Women, working through their local affiliates, have focused on juvenile justice issues. They have examined state juvenile codes, observed court hearings, interviewed juvenile justice personnel, toured juvenile institutions, published their findings,[47] and worked to implement study recommendations. Numerous local chapters of the League of Women Voters and the Junior League have also addressed juvenile court–juvenile justice concerns. Certain citizen organizations interested in judicial sentencing practices have observed and recorded hearings and issued public reports (often critical that sentences are too lenient). On an informal basis, bar associations frequently conduct citizen courthouse tours, more for interpretation than study.

Internal court management studies are accelerating as courts employ more trained administrative personnel. Improved data collection systems allow examination of caseflow—how long it takes for cases to move from one processing point to another. For example, an increasing number of courts maintain up-to-date information on the length of time required for criminal and civil caseflow, along with case filing trends. This information can then be used to facilitate the caseflow process and can be applied to broader planning efforts. A number of private management consultant firms have been used to develop or redesign court record or information systems, to structure or revise court personnel systems, and to ascertain facility needs. However, private firms may lack intimate knowledge of the courts, a deficiency that may limit the practicality of their formulations. Familiarity with the courts helps in obtaining the critical ingredient of judicial support.

Weighted judicial caseload measures, based on the average length of time judges need for hearing different types of cases, are utilized in California, Florida, and in other states to determine whether additional judges may be required, and how many. Recidivism studies are common, and measure the repeat offense rate of probationers, or offenders ordered into particular rehabilitation programs. Other court processes and issues receiving study include the implementation of the right to counsel, computerization of data systems, alternative approaches to calendaring cases before judges, juror selection and utilization, improved notification approaches to trial witnesses, and the administration of traffic offenses by noncourt agencies, to name but a few.

Several elements, over and above the technical skills of the researchers, are seen as basic to a successful court study and implementation of findings and directions:

1. Extensive preplanning leading to a clear definition of study goals;
2. Broad, continuing involvement of the people in the court system in the study process;
3. A regular and organized exchange of information, on a national basis, about court study projects, techniques, and management and procedural advances.[48]

Preplanning is necessary since courts frequently lack experience with studies, do not administer their systems on a goal basis, and need assistance in delineating the purposes of the study. Also, the courts to be studied may not have initiated the study process. A state court system or a criminal justice planning agency frequently sponsors research in local courts. Further, preplanning provides an opportunity for researchers to gain knowledge of the court and its processes. Involvement of court personnel in the planning is a several-faceted prerequisite. The study is on court turf, and a participatory process gains support for and reduces resistance to recommended changes. It also reveals to the researcher that court processes include clients, private and public attorneys, bail, probation, and corrections systems, and a variety of governmental agencies. Study recommendations must assess the impact of change on such individuals and organizations. Finally, the experience derived in studies of other court systems may be used beneficially in a current project.[49]

Causes of Public Concern

There is no particular romance between the courts and the community. The public has widespread concern over the courts, some based on misunderstandings, others justified. Certain of these concerns require comment.

Unrealistic Expectations

In reality the courts (including the probation function) are not a major deterrent to or preventor of crime. And when crimes are committed the courts handle only a small fraction of all criminal offenders. Courts by definition are an obstacle course antagonistic to summary procedures. Instant disposition of a contested case is contrary to the rule of law. Courts are mandated to provide careful protections for the individual against the state. Our heterogeneous and rapidly changing society contains, inherently, a wide variety of behavior, some which violates commonly accepted legal standards, some which violates debated legal standards which embody moral standards. The public is only beginning to become aware of the complexity of the criminal justice process, and of the extent of a) unreported crime, and b) reported crime not cleared by police arrest, as reflected in Figure 2. No one is particularly proud of what is shown by this chart. But understanding this helps refine our perceptions of the limited role of the courts.

Insufficient Public Understanding of the Procedures and Problems of Courts

Most judges acknowledge that courts have neglected their responsibility to provide public information to the community. While the courts are public instruments, courts have not encouraged the citizenry to look into their workshops. When a Massachusetts citizen group decided to assign court watchers to record bail procedures and decisions, judges were hostile to their presence. When one

Figure 2. Crime and Law Enforcement

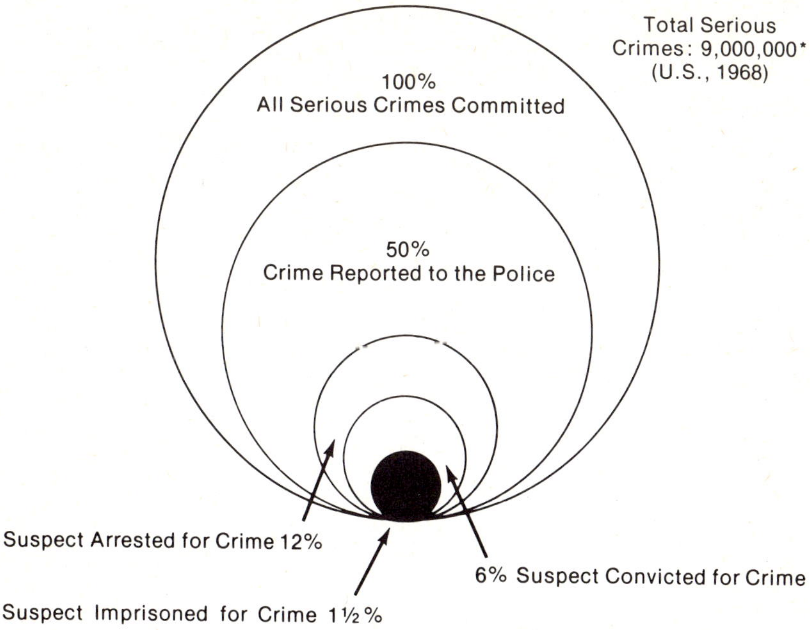

*Based on estimated aggregate of homicide, forcible rape, robbery, aggravated assault, burglary, larceny over $50, and auto theft.

SOURCE: Adapted from *To Establish Justice, To Insure Domestic Tranquility,* Report of the National Commission on the Causes and Prevention of Violence (New York: Award Books Edition, 1969), p. xviii.

experienced newsman began coverage of the Denver court system, he noted that the judges and the lawyers were sitting in padded chairs, while he and thc general public sat on hard wooden benches in the back half of the courtroom.[50] This reporter detailed his interest in covering the courts following eight years of other types of reporting: he had decided that so many issues, important to society, ended up in the courts, but neither he nor the general public adequately understood the processes or ramifications of the court system. He was concerned that to cover all the courts in Denver would result in a mediocre reporting achievement. Instead, he would bring to public knowledge and concern the more significant case; the less visible problem; the interrelationship between the courts, the police, and other criminal justice agencies; and a more studied examination of court strengths and shortcomings. One conference participant, a Florida judge, pushed the reporter to spell out his more critical views of the bench. The writer responded, "This will probably shock you, but I have been impressed with the quality of the criminal court judges in Denver." Yet the community of

Denver, he admitted, hardly shared his positive perceptions of the judiciary. In general, the media have not sufficiently widened or deepened public knowledge of the courts. But the courts and the media have increased awareness of this need, and the growth of bench, bar, and media committees in a number of communities augurs for stronger public understanding.

Court Concern for the Rights of Defendants

The extension of defendant rights by the Warren court, the expansion of the right to counsel by the Burger court, increased judicial activism in response to suits challenging existing institutions, along with the overall crime problem, have brought negative public backlash. There has been as well public uproar over civil suits initiated by impoverished citizens through publicly paid counsel, where large judgments have been won against governmental entities. Americans are concerned, somehow, by assaults on the established order, even where brought by legal means to fulfil the provisions of our laws. While we take pride that we are a "government of laws and not of men," we resist efforts to apply the full measure of our constitutions and statutes to our poor, our minorities, and to criminal defendants.

Court Delays and Inefficiencies

Here, the public concern has its most substantial merit. Courts have been inattentive to delays and inefficiencies. Chicago auto accident suits still require thirty-two months from filing to disposition, although a few years ago they required nearly double this time. The appellate process is slow. The technicalities of legal procedure require a myriad of time-consuming hearings. Court scheduling deficiencies cause too many continuances, along with the discouraging need for witnesses to appear and then reappear. More cases than should be are plea-bargained to cope with inordinate caseloads. In the face of systemic breakdown, lawyers out-manipulate the judges. We have countenanced too many judges who are prima donnas, too many attorneys lacking in professional ethics, too many court employees performing below minimum standards.

Public Intolerance of Judicial Sentencing Practices

The public sees defendants in the abstract. The courts, hopefully, see them as persons. Judges have a Hobson's choice between sentencing an offender to a debilitating prison experience, or taking the risk of a probation sentence when probation personnel are overloaded and underimaginative and lack the community resources to "make it" with defendants who could succeed in the community if probation and community agencies could put it all together. The community fails to appreciate the mitigating factors which judges discern during the course of a trial or in the presentation of a probation presentence study.

Defects in Related Criminal Justice Agencies Rub Off on the Courts

The courts, as the fulcrum of the justice system, not only receive public criticism for their own inefficiencies, deficiencies, and actions, but it appears they absorb as well additional public concern which should be addressed directly to component agencies of the justice system. Problems in law enforcement affect the public image of the courts. Further, police not infrequently criticize the courts, blaming them both appropriately and inappropriately. Probation services are grossly ineffective in many communities. The failure of probation intake officers and prosecutors to communicate effectively with victims and complaining witnesses about the reasons for rejecting case referrals has added further scars. Disparate psychiatric evaluations of the same defendant further diminish public respect for the law. The program deficiencies of mental health services and drug treatment agencies, in their work with offenders, additionally weaken support for the courts.

Both the courts, and the community support for the courts, have a long way to go.

Questions for Discussion

1. If you were employed as a court public information officer, what programs would you develop to improve the court system's relationship with the community?
2. Clip all newspaper references to the courts for one week and analyze their content and the probable citizen response to these articles.
3. Distinguish between court reorganization, court reform, and court improvement.
4. Discuss with a local jury commissioner how potential jurors are selected. Talk with a public defender about his criticisms of juror selection methods.
5. Consider the interaction between changing societal mores, police enforcement of the laws, legislation, and the courts, as to a) marriage and divorce, adultery and fornication; b) drug use.
6. Consider the United States Supreme Court's impact upon the public, and the public's impact upon the Supreme Court.
7. How should the courts contribute to the reduction of crime?
8. Is it sufficient or overly sufficient for a state court system to provide one trial and one appeal?

9. Why must criminal trials be public trials?
10. Interview a criminal court judge to obtain his views on problems in judicial and correctional administration.
11. Why is it considered preferable for judges rather than jurors to sentence convicted defendants?

References

1. Robert A. Martin, "Giving Light to the People: Public Relations for the Courts," *Judicature* 57 (December 1973): 190–93.
2. Hernandez v. Texas, 347 U.S. 475 (1954); Alexander v. Louisiana, 405 U.S. 625, 92 S.Ct. 1221 (1972).
3. See *Juror Utilization Study, Cuyahoga County Court of Common Pleas* (Cleveland: Court Management Project, 1972).
4. *Quarterly Survey of Judicial Salaries in State Court Systems* (Denver: National Center for State Courts, 1975).
5. Carl Baar, "The Limited Trend Toward State Court Financing," *Judicature* 58 (1975): 325.
6. *Code of Judicial Conduct* (Chicago: American Bar Association Special Committee on Standards of Judicial Conduct, 1972), Canon 3 A(1).
7. For reviews of the Warren court, see Archibald Cox, *The Warren Court: Constitution Decisions as an Instrument of Reform* (Cambridge, Mass.: Harvard University Press, 1968); Alexander M. Bickel, *The Supreme Court and the Idea of Progress* (New York: Harper and Row, 1970); Philip B. Kurland, *Politics, the Constitution and the Warren Court* (Chicago: University of Chicago Press, 1970); Anthony Lewis, "Earl Warren," *The Warren Court: A Critical Evaluation,* ed. Richard Sayler (New York: Chelsea House Press, 1969).
8. Mapp v. Ohio, 367 U.S. 643, 81 S.Ct. 1684 (1961).
9. Escobedo v. Illinois, 378 U.S. 478, 84 S.Ct. 1758 (1964); Miranda v. Arizona, 384 U.S. 436, 86 S.Ct. 1602 (1966).
10. Gideon v. Wainwright, 372 U.S. 335, 83 S.Ct. 792 (1963).
11. In re Gault, 387 U.S. 1, 87 S.Ct. 1428 (1967).
12. Brown v. Board of Education, 347 U.S. 483, 74 S.Ct. 686 (1954); Levy v. Louisiana, 391 U.S. 91 (1968); Glona v. American Guarantee Co., 391 U.S. 73 (1968).
13. School District v. Schempp, 374 U.S. 203, 83 S.Ct. 1560 (1963).
14. Griswold v. Connecticut, 381 U.S. 479, 85 S.Ct. 1678 (1965).
15. Baker v. Carr, 369 U.S. 186, 82 S.Ct. 691 (1962).
16. See Leonard W. Levy, *Against the Law: The Nixon Court and Criminal Justice* (New York: Harper and Row, 1974).
17. Argersinger v. Hamlin, 407 U.S. 25, 92 S.Ct. 2006 (1972).
18. United States v. United States District Court, 407 U.S. 297, 92 S.Ct. 2125 (1972).
19. Papachristou v. City of Jacksonville, 405 U.S. 156, 92 S.Ct. 839 (1972).
20. Tate v. Short, 401 U.S. 395, 91 S.Ct. 668 (1970).
21. Furman v. Georgia, 406 U.S. 238, 92 S.Ct. 2726 (1972).
22. Morrissey v. Brewer, 408 U.S. 471, 92 S.Ct. 2593 (1972).
23. Mayer v. City of Chicago, 404 U.S. 189, 92 S.Ct. 410 (1971).
24. Peters v. Kiff, 407 U.S. 493, 92 S.Ct. 2163 (1972).
25. Roe v. Wade, 410 U.S. 113, 93 S.Ct. 705 (1973).

26. Eisenstadt v. Baird, 405 U.S. 438 (1972).
27. Boddie v. Connecticut, 401 U.S. 371, 91 S.Ct. 780 (1971).
28. Wisconsin v. Yoder, 406 U.S. 205, 92 S.Ct. 1526 (1972).
29. Kirby v. Illinois, 406 U.S. 682, 92 S.Ct. 1877 (1972).
30. Harris v. New York, 401 U.S. 222, 91 S.Ct. 644 (1971).
31. Lego v. Twomey, 404 U.S. 477, 92 S.Ct. 619 (1972).
32. Adams v. Williams, 407 U.S. 143, 92 S.Ct. 1921 (1972).
33. Johnson v. Louisiana, 406 U.S. 356, 92 S.Ct. 1620 (1972).
34. Williams v. Florida, 399 U.S. 78, 90 S.Ct. 1893 (1970).
35. Branzburg v. Hayes, 408 U.S. 665, 92 S.Ct. 2646 (1972).
36. Lloyd Corporation v. Tanner, 407 U.S. 551 (1972).
37. Miller v. California, 413 U.S. 15, 93 S.Ct. 2607 (1973).
38. Goss v. Lopez, 95 S.Ct. 729 (1975).
39. Wood v. Strickland, 95 S.Ct. 992 (1975).
40. O'Connor v. Donaldson, 95 S.Ct. 2486 (1975).
41. Aryeh Neier, "Protest Movements Among the Disenfranchised," *The Civil Liberties Review* 1 (Fall 1974): 49–51.
42. Procunier v. Martinez, 94 S.Ct. 1800 (1974).
43. O'Brien v. Skinner, 94 S.Ct. 740 (1974).
44. Richardson v. Ramirez, 94 S.Ct. 2655 (1974).
45. Pell v. Procunier, 94 S.Ct. 2800 (1974).
46. United States v. Nixon, 94 S.Ct. 3090 (1974).
47. *Children Without Justice* (New York: National Council of Jewish Women, 1975).
48. *The Court Study Process* (Denver: Institute for Court Management, 1975), p. 5.
49. Ibid.
50. Statement of Richard O'Reilly, *Rocky Mountain News* reporter, to Institute for Court Management, Conference on Public Information and the Courts, Snowmass-at-Aspen, Colorado, March, 1974.

2 The Felony Courts

The felony court is the forum where the most critical crimes are processed. This is the court of the murder trial, the place where arson, aggravated assault, burglary, rape, robbery, kidnapping, forgery, drug sales, grand larceny, and other charges are adjudicated. This is the status court of the criminal system. Newspaper reporters cover its more important hearings. Its juries may be locked up for weeks, or even months, in hearing and deliberating upon cases.

A felony is a crime punishable by incarceration in a state prison or correctional institution for a minimum period of one year. The sentence for a felony offense may also be imprisonment for life, or the death penalty. Penalties short of incarceration, such as probation, may also be imposed upon convicted felons.

While a felony represents in theory a more serious offense than a misdemeanor, this is not always true. A misdemeanor assault may result in serious physical injury, while an auto theft may cause only minor inconvenience where the auto is later recovered intact. Further, since the definition of what is a felony or a misdemeanor is made by a legislative body, statutory definitions differ between the states. As an example, the felony of grand larceny is defined by Oklahoma statute as the theft of property valued in excess of $20, while in Oregon, the dividing line between the misdemeanor of petty larceny and the felony of grand larceny is $200. In both states, grand larceny is punishable by a penitentiary term not to exceed five years.

In a discussion with the author in September, 1973, a felony court judge commented:

> I naturally work hard. I schedule five felony jury trials each Monday, and four each Wednesday. Many of these cases end up with a plea bargain and no trial, but sometimes two cases are ready to go. I call up the chief judge, and he sometimes is able to assign another judge to hear the second case. Otherwise, I must continue it. Usually, I proceed to hear the case that is oldest.
>
> The trouble with young prosecutors and public defenders is that they're reluctant to go to trial for fear they'll lose. Defenders seek too many continuances, and prosecutors prefer to bargain. Both offices lack enough experienced senior staff who have good common sense and could advise younger staff members in making better decisions. Both offices make mistakes in selecting the cases they want to try. When they question the jury to rule out persons they consider may be partial, they sometimes take a very long time. Jurors have come to me after a trial to say an attorney "turned them off" asking them so many questions, and that it was difficult for them to objectively weigh the merits of the case because they had been irritated by the attorney. So except in highly publicized cases, I enforce a rule that I will question the jury, which takes about an hour and a half, and then each counsel has one-half hour to ask further questions. But when a jury trial begins, I have the lawyers run the trial, and I ask very few questions of the witnesses.
>
> We have a six-months-to-trial rule, and that is working. There are five regular criminal division judges in our court. We're all conscientious, but we don't seem to get anywhere. A basic problem is that too many cases are filed. And there are all kinds of preliminary motions to be decided before trial. But I believe in full disclosure before trial, and have made this a rule of my court, although I will consider prosecutor motions to prohibit disclosure in special cases. I get appealed from both sides, three times last week. Appeals are increasing. There were fifty-five felony case appeals the first five months of this year, but only sixty-five all of last year.
>
> Our prison is poor, but I still have to send some people there. Probation caseloads are too high, and they're swamped with paperwork. Over a given period I might differ with the probation officer's recommendation against probation as much as 50 percent of the time. Today I held seven sentencing hearings, and probation recommended against imprisonment in all seven cases.[1]

The major U.S. Supreme Court decisions concerning criminal law and procedure have usually developed from felony cases in the state courts. Decisions arising from felony cases in the federal court system, related to violations of federal statutes, have also been significant, but practice and procedure in the federal courts is far more uniform since it is one system, as compared with fifty systems of the fifty states and their differing statutes and rules.

Because of the potential gravity of a sentence in a felony court, trials are often vigorously contested, and prosecution and public defense offices assign to these courts their more experienced trial lawyers. But contrary to what much of the public believes, the majority of felony cases do not really go to trial. Somewhere along the criminal justice process, most defendants enter a plea to one of the charges lodged against them, or to a substitute count of a lesser offense than previously charged. This is known as "plea bargaining," and it is a dominant characteristic of today's criminal courts. While a prominent national commission has urged its abolition by no later than 1978,[2] another influential body prefers its retention and refinement.[3] For example, the annual report of the Criminal Division, Court of Common Pleas, Cuyahoga County (Cleveland), Ohio, revealed for the year 1970 the following dispositions as to felony cases:

Guilty Pleas	2,178
Trial by Court (Judge)	42
Trial by Jury	260

The court with felony jurisdiction in Houston, the Harris County Criminal District Courts, reported that 12,243 felony indictments were filed in 1970. That year, Houston felony judges conducted the following number of trials:

Trial by Court (Judge)	631
Trial by Jury	493

In both of these courts a significant number of additional cases were dismissed by the court without trial, or dismissed upon the request of the prosecutor. Some of this occurs when two or more separate felony cases are pending against a defendant, and upon a plea or finding of guilt followed by a sentence the other case or cases are dismissed as unnecessary for further prosecution. The 1974 report of the courts of Oregon revealed a 12.4 percent statewide felony trial rate, down from 20 percent in 1969. These data suggest an increase in the use of plea bargaining.

Structure of the Felony Courts

The lower criminal courts, which hold jurisdiction over misdemeanors and local ordinance violations, are seen as inferior to the felony courts. All felony courts are presided over by lawyer judges, and they are all courts of record. All proceedings are recorded verbatim by court reporters, electronic tape recordings, or some other system. Invariably, felony court judges receive higher pay than lower criminal court judges. Their courtrooms are usually more ample, and they are less inundated by vast numbers of defendants flowing through their system.

In many states, when a defendant wishes to appeal an adverse ruling in the lower criminal court it is appealed to the felony court. Appeal from a felony court decision is taken to the state's appellate court system.

The felony court in each state is a part of the state's highest court of general trial jurisdiction. It is known by different names in different states, as shown by Table 1. The general trial courts also consider civil cases where unlimited money claims are requested. Most of these courts also hear domestic relations matters such as divorce; they may include probate divisions which supervise the administration of the estates of deceased persons and persons declared mentally incompetent. Sometimes these courts include a juvenile division. Several states, such as New York and New Jersey, structure an appellate division of these courts in lieu of the more general pattern of a separate intermediate appellate court. (See Appendix A for representative examples of state court system structures.) It can be expected that these courts will play an increasingly powerful role in the future administration of justice in this country. In some states the presiding or chief judge of these courts has now been given various supervisory powers over both his own court and certain lower courts within his district. Similarly, these courts have begun to

Table 1. The Felony Court in the Different States

CIRCUIT COURT	Alabama, Arkansas, Florida, Hawaii, Illinois, Indiana*, Kentucky, Maryland, Michigan, Mississippi, Missouri, Oregon, South Carolina, South Dakota, Tennessee, Virginia, West Virginia, Wisconsin
COURT OF COMMON PLEAS	Ohio, Pennsylvania
DISTRICT COURT	Colorado, Idaho, Iowa, Kansas, Louisiana, Minnesota, Montana, Nebraska, Nevada, New Mexico, North Dakota, Oklahoma, Texas, Utah, Wyoming
SUPERIOR COURT	Alaska, Arizona, California, Connecticut, Delaware, District of Columbia, Georgia, Indiana*, Maine, Massachusetts, New Hampshire, New Jersey, North Carolina, Rhode Island, Vermont, Washington
SUPREME COURT	New York

*Concurrent jurisdiction for felonies.

SOURCE: U.S. Department of Justice, U.S. Bureau of Census. *The National Survey of Court Organization* (Washington, D.C.: Government Printing Office, 1973).

employ trial court administrators who work under the supervision of the presiding or chief judge, but who have responsibility for the administration of the lower courts as well.

Generally, the number of these courts in a state is less than the number of lower courts. The lower courts were organized on a town, city, or county basis, while courts of general trial jurisdiction requiring lawyer judges were organized on a district or circuit basis. Except in more populous counties these latter courts may encompass two or three or even a half dozen counties. In many districts of many states today these judges still "ride circuit." They may hold court in one county's courthouse on Monday and Tuesday, and then travel to a contiguous county to hold court on Wednesday. Or, for example, they may center in one county for a week, and then travel to another county or counties to handle judicial business the following week. Many of these judges become long-term judges, making this their career after a number of years of law practice. The position is prestigious, and is sometimes a stepping-stone for election or selection to a state appellate court, or for appointment to the federal bench. A number of these judges came into their positions through earlier political careers. A substantial number are former prosecutors. The developing movement in a number of states to eliminate election of judges by voters, and to substitute appointment by the governor from two or three names submitted by a judicial nominating commission, more frequently results in the selection of judges who had not earlier engaged in extensive political activity.

The annual salaries of these judges, in June, 1975, ranged from a low in Utah of $22,000 to a high in New York of $48,998.[4] These judges are not permitted to engage in private law practice. Organizations interested in a strengthened judicial system urge that the judges of these courts should be drawn from the better law practitioners and from the best of the lower court judges, and that their salaries should approximate those of state executive department officials, and rival the income of reasonably successful lawyers and senior professionals such as doctors, engineers, and accountants.[5] Yet these are the judges who are frequently unmoved by the reformist proposal for a single-tier court system, blanketing into their court the lower criminal and civil courts, traffic courts, and where not already so structured, the juvenile and probate courts. The Superior Court for the District of Columbia, as reorganized in 1970, is perhaps the best example of the one-tier system. It is a total trial court.[6]

As will be described later, the unification of courts is seen as particularly critical to the improvement of the lower level courts;[7] administrative efficiencies should follow, and the fragmentation of jurisdiction between different courts should be substantially reduced. Interestingly, back in 1920, Detroit took the then bold step of creating a single criminal court to hear all ordinance, misdemeanor, and felony offenses which arose in that city. Called the Recorder's Court, it was created separate from the general court structure. But today's court reformers would prefer to see the Detroit model reformulated. A single trial court with jurisdiction over all criminal, civil, juvenile, and other matters, is seen as a preferable structure offering a more flexible and efficient management potential.

History of the Felony Courts

The term "felony" comes from the old English law. It referred to a forfeiture of one's land and goods to the crown, or to the lord, following conviction of a crime. Capital punishment could be meted out as well. The felony was distinguished from a misdemeanor, and no forfeiture of lands or goods followed conviction of a misdemeanor. Over a period of time forfeiture was abolished, although present criminal law permits the assessment of a fine. Also, over time, the early English procedure of rather summary and arbitrary justice by a king or lord yielded to the public magistrate and jury. Criminal cases were initiated by a grand jury system, structured to provide a relatively unrestricted citizen inquiry as to whether there was a reasonable basis for believing a certain individual had committed a crime. No rigid rules of evidence restricted the grand jury inquiry, which also operated free of judicial supervision.[8]

The Fifth Amendment incorporated this process into the American legal system, and required a grand jury indictment for anyone charged in federal court with a capital crime or felony. The Fifth Amendment requirement has been held not to bind the states from instituting felony charges by other means. The U.S. Supreme Court ruled in 1884 that a criminal information initiated by a prosecutor was a constitutionally permissible substitute.[9]

As shown in Table 2, nine states today require that all felonies be initiated by grand jury indictment; fifteen states authorize defendant waiver of grand jury indictment; twenty-six states provide prosecutor discretion whether to invoke grand jury processes. Prosecutors in the third category routinely file criminal informations, but invoke grand jury inquiries in organized crime cases, in cases where a law enforcement officer has killed a citizen, cases involving public officials, and other sensitive matters. Court reform advocates urge the abolition of the grand jury indictment requirement. Opponents of this change claim the grand jury is a protection against arbitrary prosecution. Yet in many jurisdictions one hears the recurrent complaint that the grand jury is nothing but a "rubber stamp for the prosecutor."

Table 2. The Requirement of Grand Jury Indictment for Felonies: A State Analysis

MANDATORY GRAND JURY INDICTMENT	Hawaii, Kentucky, Maryland, Massachusetts, Mississippi, New York, Tennessee, Texas, West Virginia
GRAND JURY INDICTMENT MAY BE WAIVED BY DEFENDANT	Alabama, Alaska, Delaware, Georgia, Illinois, Maine, New Hampshire, New Jersey, North Carolina, Ohio, Oregon, Pennsylvania, Rhode Island, South Carolina, Virginia
GRAND JURY MAY BE WAIVED BY PROSECUTOR	Arizona, Arkansas, California, Colorado, Connecticut, Florida, Idaho, Indiana, Iowa, Kansas, Louisiana, Michigan, Minnesota, Missouri, Montana, Nebraska, Nevada, New Mexico, North Dakota, Oklahoma, South Dakota, Utah, Vermont, Washington, Wisconsin, Wyoming

SOURCE: Samuel Dash, "The Indicting Grand Jury: A Critical Stage?" *The American Criminal Law Review* 10 (1972): 812–13.

The 1970 Cuyahoga County (Cleveland), Ohio, grand jury report reflected that all but 7 percent of more than 4,400 felony cases presented to the grand jury resulted in true bills (indictments). The range of grand jury "no bill" decisions generally runs less than 10 percent. With so little overruling of the prosecutor by the grand jury many consider that the extra cost and delay, and the extension of pretrial jail time that the grand jury process entails for many defendants, outweigh any benefits.

In grand jury states, jury size ranges from twelve to twenty-three persons. In Ohio, for example, the grand jury consists of fifteen persons. At least twelve must concur in returning a true bill. Each grand jury in Cleveland sits for about four months, and meets two or three days each week.[10]

Also carried over from old English practice is the petit or trial jury. England, sometime during the fourteenth century, fixed the size of this jury at twelve persons. Determination of guilt at trial by one's peers, i.e., other citizens who lived in the general vicinity, evolved as a basic trial feature and was incorporated into the U.S. Constitution's Sixth Amendment. The petit jury system provides an option for the defendant to choose between trial before a judge, or a trial before a twelve-person jury. The motivation for a defendant to choose a jury trial has weakened, however, in recent years. While in 1968 our highest court ruled that even misdemeanor and petty offense trials must permit the right to jury if the potential penalty exceeds six months,[11] the court later decided that the Florida law permitting a six-member felony jury was constitutional.[12] Two years later the Oregon constitutional provision which authorized a guilty verdict when ten members of a twelve-member jury found the defendant guilty was also upheld.[13] A dissenting opinion in the Oregon case by Mr. Justice Douglas stated:

> I had . . . assumed that there was no dispute that the Federal Constitution required a unanimous jury in all criminal cases . . . Today . . . two centuries of American history are shunted aside.

A further opinion that year approved the Louisiana provision that a defendant could be found guilty if nine of the twelve jurors returned such a verdict.[14]

American legal history reflects the names of great trial lawyers, such as Clarence Darrow and Samuel S. Liebowitz, who earned their reputations through criminal defense work in the felony courts where the predominant group of defendants has historically been the poor and members of immigrant and minority groups.[15] Of course, the middle and upper classes also commit felonies, and their charges are tried in these courts as well. The more recent history of these courts has been strongly impacted upon by Supreme Court decisions. During the late 1950s and throughout much of the 1960s the procedural rights of criminal defendants were strongly extended by the Warren court. A long string of decisions required that the states adhere to basic tenets mandated upon the federal court system by the first ten amendments to the Constitution. The Fourteenth Amendment has been the vehicle through which these protections have been made mandatory upon the states. Despite the numerous critics of these decisions, and the concern that the rights of defendants have taken precedence over the rights of victims, many observers believe the decisions have improved police investigative work, enhanced the fairness of judicial proceedings, and provided valuable protections to all citizens against arbitrary governmental action.[16]

The Processing of Felonies

Felony cases generally receive more careful attention from police, prosecutors, and judges. Bail is generally set at a higher amount than with misdemeanors; courts are insistent that the felony defendant have a lawyer, retained or appointed; and the sentence meted out to convicted felony defendants is frequently long-term imprisonment or long-term probation.

A defendant's first felony may result in a grant of probation, but this seldom occurs following a second felony offense. While we have little confidence that imprisonment will achieve major rehabilitative gains, sentences to prison are frequently invoked as a means of temporary community protection. It is a challenge of the 1970s to strengthen probation services for felony offenders, and to provide a wider range of community based alternatives to imprisonment.

Initial Discretion: The Police-Public Interface

The old common law of arrest took note of the greater concern for felony offenses. The police officer did not have to witness a felony to arrest a suspect if he had reasonable cause to believe the suspect had committed a felony. By contrast, a misdemeanor offense had to be witnessed by a law enforcement officer in order to authorize arrest. The alternative, when there was reasonable cause to believe a misdemeanor had been committed in his absence, was for the police officer to appear before a judge or magistrate and document a basis for the issuance of a warrant for arrest. A number of states, during the past two or three decades, have modified their arrest statutes to permit misdemeanor arrests as well as felony arrests for offenses committed in the absence of the police officer, where there is reasonable cause.

Certain judges and legal observers state a general preference that arrest warrants be issued by a judicial officer before any arrest is made. This is a minority view, and probably an impracticable one. In part, this view is influenced by the desire to eliminate the not uncommon police practice of arresting persons for investigation and interrogation where, although reasonable cause for arrest may be lacking, the pressures of temporary incarceration and questioning may produce a confession. Not all such statements made are reliable, however, and harassment is an inadequate substitute for professional investigation. Also, legal arguments frequently arise as to the validity of the arrest and the admission. This view also suggests that the Fourth Amendment, protection of one's home from unreasonable search, and its general requirement of a judicially issued search warrant prior to entry, should extend to the seizure of a person. The Fourth Amendment, however, does not use the term "arrest," and courts have consistently upheld warrantless arrests. A warrantless arrest is clearly the norm. During 1966 New York City police officers arrested more than 171,000 persons for all types of offenses. Only 366 of these were arrested following judicial issuance of an arrest warrant.[17]

While the public is aware that false arrest suits may be brought against police officials who may have lacked a sufficient legal basis for an arrest, it is also commonly recognized that far more illegal arrests are executed than false arrest suits are instituted. Further, the test for validity of an arrest is "reasonable cause to believe the offense was committed by this person," not the actuality that this person had committed the offense.

Police discretion as to whether or not to forward an arrested offender for formal prosecution is more narrowly applied with felonies than with misdemeanors and ordinance violations. Yet there is a use of discretion: whether to value a stolen article higher (grand larceny—felony) or lower (petty larceny—misdemeanor); whether a minor stabbing of a husband by his wife should receive the further attention of the criminal justice system? One national commission recommended that police officials divert from the criminal justice system an offender for whom the purpose of the criminal process "would be inappropriate, or in whose case other resources would be more effective. All diversion dispositions should be made pursuant to written agency policy that insures fairness and uniformity of treatment."[18] All too few police agencies have clear standards guidelining the use of their discretion. And critics of the exercise of police discretion contend it is exercised prejudicially against the poor and minority groups.[19]

Felonies occur less often than misdemeanors. Hennepin County (Minneapolis), Minnesota, reported in 1968 more than ten times as many misdemeanors as felonies.

The Bail-Jail Alternative

The Eighth Amendment of the U.S. Constitution sets forth: "Excessive bail shall not be required nor excessive fines imposed, nor cruel and unusual punishments inflicted." Since under our system of law an accused is presumed innocent, the purpose of bail is to serve as a lever to insure his appearance at trial. Its purpose is not to punish the defendant by jailing him pending trial, or to prejudge that an alleged offender may well commit a second offense before the disposition of the first offense is concluded. Yet theory is tarnished with the practical, and many judges set higher bond for persons who have prior records, or for those they consider likely to repeat.[20] The right to bail, generally, does not apply to offenses punishable by the death penalty.

In many jurisdictions the arraigning judge, along with the prosecutor, dominates the bail-setting decision. Some courts promulgate a bail schedule for different offenses, and this represents a guide to the judge. Elsewhere, prosecutors have developed bail schedules, often worked out informally with arraigning judges over a period of time. Occasionally the judge sets a lower bail than recommended by the prosecutor. Defense counsel, if present, typically recommends a lower amount than envisioned by the judge or prosecutor. Judges' bail-setting decisions more closely follow prosecutors' recommendations; they prefer to buffer these decisions with the concurrence of the prosecutor.[21] Not infrequently defense counsel files a motion to reduce bail, to be heard at a subsequent hearing, accompanied by a statement that the original bail cannot be met and is causing undue hardship on the defendant.

In recent years certain communities have authorized a bail and pretrial release agency to conduct the intitial determination of bail, to conduct the investigation as to whether the defendant can qualify for release without bail, and even to provide certain counseling services for the defendant pending court processing. Background checks on an arrested defendant are useful and broaden out the release-bail-jail decision beyond the simple measure of the seriousness of a particular offense. It is likely that this movement will continue, and that the court's major responsibility will be to review attorney motions to modify the previously determined bail amount. The growth of pretrial release agencies is diminishing the system's reliance upon the commercial bail bondsman. American Bar Association Standards take the following advanced positions:

> Reliance on money bail should be reduced to minimal proportions. It should be required only in cases in which no other condition will reasonably ensure the defendant's appearance. Compensated sureties should be abolished, and in those cases in which money bail is required the defendant should ordinarily be released upon the deposit of cash or sureties equal to 10 percent of the amount of the bail.[22]

Yet today the system relies heavily on the commercial bail bondsman, and courts have not effectively policed the bondsman. A court administrator in Seattle, in late 1973, told this author that he had demanded a bondsman make good on the total amount of the bond since the defendant had not appeared in court as scheduled. The bondsman registered shock that the court had demanded he make payment in the amount of the bond. In 1971, in Cleveland, the felony court discovered that a number of bondsmen had posted bonds in excess of their authorization and their insurability. This was discovered when the Court of Common Pleas checked out the bonds posted not only in its court, but in the lower courts and in suburban courts as well.

The Prosecutor-Grand Jury Screen

Criminal justice standards interpose the prosecutor's office between the police officer and the courts, to provide a lawyer-oriented evaluation of the merits of a proposed charge. Following this stage, a preliminary hearing before a judge is a further method for shortstopping the weak case or the wrong charge. The mandatory use of the grand jury as a screening approach in some states represents an alternative screening device. There, grand jury consideration frequently follows a preliminary hearing where evidence is sufficient to bind over for the grand jury. But practices differ in different communities, and even within the same community. In Chicago, for instance, a 1968 study showed that police did not screen felony cases through the prosecutor's office, but instead prepared and filed their own complaints. The big screening device in that city was the judge at the preliminary hearing. One study revealed that only about 20 percent of felony offenses were bound over to the Cook County grand jury for further consideration; the remainder were disposed of by dismissals, convictions of lesser (misdemeanor) offenses, or by other alternatives to felony prosecution.[23] The study suggested that the Chicago system accommodated a number of factors: the police preferred to file more cases since this increased their clearance rate; they accordingly accepted a judge's dismissing or reducing the charge on many cases; the grand jury process would bog down if many more cases were bound over to it; the prosecutor's office was not staffed to handle a substantial increase in formal felony prosecutions. Since this study, the Cook County State's Attorney (prosecutor) has undertaken extensive felony screening. The preferable approach is to invoke the prosecutor as a strong screening agent to determine whether there is a likelihood of conviction if a case is filed, and to ascertain what particular charge or charges are justified by the evidence.[24] Good prosecutor screening involves questioning the arresting officer and witnesses, and a careful examination of police procedures incident to arrest, interrogation, and search.

The 1971 Cleveland study, conducted by this author, initially examined thirty-five felony arrests and discovered that the charges listed by the police at the time of arrest differed from the charges formally filed by the prosecutor in at least seven of thirty-five cases.[25] For example, charges of armed robbery and forgery in one case were changed to carrying a concealed weapon and possession of firearms; carrying a concealed weapon was changed to assault and battery; grand larceny was changed to petty larceny. Also in the study, prosecution screeners were asked to record what actions they had taken on 100 cases brought to them by police. The responses indicated different attitudes by different screeners. The senior deputy recorded that as to sixty police referrals he had certified all sixty for filing without any change in charge. Police officers more often brought their cases to him, expecting approval of virtually anything they presented. The junior deputy rejected one of twenty complaints he screened, deciding that one case represented an accidental shooting rather than a crime. The chief police prosecutor, as to twenty cases, rejected three and reduced one to a misdemeanor. It would seem that due to this more powerful position, he chose to exercise greater latitude in the screening process.

Overcharging bogs down a system. It encourages excessive plea bargaining. Each step in the system requires careful screening. Yet the police too often bring doubtful cases to the prosecutor or preliminary hearing judge, the prosecutor transfers the real screening responsibility to the court, the preliminary hearing judge binds over cases which could be disposed of through a more rigorous hearing or negotiation process, the grand jury rubber-stamps the prosecutor's evidence, and the result is heavier criminal court dockets, delays in processing, more defendants waiting longer in jail before disposition, and increased costs which accompany this "back ending" of where the buck finally stops.[26]

The Preliminary Hearing

A major purpose for the preliminary hearing is to obtain a speedy review by a judicial officer as to whether the evidence is sufficient to warrant the case going further into the system. The preliminary or bindover hearing frequently occurs in the lower criminal court. It is required in many states for felonies, but not for misdemeanors. It is the right to such a hearing which is required in these states; the defendant may waive the hearing.

During his 1971 Cleveland study, this author timed thirteen preliminary hearings in the Cleveland Municipal Court. The median time for preliminary hearings was seven minutes. All thirteen were bound over. Cleveland prosecutors commented informally that 98 or 99 percent of preliminary hearings resulted in bindover decisions. Observation of other hearings in that court, clocked at a median time of less than two minutes each, found seventeen defendants waiving the preliminary hearing in what the author recorded as "a rather informal procedure doubtfully understood by the defendant." Yet in some courts the preliminary hearing is a vigorously contested process providing significant benefits. It serves at least five additional functions: (1) A discovery device where a defendant can learn certain of the evidence and may obtain approval to inspect certain reports and physical evidence in the prosecutor's possession; (2) As a substitute for a full trial—notably in Los Angeles County, the verbatim transcript of the preliminary hearing may be submitted to the felony court judge with the stipulation that no evidence other than the transcript is offered; (3) To determine the legality of detention; it is a seizure when one is jailed and a judicial body may consider whether or not the arresting officer had reasonable cause to arrest; (4) To determine the constitutionality of certain procedures used in acquiring evidence against the defendant; (5) An opportunity for a defendant to enter a guilty plea prior to the hearing or after the hearing, to the charges presented or to modified or lesser charges.[27]

The Trial

Plea bargaining often continues up to the moment a trial is to begin. The pressure of an imminent trial brings a new reality to negotiations between lawyers. Analyses of the percentage of felony defendants who actually go to trial on felony charges reflect a range from 2 to 20 percent in various jurisdictions.[28]

A felony jury trial generally takes two or more days to complete. The same case tried before a judge would be briefer, since there is no need to impanel a jury or provide for jury deliberations. A felony jury may be isolated or "locked up" throughout a trial. This process seeks to immunize the jury from outside media and from the comments of friends and family, and to restrict juror input to what they actually hear in court. Major legal arguments are heard by the judge in his chambers outside of the hearing of the jurors.

A trial is constitutionally required to be public, in recognition that this is the public's business, and that fewer arbitrary trials will occur when the trial process is exposed to public view. The defendant must be present but need not testify. The burden is on the state to prove the offense. The judge may dismiss the charge following the completion of the prosecutor's case if insufficient evidence was presented to permit the case to go forward. When a defendant is found innocent, the charge must be dismissed even if serious errors were made in the conduct of the trial. Our Fifth Amendment provides, ". . . nor shall any person be subject for the same offense to be twice put in jeopardy of life or limb." A defendant may appeal a guilty conviction, initially to the court where he was convicted, then to a higher court.

Sentencing

In most states sentencing is the responsibility of the trial judge. But as to capital cases, most states vest the decision as to death or life imprisonment with the jury. Jury decision power over the question of life or death represents a societal preference to spare the judge of this awesome responsibility. Some states provide for jury sentencing for lesser crimes, although this is not a wise policy.[29] Greater equalization of sentences can be achieved where judges have the sentencing power. A probation presentence investigation should be conducted, and presented at a sentencing hearing where defense counsel may cross-examine the probation officer or other witnesses, and where the prosecutor may comment. Typically, the felony sentencing hearing is briefer and less elaborate than the dispositional hearing in juvenile court. There are, however, serious disparities in sentencing practices among judges of the same court, and among judges of different courts.[30] This creates critical morale problems in a prison which mixes defendants from all over a state, who typically discuss their offense and court experience. Two defendants with similar offense records may receive grossly disparate sentences, incarcerating one for ten years or more than the other.

Sentencing reform efforts take the following directions:

a. Statutory simplification and standardization of crimes and sentences;
b. Statutory elimination of, or restrictions on, sentencing discretion;
c. Legislation or court rule specifying that a sentence must be the least restrictive alternative compatible with community welfare;
d. Improved presentence investigation reports;
e. Judicial sentencing institutes;
f. Provisions for review of sentences by other judges;
g. A sentencing council where the sentencing judge consults with two other judges before entering his disposition;
h. Extended research which feeds back the results of the use of various types of sentences;
i. Requiring judges to record their reasons for each sentence.[31]

Judicial resistance to severely impaired sentencing discretion and sentence review is anticipated since judges, at the top of the system's status ladder, experience job satisfaction due to the broad sentencing powers they hold.[32]

Judges, asked to list the major factors they consider in sentencing, typically record the severity of the present offense, the prior criminal record, the defendant's employment record and present employment, and whether he is confined at the time of sentence. There are other factors: the defendant's attitude, his lawyer's skills, his racial and ethnic background, his socioeconomic status, the use of weapons, and more. The Administrative Office of the United States Courts reported for fiscal year 1965 that judges in one circuit used probation as a sentence 44 percent of the time, while judges in another circuit sentenced defendants to probation 64 percent of the time. When federal probation officers recommended that the judge grant probation, it was in fact granted in 94 percent of such hearings. But when these probation officers recommended incarceration, judges were less prone to accept the recommendation, and 20 percent of these defendants were nonetheless granted probation.[33] When a defendant has been found guilty of more than one offense and is ordered incarcerated, the judge may order the sentences to be served either concurrently or consecutively. A concurrent sentence means that two sentences are combined into one, and the defendant really serves just one sentence. A consecutive sentence means that when the defendant completes his first sentence, he then begins to serve the second.

Appeals and Post-Conviction Remedies

Criminal case law is made in the appellate courts and not in the trial courts. A trial judge's opinion is limited in its effect to his own division of the court. Fellow criminal judges in the same court are not bound by his decision, although they may be influenced by it. The appeals of cases to state appellate courts and to federal courts result in written opinions which have binding application. Convicted defendants have a right to counsel, and to free counsel, to assist them in the preparation of appeals. These appeals litigate countless police and trial processes, as well as the substance of the crime itself. Certain victories by defendants raise the further issue as to whether the new decision will have retroactive effect upon other persons previously convicted under similar circumstances. The mandatory right to free counsel for indigents is one type of case which was held to have retroactive effect because of the intimate connection between the absence of counsel and the fact-finding process in trial.

Recent years have also seen rigorous judicial review concerning the administration of prisons. Through this process, as well as through legislative enactment, prisoners have acquired certain rights. Further, the processes by which incarcerated defendants are considered for parole release, or, when paroled, experience revocation of parole status, have also been subjected to critical court review, and an enunciation of further procedural rights for a defendant.[34]

The Felony Courts—Internal and External Issues

Probably no one considers that the felony processing system cannot be substantially improved. And more people are beginning to understand that the whole of the system requires improvement and enrichment, and that change in one part of the process has impact on other parts. The present reform thrust owes substantial measure to input of funds through the U.S. Law Enforcement Assistance Administration (LEAA). The allocation of these funds, however, has sometimes caused further imbalance to the system. For some years the courts failed to aggressively seek funds for major improvements. Law enforcement agencies vigorously snared substantial monies from this source. Neither the courts nor correctional agencies were prepared to handle an increasing criminal caseflow with effectiveness.

An enormous number of issues confront the criminal justice system. Within the context of the felony court, certain issues should be emphasized:

"Front End" the System

It is important that each functionary at each stage of the system take greater responsibility for the thoroughness of his investigation and for researching ways for more flexible and speedier decision processes. Better police training and supervision produces more legally sound cases. Doubtful cases should be shortstopped. Prosecution screeners should be highly experienced lawyers. The early appointment of defense counsel, and a mandatory prosecutor–defense counsel conference prior to the filing of a case, could lead to more speedy dispositions.[35] A rigorous rather than a casual preliminary hearing has been shown to force out at that stage 37 percent of felonies, either through dismissal or reduction to misdemeanors.[36]

Diversion programs will grow, and will at times be extremely controversial, although society is recognizing it may be in its best interest to keep more offenders out of a justice system which may be destructive in itself. The issue is to develop the alternative service programs which offer more rehabilitative gains than a justice system may directly provide. It is extremely significant that American Bar Association Standards set forth:

> a. The prosecutor should explore the availability of non-criminal disposition, including programs of rehabilitation, formal or informal, in deciding whether to press criminal charges; especially in the case of a first offender, the nature of the offense may warrant non-criminal disposition.
> b. Prosecutors should be familiar with the resources of social agencies which can assist in the evaluation of cases for diversion from the criminal process.[37]

Strengthen Public Defender Services

It would seem that neither the public at large nor its elected officials have yet been willing to accept the supposition that the effective provision of legal defense services is as important as the effective provision of prosecution services. That the Supreme Court has repeatedly had to define due process as compelling the right to free counsel if indigent, symbolizes our reluctance to expend monies for those charged with breaking the law. The slowness with which state and local courts have implemented this right to counsel is an even graver disgrace. The right to counsel arises at the point of arrest, covers the interrogation and investigation phase, and continues throughout court proceedings and the appellate process. All too few communities provide counsel at the earliest stages of the process, or provide sufficient funds to enable an appropriate staffing of its public defense agency. Yet despite numerous problems public defender organizations appear to offer the most efficient and most economical approach for the provision of legal defense services. Many communities still appoint private attorneys to perform the basic representation of indigent offenders.[38] Such an approach has serious disadvantages—it cannot effectively provide the needed services, but it should be retained, in part to complement an organized defender service, and partly to retain the interest of the private bar in searching for improvements to the criminal justice system. Such a joint approach was recommended by the National Advisory Commission on Criminal Justice Standards and Goals.[39]

Pretrial Release Alternatives

Despite progress in implementing alternatives to the commercial bail bondsman, the great majority of communities have failed to implement suitable alternative systems. The evidence is clear that a well-conceived and well-administered approach for determining eligibility for release on recognizance, backed up with a 10 percent deposit plan for those defendants not eligible for "ROR," for regularizing notice to defendants to appear at court hearings, for providing interim counseling and assistance, and for speedily searching out the defendant who fails to appear, is both more humane and less costly than traditional money bail practices. There are of course risks to this approach, such as when a released defendant may commit a heinous crime while pending initial trial. But the present bail system does not bail out only those least likely to commit another offense. And retaining countless persons unnecessarily in jail is expensive and often self-defeating.

Speedy Trial

State after state is now enunciating mandatory time frames within which defendants shall be processed. Failure to bring an offense to trial within this time limit, except where delay is occasioned by the defendant's inability to go to trial, may result in dismissal of the charge. Usually, for felonies, these rules mandate time limits of from two to six months. Despite the immensity of the processing problems which must be solved the constitution guarantees a speedy trial, and the mechanisms and the administration must be discovered and implemented.[40]

Caseflow Management and Management Information Systems

We now know how to track cases through the system and to ascertain at any time where the delays occur. We know, if we will only implement, how to improve the scheduling of judge time, how to make better use of juror time, and how to reduce delays. Larger jurisdictions have computerized information systems to provide the data to systematically tell us what is happening, and to permit court management to take the necessary steps to eliminate the problems. Smaller courts can use manual systems or other less complicated approaches to getting the information they need to manage effectively. While computers raise certain issues and problems, our present system is loaded with problems, some of which can be remedied by computer.

Statutory and Rule Revision

Too many states have failed to comprehensively update their criminal codes and their rules of criminal procedure. Statutory sentences are frequently far too long; certain lesser offenses actually permit a lengthier penalty than certain more severe offenses. Moral viewpoints still pervade the law, and we label behavior which may not injure others but which we dislike as a crime, and clutter the courts with unnecessary felony causes. Drug use exemplifies this problem. Certain matters should be decriminalized, sentences should generally be briefer, the courts should accept still greater responsibility for monitoring their sentences and issue orders to insure that maximum treatment and reform are actually achieved.

Strengthened Community Alternatives

We have begun to enrich probation services, and a variety of other community agencies are providing more employment, counseling, mental health services, and other forms of assistance which reduce the need for imprisonment, and probably offer more hope for an individual's reordering his own life. But we hope for more than these programs can now deliver. The defendant, retained in the community and offered a supportive counselor, is often still far removed from opportunity, from having any real chance for upward mobility, from finding the strength to say no to the destructive environment and confused value system which surround his daily life experience. We know that big prisons don't work, and that small prisons are not much better. Yet certain people do require incarceration. But the future lies in community corrections, and the more sentencing alternatives available to the judge, the less we will need to continue our overreliance upon the prison. Many of these issues apply to the lower criminal courts as well.

Questions for Discussion

1. Discover what offenses are felonies and misdemeanors in your state, and how these are classified. Which are victimless crimes? Which felonies may appear less serious than certain misdemeanors?
2. Learn from an official of the nearest felony court the number

of felony informations and/or indictments filed during the previous year, and the number of felony trials heard by the court (judge) and by a jury.
3. Are grand juries used routinely in your state for all felony indictments, or used only in special cases? Discuss grand jury proceedings with the prosecutor responsible for this function.
4. Should plea bargaining be abolished?
5. Observe a preliminary hearing of a felony case in a local court. What did defense counsel learn from the hearing which may be useful to him in a later proceeding involving the defendant?
6. What factors should a judge use in determining the sentence of a convicted felon?
7. What amount of time lapse, between the filing in court of a felony charge and the trial of a felony charge, should be tolerated under the constitutional requirement of a speedy trial? Find out your state or local court rule governing the time space prior to a felony trial.
8. What is the purpose of bail?
9. Observe several bond and bond reduction hearings to understand the interaction of the judge, lawyers, and defendant.
10. Should jailed defendants awaiting trial be required to perform work by jail authorities?
11. Should indigent defendants who plead or are found guilty be required to pay, at a later date, for their free lawyer? What if they are found innocent, or if their case is dismissed?
12. Following a plea or finding of guilty, how much time should be necessary for a probation officer to complete a presentence investigation, and for the sentencing hearing to be completed?

References

1. Interview with Judge Joseph Quinn, Denver District Court, September 13, 1973. For two weeks prior to this discussion, a Denver newspaper carried page one and other prominent stories concerning management scandals in the state prison, the firing of the acting warden, violence between different inmate groups, photos of the confiscation of inmate weapons, a report that one inmate had died of drug overdose, a report of the attorney general's investigation, a prominent state legislator's urging of a grand jury probe of the prison, and the governor's suggestion that the state embark on a program of decentralized, smaller imprisonment facilities around the state. It may have been that the prison crisis influenced this probation department to recommend against imprisonment in the seven cases.
2. National Advisory Commission on Criminal Justice Standards and Goals, *Courts,* Standard 3.1 (Washington, D.C.: Government Printing Office, 1973).
3. American Bar Association Project on Minimum Standards for Criminal Justice, *Standards Relating to Pleas of Guilty,* Standards 3.1–3.4 (Chicago: American Bar Association, Approved Draft, 1968).

4. *Quarterly Survey of Judicial Salaries in State Court Systems* (Denver: National Center for State Courts, June, 1975).
5. American Bar Association Commission on Standards of Judicial Administration, *Standards Relating to Court Organization* (Chicago: American Bar Association, Approved Draft, 1974), p. 60.
6. 11 D.C. Code Ann., Sec. 11–101 et seq. (1972 supp.).
7. National Advisory Commission, *Courts,* Standard 8.1; President's Commission on Law Enforcement and Administration of Justice, *The Challenge of Crime in a Free Society* (Washington, D.C.: Government Printing Office, 1967), pp. 128–29.
8. Frederic W. Maitland and Francis C. Montague, *A Sketch of English Legal History* (New York: Putnam, 1915).
9. Hurtado v. California, 110 U.S. 516, 4 S.Ct. 111 (1884).
10. Ted Rubin, *The Felony Processing System, Cuyahoga County, Ohio* (Denver: Institute for Court Management, 1971), pp. 31–32.
11. Duncan v. Louisiana, 391 U.S. 145, 88 S.Ct. 1444 (1968).
12. Williams v. Florida, 399 U.S. 78, 90 S.Ct. 1893 (1970).
13. Apodaca v. Oregon, 406 U.S. 404, 92 S.Ct. 1628 (1972).
14. Johnson v. Louisiana, 406 U.S. 356, 92 S.Ct. 1620 (1972).
15. See the following works by or about great American trial lawyers: *Attorney for the Damned* (Clarence Darrow), ed. Arthur Weinberg (New York: Simon and Schuster, 1957); Quentin Reynolds, *Courtroom—The Story of Samuel S. Liebowitz* (New York: Farrar, Straus and Young, 1950); Lloyd Paul Stryker, *For the Defense* (New York: Doubleday & Co., 1947); Arthur Garfield Hays, *City Lawyer* (New York: Simon and Schuster, 1942).
16. Herbert L. Packer, "The Courts, the Police and the Rest of Us," *Journal of Criminal Law, Criminology, and Police Science* 57 (September 1966): 238. Lawrence P. Tiffany, "The Fourth Amendment and Police-Citizen Confrontations," *Journal of Criminal Law, Criminology, and Police Science* 60 (December 1969): 442.
17. *A Model Code of Pre-Arraignment Procedure,* Tentative Draft No. 3 (Philadelphia: American Law Institute, 1970).
18. National Advisory Commission on Criminal Justice Standards and Goals, *Police,* Standard 4.3 (Washington, D.C.: Government Printing Office, 1973).
19. American Bar Association Project on Minimum Standards for Criminal Justice, *Standards Relating to the Urban Police Function,* Standards 4.2 and 4.3 (Chicago: American Bar Association, Approved Draft 1973).
20. Daniel J. Freed and Patricia M. Wald, *Bail in the United States: 1964* (Washington, D.C.: National Conference on Bail and Criminal Justice, 1964).
21. Frederic Suffet, "Bail Setting: A Study of Courtroom Interaction," *Crime and Delinquency* 12 (October 1966): 318.
22. American Bar Association Project on Minimum Standards for Criminal Justice, *Standards Relating to Pretrial Release* (Chicago: American Bar Association, Approved Draft, 1968), p. 26.
23. Donald M. McIntyre, "A Study of Judicial Dominance of the Charging Process," *The Journal of Criminal Law, Criminology, and Police Science,* 59 (December 1968): 463.
24. National Advisory Commission, *Courts,* Standard 4.4.
25. Rubin, *Felony Processing,* p. 13.

26. Lewis Katz, Lawrence Litwin, and Richard Bamberger, *Justice is the Crime, Pretrial Delay in Felony Cases* (Cleveland: The Press of Case Western Reserve University, 1972).
27. Kenneth Graham and Leon Litwin, "The Preliminary Hearing in Los Angeles: Some Field Findings and Legal-Policy Observations," *U.C.L.A. Law Review* 18 (May 1971): 916.
28. Sol Rubin, *Law of Criminal Corrections* (St. Paul, Minn.: West Publishing Co., 1973), p. 54.
29. National Advisory Commission, *Courts,* Standard 5.1.
30. Leonard Cargan and Mary A. Coates, "The Indeterminate Sentence and Judicial Bias," *Crime and Delinquency* 20 (1974): 144–56; Marvin E. Frankel, *Criminal Sentences: Law Without Order* (New York: Hill and Wang, 1973); John Hogarth, *Sentencing as a Human Process* (Toronto: University of Toronto Press, 1971).
31. Frankel, *Criminal Sentence;* Hogarth, *Sentencing;* Norval Morris, *The Future of Imprisonment* (Chicago: University of Chicago Press, 1975); Joseph D. Tydings, "Ensuring Rational Sentences—The Case for Appellate Review," *Judicature* 53 (1969); 68–73.
32. Gerald D. Robin, "Judicial Resistance to Sentencing Accountability," *Crime and Delinquency* 21 (1975): 201–12.
33. Robert M. Carter and Leslie T. Wilkins, "Some Factors in Sentencing Policy," *The Journal of Criminal Law, Criminology, and Police Science* 58 (December 1967): 503–14.
34. Morrissey v. Brewer, 408 U.S. 471, 92 S.Ct. 593 (1972).
35. Katz et al., *Justice is the Crime.*
36. *Felony Processing System in Denver* (Denver: Institute for Court Management, 1971).
37. American Bar Association Project on Minimum Standards for Criminal Justice, *Standards Relating to the Prosecution Function and Defense Function,* Standard 3.8 (Chicago: American Bar Association, Approved Draft, 1971).
38. *The Other Face of Justice, A Report of the National Defender Survey* (Chicago: National Legal Aid and Defender Association, 1973).
39. National Advisory Commission, *Courts,* Standard 13.15.
40. See National Advisory Commission, *Courts,* Standard 4.1, which urges "The period from arrest to the beginning of a felony prosecution generally should not be longer than 60 days." Six years earlier, the recommended standard was four months. See President's Commission, *Challenge,* p. 155.

3 The Lower Criminal Courts

The lower criminal courts represent a stepchild of the American judicial system. In these frequently worn and cramped quarters, millions of Americans annually appear before the bar of justice.

Of the three basic courts which are organized to consider an individual's violation of criminal law—the felony court, the lower criminal court, and the juvenile court—the court which bears the greatest volume, the court which is daily faced by more alleged law violators than any other, is the lower criminal court. The President's Commission on Law Enforcement and Administration of Justice pointed this up: "While public attention focuses on sensational felony cases and on the conduct of trials in the prestigious felony courts, 90 percent of the nation's criminal cases are heard in the lower courts."[1] Probably only the traffic courts of this country hear more cases involving law violations than do the lower criminal courts. But traffic courts are expressly organized to consider alleged violations of motor vehicle laws, and while traffic courts do have the power to sentence a defendant to jail for certain violations, they are not considered within the definition of the lower criminal courts. They are, however, considered within the definition of lower courts, which is a generic term referring to courts whose jurisdiction, or range of authority, is limited to lesser violations of law, and lesser claims in civil actions.

The lower courts, then, include the lower criminal courts, the traffic courts, and civil courts which handle a range of disputes involving claims up to $5,000 or $10,000, and other civil issues such as landlord-tenant matters and complaints for return of property.

A lower court is generally seen as an inferior court, "inferior" for a variety of reasons:

1. The judge is not always required to be a lawyer;
2. The judge frequently receives an inferior salary in comparison with judges of a court of general trial jurisdiction;
3. A verbatim record is not always made of the proceedings;
4. Appeal from a lower court decision is typically heard in a court of general trial jurisdiction, not in a state's appellate court system;
5. The physical facilities of the lower court are frequently inferior to those of a court of general trial jurisdiction.

The lower criminal courts are the forums which still receive the countless cases of public drunkenness, except in those states which in recent years have repealed these statutes or ordinances. These are the courts which process the innumerable violations of state misdemeanor statutes and local ordinance violations; they are the court of the prostitute, the petty gambler, the lesser thief, the shoplifter, and the disturber of the peace.[2] Here is where disorderly conduct cases are reviewed, and where vagrants are sentenced, although vagrancy statutes have increasingly been held unconstitutional as punishing an ill-defined status rather than a specifically described act. These are the courts typically associated with impoverished defendants; probation services offered in these courts are generally inferior; the jails receiving these defendants provide little in the way of rehabilitation.

A former U.S. Supreme Court Chief Justice, Charles Evans Hughes, stated more than fifty years ago:

> The Supreme Court of the United States and the Court of Appeals will take care of themselves. Look after the courts of the poor, who stand most in need of justice. The security of the Republic will be found in the treatment of the poor and the ignorant; in indifference to their misery and helplessness lies disaster.[3]

While the average criminal defendant in this court has been charged with a violation of a state misdemeanor or a local ordinance, or of a more serious motor vehicle violation which has been defined as a misdemeanor, such as driving while intoxicated, this court also frequently exercises a limited role with the felony offender. It does not adjudge the guilt or innocence of the felony offender, nor does it generally mete out a sentence, but in many jurisdictions the judge of this court advises the felony defendant of his rights, determines the amount of bail, and conducts a preliminary hearing on the charge. The preliminary hearing occurs within a relatively short time following arrest. The purpose of this hearing is to ascertain, following a presentation of evidence against the defendant, whether there is probable cause to believe that a crime has been committed, and probable cause to believe that this defendant has committed the crime. Theoretically, this is a protection for the defendant. If the evidence is insufficient, the charge is dismissed. If sufficient evidence is found, the defendant is bound over for consideration by a grand jury as to whether an indictment shall issue, or in some states, he is bound over for a criminal information to be filed by the prosecutor in the felony court. In practice this hearing is frequently cursory.

Structure of the Lower Criminal Courts

Across the nation the lower criminal courts include municipal courts, city courts, county courts, justice of the peace courts, mayor's courts, and similar forums. Not infrequently there are two or even three such courts within one county of a given state. The administration of justice in these courts has been criticized for decades.[4] Court reorganization in some states has abolished the justice of the peace court, but has left municipal courts and county courts to exist side by side. Other states have consolidated their lower courts to achieve a simplified structure. Connecticut, for example, in 1961, reorganized a variety of courts into a single lower court system, uniform throughout the state, made up of lawyer judges. Florida, Hawaii, and Alaska represent structurally advanced states where there is only one lower trial court along with one upper, general trial court.

Just as there is a movement to enhance the status of the juvenile court, and generally to promote its becoming a specialized division of the court of highest general trial jurisdiction, so is there also a development, as has occurred in Illinois, to absorb the lower courts into the court of highest general trial jurisdiction.[5] This latter court is known by different names in different states: the district court, the circuit court, the superior court, and in New York, the supreme court. It is further confusing that in some states the title "district court" or "circuit court" refers to an inferior, lower court, while in all but a few states the supreme court is the highest appellate court.

Advocates of court restructuring urge one of two basic models for the trial courts. Both approaches, however, urge a single trial court:

1. A one-tier trial court system where there is a single level court, comprised of a number of divisions, presided over by judges of equal status. This is the District of Columbia model. For example, there may be a juvenile or family division, criminal division, civil division, traffic division, probate division, and other divisions. All judges would need

to be lawyers. This would be the only court other than the appellate court system. Judges would be elected or appointed to the total court rather than to one of the divisions. They would then be assigned to a division. The basic concept of the inferiority or superiority of trial courts would largely be erased. A judge in a criminal division might hear felony as well as misdemeanor cases. Theoretically the most prestigious judge of the court could be assigned to hear minor traffic, civil, or criminal matters.

2. The two-tier trial court system. This is the Illinois model. Within this single trial court there would be two levels. The higher level might include a felony division, a civil division with jurisdiction over larger money claims, a probate division, and a juvenile or family division. A lower tier would include traffic, lesser civil claims, and lesser criminal violations. Judges of the upper level would be accorded a higher rank and higher pay than lower level judges. A variation of this latter approach was enacted in Florida during the past several years. There, county courts are the inferior courts, and are separate from the circuit court, which is the court of highest general trial jurisdiction. But the Florida circuit court is given supervisory and administrative authority over the various county courts within its circuit.

The ultimate goal should be the one-tier system, and this has been recommended by both the American Bar Association[6] and the National Advisory Commission on Criminal Justice Standards and Goals.[7]

History of the Lower Criminal Courts

Legal historians, in describing the historical development of the lower criminal court, typically refer to two models: the more rural court, frequently titled the justice of the peace court, and the more urban court, frequently called the municipal court. Neither setting received many charitable reviews. The justice of the peace was generally not required to be an attorney, and was sometimes best known as one who performed marriages. A neighbor, and one with strong community ties, he was frequently short on law and long on enforcing established local behavior norms. He heard ordinance violations, issued search and arrest warrants, determined bail, arraigned defendants, and processed civil cases involving limited dollar amounts. Traffic violation cases became in time a strong focus of his duties. This functionary was necessary in the development of America, with its isolated pockets of population, its absence of modern transportation, and the need to hear minor criminal matters speedily, which meant locally.

One problem with this judicial system was that justices of the peace, often called JP's, heard legal matters in undignified settings. Cases would be heard in the living room of the justice's house, or at the gas station where he was employed. He was on call at all hours, and defendants were taken by law enforcement officials to wherever the justice was at that time. Lawyers who practiced in more urban settings, but who might represent an occasional defendant before a JP, were frequently appalled by the latter's lack of legal knowledge. This justice had little opportunity to know that a state supreme court had entered a ruling on a certain matter. If he did know of the ruling, the decision often appeared irrelevant to him.

The method of compensating the justice for his services created further indefensible problems. In some states the justice was paid from the court costs he would assess against a defendant found to have violated a law. If he found the defendant innocent, he would not assess court costs. Therefore he had a clear interest in convicting any defendant who appeared before him, since otherwise he would receive no compensation.[8] Countless defendants protested that under this system they had not really had their day in court.

Further, this justice frequently felt a responsibility to the local community which had appointed or elected him to the position. The more defendants he found guilty, the more fines he could assess, and the more income he could generate for local governmental cash registers, the greater likelihood he would continue in office. Further, law enforcement officers could often select the particular justice they wished to have hear a particular case—justices with little respect for law or the Constitution but with great rapport with their community establishment would frequently receive more than their share of the cases. It was not common for justices to overrule police judgment or the desires of the local prosecutor. Defendants learned that it was often easier and cheaper to simply enter a plea of guilty rather than contest a charge, since in effect they were presumed guilty and would have to pay additional court costs for a "trial."

The incompetencies and inequities of these legal forums led many states to develop a somewhat more sophisticated local area court in place of the justice of the peace. But JP's still exist in a decreasing number of states where they have convinced elected lawmakers that their closeness to their community and their interest in its residents are advantages and that justice would deteriorate were this system to be eliminated.

States like Louisiana have in recent years sought to do away with their justice of the peace system, but political complaints have presented strong resistance to change. In that state the first justices of the peace were appointed by the governor, following legislative authorization in the second decade of the nineteenth century. The Louisiana Constitution of 1845 shifted this position to a two-year elective post. The justices were given authority over municipal and parish (county) criminal ordinances where penalties did not exceed $100. But a subsequent Constitution in 1898 created mayor's courts, and legislation transferred jurisdiction over lesser criminal matters to them. The mayor also served as a judge on traffic matters and certain other legal suits. As of 1973 there were 252 mayor's courts in that state serving towns of less than 5,000 population, and approximately 465 justices of the peace.[9] The Louisiana Constitution of 1921, still in effect in 1973, provided, "Justices of the Peace shall be of good moral character, freeholders and qualified electors, able to read and write the English language correctly, and shall possess such other qualifications as may be prescribed by law."[10] Court reorganization proposals in that state have urged doing away with both justices of the peace and mayor's courts. In 1972 the U.S. Supreme Court held that serious constitutional problems arose when an elected mayor also served as the judge of a local court, and particularly when the court was the income source for a substantial portion of municipal revenue, through fines, forfeitures, costs, and fees. The court in that case held that a citizen was denied a fair trial before a disinterested and impartial tribunal, as guaranteed by the Fourteenth Amendment, when the judge was also the mayor who was also responsible for administering municipal finances.[11]

The urban analogy to the justice of the peace and the mayor's court is the municipal court. Municipal courts in our large urban centers have attracted the most public attention, and certainly the most critical attention. The origins of this court seem to lie in the early development of the position of magistrate, who was in effect the supervisor of local police officials. Police officials would bring allegations to the magistrate, who often personally continued and deepened the investigation into the crime and decided whether the defendant should be bound over for trial, often appearing at the trial himself, prosecuting the defendant, and testifying against the defendant based on his investigation. As time went by the magistrate withdrew from making direct investigations and the police came to be headed by their own chief, but the magistrate, clearly now within the judicial branch, held bind-over hearings where police and other witnesses presented evidence, and the magistrate decided whether or not the evidence was sufficient for the cause to proceed.

All municipal courts hold authority to hear violations of municipal ordinances, and while many of them hear traffic cases, others also conduct the preliminary or bindover hearing to ascertain whether there is sufficient evidence on a felony charge to bind over the defendant to the felony court. The "system" is further complicated in that in many jurisdictions violations of state misdemeanor laws are handled in lower county or district level courts, which may also hear preliminary hearings. In analysis of the criminal justice processing system, analysts often lump the municipal ordinance violation courts and the state misdemeanor violation courts together, whether they are joined as one court or are separate, since together they represent the forums where millions of petty offenses are heard each year.

The world of the lower court criminal magistrate has been characterized by an enormous people flow, a speedy "justice," a great deal of noise, and relatively little legal defense. In most states the maximum punishment for a municipal ordinance violation or a misdemeanor offense has been one year in a local jail. The more established lawyers have generally avoided these courts, and though there were many exceptions, the criminal bar which practiced there was often held in relatively low regard within the legal fraternity. Until recent years many of these courts made no official verbatim transcript of what transpired there. A defendant could appeal an adverse decision to a higher status trial court where he would receive a "de novo," or completely new, trial, since there was no record to be reviewed.

While in 1963 the U.S. Supreme Court had ruled that an indigent defendant was entitled to a free lawyer in a felony prosecution,[12] and while in 1967 the same court ruled that a juvenile charged with a law violation was also entitled to free counsel if indigent,[13] it was not until 1972 that the court ruled in *Argersinger* v. *Hamlin* that an adult defendant charged with an ordinance violation or a misdemeanor offense was also entitled to free counsel if indigent.[14] In these three cases the court reasoned that the issue was the threat to liberty, and in such circumstances the guiding hand of legal counsel was constitutionally necessary to provide fair protection for the defendant. The court recognized that deprivation of freedom, even for a short time, had important impact upon the defendant, upon how others viewed him, and upon his record. The court decreed that the administration of justice must be a balanced system where, since the interests of the state are represented by a prosecuting attorney and by police officials, the interests of justice must provide rich and poor defendants alike with the opportunity to be represented. Prior to the *Argersinger* decision, defendants could be represented by attorneys in these courts if they had the funds to employ counsel. Also, some jurisdictions had previously appointed publicly paid counsel for defendants charged with nonfelony offenses. Most observers believe that the presence of counsel has been generally helpful to defendants. The defendant may still be convicted, but frequently counsel is able to negotiate a plea of guilty to a lesser offense, or his advocacy may result in a sentence of probation rather than incarceration.

In many communities a municipal court is physically a part of the police and jail building, or adjacent to it. Many urban jails are filled beyond their capacity, represent a demeaning milieu to residents and to staff, and warehouse people there unnecessarily, inadvisably, and detrimentally. While we do need jails, their presence has diverted our energies from finding suitable alternatives to pretrial and post-trial jailing.

Historic bail bond systems, often using disreputable commercial bail bondsmen, have permitted those who could afford bond to be released while the impoverished defendant has languished in his cell awaiting trial or disposition. It has been difficult, even for our best judges, to consistently adhere to the presumption of innocence when a disheveled defendant appears before him without counsel, with a jail guard or law enforcement official attached to him or standing nearby.

The urban political machine frequently viewed the lower courts as a center for party patronage, and not infrequently controlled the appointment or election of the judge. His bailiff and clerk were often political functionaries, more dedicated to the party and to enhancing their judge's ego than to the administration of justice. The prosecuting attorneys were often the newest or most inadequate members of the prosecutor's staff. Defense counsel who did appear were often more interested in maintaining their relationship with the judge than in vigorously advocating their client's cause. The courtroom was often ill-lit, with paint-flaked walls and ceilings, hard benches, and little dignity, and the judges, if they were lawyers, were typically low status members of their profession.

However, these magistrates often dominated their settings more than their rural counterparts did theirs. The judge was the key person in the urban lower court, and in the face of an enormous caseflow exercised rather wide discretion in ordering certain cases dismissed, or in abbreviating the law, or in issuing sarcastic or humorous remarks to gain laughs from police and court functionaries.

In the early 1920s two great legal scholars, Roscoe Pound and Felix Frankfurter, surveyed the administration of criminal justice in Cleveland, Ohio, and entered a rather scathing denunciation of the Municipal Court of that city. There they found the assembly line of justice broken down by quantity and devoid of quality.[15] Fifty years later, this author returned to the Cleveland Municipal Court to conduct a study which included direct observation of ninety-eight cases heard in that court. This author recorded:

> The Criminal Division of the Cleveland Municipal Court is located in the Police Building at 21st and Payne. The courtroom is well worn, crowded, and noisy. Row on row of benches are peopled with defendants out on bail, witnesses, friends and relatives of

> defendants, attorneys, social service personnel, and others. Most attorneys sit at the several counsel tables at the front of the room. The judge is flanked by a representative of the clerk's office to his right and two police officers. To his left is his bailiff. An assistant police prosecutor is present on one end of the judge's bench, an assistant county prosecutor on the other. A stenotype reporter was added during April, 1971, and sits along the bar in front of the judge immediately next to the defendants and counsel who appear. The arraignments, hearings, and conferences which occur at the bench are largely inaudible beyond the second or third row of the spectator gallery. Witnesses generally testify from standing positions off to the side of the judge. There is little dignity to the setting. Jailed defendants are brought in and out from a door behind the judge and off to his right. People leaving the courtroom go out a door in the front of the room and off to the judge's left, where outside noise enters the courtroom as the door opens and closes.[16]

Part of the problem in Cleveland and elsewhere is numbers. The President's Crime Commission reported that in 1962 over four million misdemeanor cases were brought to the lower criminal courts of the nation. The commission found that prior to 1966, in the District of Columbia, four judges processed the preliminary stages of more than 1,500 felony cases, and heard 7,500 serious misdemeanor cases, 38,000 petty offenses, and an equal number of traffic offenses annually. Further, that in Detroit, over 20,000 misdemeanor and non-traffic petty offense cases were handled by a single judge sitting in one division. In Atlanta, in 1964, three judges of the Municipal Court disposed of more than 70,000 cases.[17]

Another problem is language. The employment of court interpreters has not kept pace with the number of defendants who lack a basic competency in understanding the English language.

The Processing of Lesser Criminal Offenses

Differential decision-making accompanies the processing of persons alleged to have committed lesser offenses. A primary difference in processing lesser adult offenders, compared with alleged juvenile offenders, is the greater reliance by the adult system on jail or bail as a precourt process (most juvenile court acts do not provide for bail, but emphasize that children should be returned to parental custody unless retained in a juvenile detention facility because of likely danger to themselves or others were they to be released).

A further major difference is that misdemenant processing involves less attention to intake screening: social-psychological-environmental factors are less frequently considered when deciding whether a charge should be formally filed. Further, judicial sentencing in these courts is typically performed with no, or at most limited, presentence study of the defendant by probation staff. Finally, municipal and misdemeanor court probation departments have higher caseloads than juvenile probation organizations, and the probation assistance provided is more narrow and traditional. Misdemeanor probation caseloads averaged 114 in one multijurisdiction survey.[18] By contrast, juvenile probation caseloads are frequently twenty-five to fifty youths.

Initial Discretion: The Police-Public Interface

It can generally be said that law enforcement officials are more careful to have a solid case when they process a felony charge than when they bring a lesser charge, and that the more serious the felony, the more care is utilized as to legal procedures and evidence gathering. Within this simple scale of seriousness then, police officers often have less investment in the lesser offenses. For example, the common offense of disturbing the peace may require a very subjective and hasty decision by a policeman as to whether the noise, the language, or the conduct is sufficient to justify removing an individual from the scene. Disturbances are frequently ignored by policemen. A police officer may simply wish to remove an offender from the public setting, bring him to the station house, warn him, and release him. For other disturbances, and for a variety of reasons, the policeman may wish to prefer formal charges against a defendant. For some cases he may be satisfied if the defendant is jailed a few days, comes before a judge, and is then dismissed because the judge views the matter as nonserious. For others, he may strongly desire that the defendant be jailed for a more prolonged period. Disorderly conduct is another common charge somewhat similar to disturbing the peace.

Baltimore, Maryland, police, during 1964, brought 2,837 charges of disturbing the peace and 11,490 charges of disorderly conduct. Further, 9,288 charges of drunkenness were preferred among the overall 62,437 charges police brought before the municipal court that year. A significant number of persons had more than one charge preferred.[19] Multiple charging may be done because the facts support several different charges, or because in some communities there is a bargaining system where the defendant is overcharged with the expectation that one or more of these charges will be dismissed later upon agreement between the prosecutor and defense counsel. A problem for the unrepresented defendant in such a circumstance is that he knows little about plea bargaining, and more typically will admit to all offenses, thereby obtaining an expanded criminal record which may well injure him when he is brought to court on a future offense.

Not everyone who is arrested is charged. Not everyone who is charged has been arrested. Not everyone who is charged is convicted. Not everyone who is convicted is incarcerated. We have no idea how many Americans annually have police contacts at which officers decide whether or not to take the person into custody. But we do know that some police officers proportionately arrest and charge more defendants than others. Further, we know that some communities wish their police to enforce certain offenses rigorously, and other offenses less rigorously.

The first screening decision is that of the arresting officer. A further screening decision may be made by a higher level police official, who should anticipate that a prosecutor or court may throw out the charge due to insufficient evidence. Police officials are increasingly diverting lesser offenders away from court. It has been well known that police officials, when confronted with a husband-wife assault situation, frequently seek to placate the couple and dissuade the more offended party from filing a formal complaint. The increased training which police officials are receiving in interpersonal conflict resolution should reduce the number of these cases, and of similar neighbor-to-neighbor problems, which become formal complaints. Further, police are increasingly referring these parties to community social and mental health agencies for professional services.

The Bail-Jail Alternative

An accused is arrested. He is brought before a magistrate. The magistrate sets bail in a given amount, usually related to the seriousness of the present offense. If the defendant owns property with equity in excess of the amount, legal evidence of property ownership may be placed with the court to satisfy bail. More typically a defendant, relatives, or friends locate a bail bondsman and pay him a premium, usually 10 percent of the face amount of the bond. The bondsman then provides evidence to the court that he will stand behind the full amount of the bond in the event the defendant does not appear for trial. Some defendants, of excellent community standing, are released "on their own recognizance," without providing property or money bond. But enormous numbers of defendants charged with lesser offenses can provide none of these alternatives, and are detained in jail pending court disposition.

Significant bail reform activities have been underway in this country for more than a decade. The grandfather of bail reform was the Manhattan Bail Project of the Vera Institute of Justice in New York City.[20] During the early 1960s, with the cooperation of the courts and the prosecutor, this project provided a new alternative to that community's widespread overjailing. Persons charged with lesser offenses were interviewed and information was obtained as to employment history, family relations, length of time in the community, and prior criminal record. A point scale was developed to measure stability and criminality factors. Large numbers of defendants whose scores indicated a high probability of voluntary return to court were released without bond "on their own recognizance." Follow-up studies of these defendants revealed that with a small percentage of exceptions they did return to court as required.

The Vera experience had led to replication of the project in hundreds of communities throughout the nation, and has spawned extensions of this program which provide job finding assistance, social and mental health counseling, and other programs to released defendants.[21] Pretrial jail use has been significantly reduced, fewer defendants are separated from their families and their employment, fewer families apply for welfare aid, and enormous savings accrue to the community. The Seattle Municipal Court reported in 1974 that 92 percent of the 4,600 defendants released on personal recognizance through its pretrial release service did appear for subsequent court proceedings.[22] Yet many states and communities have been slow to respond to bail reform and jail alternative programs.

Bail for ordinance violations and misdemeanor offenses commonly runs from $100 to $2,000, with $500 the amount for a typical offense. Raising 10 percent of this amount, to hand over to the bail bondsman to temporarily buy one's freedom, is an impossible chore for many of our poor. Even when this money is raised it is not returned to the defendant when he shows up for trial: it is retained by the bail bondsman for his service. A number of courts now permit the defendant to deposit ten percent of the bail with the court, or with an approved public pretrial release agency, and when the defendant appears he is refunded 90 percent of the 10 percent he had deposited. The remainder is retained to help administer this program.[23]

Prosecutor Screening and Charging

The ideal system for the next stage of the criminal justice process, the involvement of the prosecuting attorney, would include the following:

Police officers would bring their report to the local prosecutor, who would pursue the adequacy of the legal case against the defendant. Prosecutors should be concerned not only with whether there is probable cause to believe the defendant committed the alleged crime, but whether there is a likelihood the defendant could be convicted at trial. This is known as the prosecutor's screen. At least as to lesser offenses, the prosecutor should consider alternatives to going to court: drug treatment services, alcoholic treatment services, community counseling, education and job training programs. The future should see increased diversion programs available to the prosecutor to provide alternatives to formal court processing.[24]

The prosecutor would then weigh all of the above information with the following additional criteria: the seriousness of the offense, the prior record of the defendant, the maximum punishment authorized for this offense, the victim's willingness to testify, community attitudes regarding this offense, and a prediction of the defendant's ability to remain out of further trouble if this charge is dropped or deferred.

But in many communities, prosecutor screening is limited to felony offenses, and the police, rather than the prosecutor, decide whether or not a case should be filed. In too many communities the prosecutor receives information as to lesser offenses the morning the defendant is to be arraigned. He has often graduated from law school within the past year, has had no formal in-service training before assuming his duties, and is overwhelmed by the number of cases he is responsible for. He is often dominated by the judge, and is even more dominated by the system which moves volumes of defendants through the treadmill and seems to take for granted that a cursory treatment of the case is all that can be done. Part of the problem is that too little care has been taken at the earlier stages of the criminal process, where many cases might better have been screened out through statutory repeal of victimless crime offenses, through increased diversion options to defendants, or through more careful legal screening. Prosecutor offices have focused heavily on the trial aspects of the system. But more prosecutors are now awakening to the realization that they no longer have to be victims of the process, but can achieve changes in the system to reduce the volume and improve the quality of individualized justice. Good prosecutor screening brings improvement to the quality of police investigations, and curbs arrests which are not well founded.

Initial Arraignment

Arraignment is the legal term for the process whereby a defendant is brought before a judge or magistrate, is given a copy of the formal charges filed against him, is advised of his constitutional rights, has his bail determined if this has not been done previously, and is asked to enter a plea. If he requests a continuance to enter a plea at a later date, so that he may obtain counsel or for other reasons, the entry of plea may be deferred. For many defendants this means a return to the local jail, and the wait until counsel is employed or appointed, the attorney conference and investigation, and the subsequent return to court.

One may enter a "not guilty" plea, and on or before the date of trial change the plea to "guilty." This is frequently done on the advice of counsel to enable the defense attorney to negotiate the dismissal of other charges. It is difficult to withdraw a guilty plea once it has been offered in open court. This has been done, however, on showing that the defendant lacked knowledge of his right to counsel, or of the extent of potential incarceration, or that a prosecutor had not adhered to a plea bargain. A defendant's waiver of rights must be "knowing and intelligent." He must know what rights he is waiving, and the consequences of such waiver.

A judge may prefer to hold as few trials as possible, and may subtly discourage a defendant's exercise of his right to counsel and to trial. More commonly, judges meticulously advise as to rights, and encourage representation by counsel. Many courts and communities are really not tooled up to provide an adequate system of defense counsel for indigents. Other courts and communities accept this responsibility as critical to a balanced administration of justice. Some courts still ask lawyers to volunteer their services to an indigent defendant. Other courts appoint private attorneys to this responsibility and compensate them from tax funds. A model used by many larger communities for the provision of defense services is the office of public defender. There, generally, full-time attorneys are publicly employed to render defense services for the indigent.

There are also mixed systems involving the appointment of private attorneys and publicly employed counsel. The public defender model is essentially independent of the judges, can employ a stable of specialists on a par with the prosecutor, and is more free to challenge judicial procedures and decisions. But a defender system can break down when its caseload overwhelms the staff attorneys, or when it lacks experienced investigators to assist the attorneys with trial preparation. The National Advisory Commission on Criminal Justice Standards and Goals recommended that larger jurisdictions maintain both approaches, a direction which would wisely retain private attorneys' interest in improving the criminal justice system.[25]

Trial

Trials of lesser offenses are often quick and abbreviated. While there are many exceptions, trials are frequently completed within a half hour, and trials are more often before a judge than a jury. Many defendants do not request counsel and plead guilty. The Hennepin County Municipal Court (Minneapolis, Minnesota), reported in 1974 a cases-arraigned-to-cases-tried ratio of less than 7 percent.[26]

The U.S. Supreme Court ruled in 1968 that any offense which may subject an adult defendant to more than six months of imprisonment must be accompanied with the right to a jury trial.[27] It is interesting that in the aftermath of this case the State of Louisiana redesigned the penalty clause attached to a number of its lesser offenses, making these subject to no more than six months imprisonment, thereby reducing the opportunity for a defendant to request a jury trial. Maine, Colorado, and other states nonetheless provide jury trials for petty offenses where a penalty of less than six months is the maximum sentence.

Sentencing

In many lower criminal courts, when a defendant enters a plea of guilty or is found guilty at trial, he is immediately sentenced. In other courts the sentencing decision is continued for several weeks to enable probation staff to complete a presentence investigation. In many communities there are essentially no probation services, presentence investigations, or community supervision services assisting the lower criminal courts. In other courts there is a separate probation arm, organized only to serve that court, and generally inferior to probation programs in the juvenile and felony courts. Caseloads for such probation officers are seldom fewer than 100 per officer, and sometimes exceed 200. Obviously, the supervision provided is minimal or nonexistent.

Another form of probation organization, organized under the county executive or administered by the judiciary, serves juvenile offenders and all adult probationers through divisions of a single department. There is at least a fourth model, with a separate juvenile probation department, and a combined adult probation department serving the lower and upper criminal courts. Figure 3 illustrates several approaches to the organization of probation services.

Figure 3. Examples of Misdemeanor Probation Organization

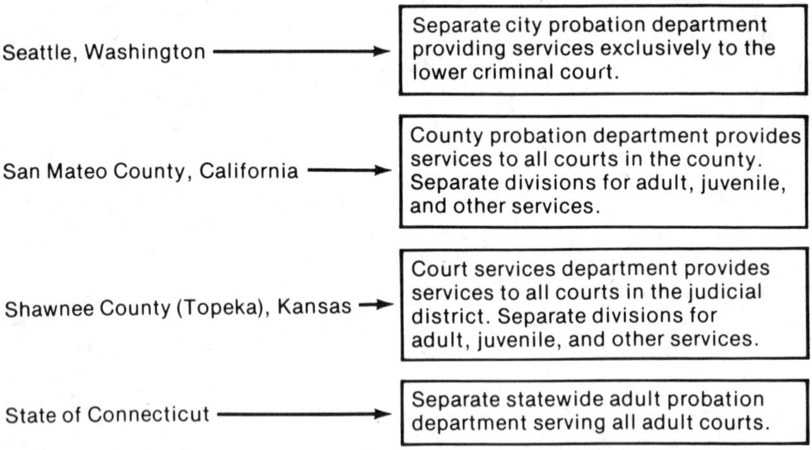

Combined probation departments generally provide better probation services than those organized solely to serve a lower criminal court. The larger organization generally affords higher standards for recruiting, training, and supervising probation officers.

Statutes and ordinances generally prescribe the outer limits of judicial sentence: not more than thirty days in jail and/or a fine not to exceed $50; not more than one year in jail and/or a fine not to exceed $500. Over the years, defendants who were unable to pay their fine served out their time in jail. But in 1970 the U.S. Supreme Court struck down this practice in the case of *Williams* v. *Illinois*. Defendant Williams was given the maximum sentence for petty theft, one year's imprisonment and a $500 fine. The Illinois statute provided that if, when the one-year sentence expired, Williams did not pay the fine, he was to remain in jail a sufficient length of time to satisfy the fine, at the rate of $5.00 per day. The court held this violated the Equal Protection Clause of the Fourteenth Amendment and represented invidious discrimination against the poor.[28] Shortly after, the court held a related practice unconstitutional. The defendant in that case had accumulated fines of $425 on nine convictions of traffic offenses in Houston, Texas. Unable to pay the fines because of indigency, defendant was required to serve eighty-five days at the prison farm and to satisfy the fines at the rate of $5.00 for each day. This, too, was held to be invidious discrimination, and violative of the Equal Protection Clause.[29]

But masses of defendants are still sentenced to grimy jails or to overloaded probation services. Despite improvements in a number of communities, the prospect for speedy and major improvement remains dim. A number of courts have added citizen volunteers to augment their limited probation programs, and more jails are also adding volunteer services, developing in-service staff training programs, and employing educational and correctional counselors.

The Lower Criminal Courts—Internal and External Issues

In 1967 the President's Crime Commission entered certain findings and concerns about the lower criminal courts:

> It has seen cramped and noisy courtrooms, undignified and perfunctory procedures, and badly trained personnel. It has seen dedicated people who are frustrated by huge caseloads, by the lack of opportunity to examine cases carefully, and by the impossibility of devising constructive solutions to the problems of offenders. It has seen assembly line justice.[30]

The commission further observed: "While jail sentences of 1, 2, or 3 months are very common, probation appears to be used less frequently than it is for presumably more serious offenses in the same jurisdiction."[31] A system that treats defendants charged with minor offenses with less dignity and consideration than it treats those charged with serious crimes is hard to justify. The unification of courts and services may provide a sound way to bring about long overdue improvement in the standards of the lower courts.

Who comes into these courts is one issue to be addressed. Substantial progress is being made to reduce the vast numbers of public drunkenness cases processed through these courts. While the alternative health and social service programs required to assist these persons remain grossly inadequate, we are at last getting through to the public that public drunkenness and criminality can no longer be equated. Further, legal challenges have resulted in the voiding of vagrancy charges as unconstitutionally vague, and we can now expect a reduction in such charges. A further large hope for reduced cases in this court lies in the prospect of diversion. While many are troubled by the concept of diversion, believing that if one has committed an offense he should be brought before a court, the diversion concept now has strong momentum, recognizes the reality of court overload and limited effectiveness, and recognizes that many lesser crimes represent personal or social adjustment problems more meaningfully addressed by noncorrectional agencies.

While court reorganization and unification moves at a slow pace through legislative halls, there is an acceleration of activity in this area. What is needed is that we address the problems of lower courts on a state basis rather than on an individual court basis. We need to lift these courts up through a comprehensive plan that enhances lower court justice on a total state basis, rather than just pushing for a particular court to improve itself. This also relates to the need to place the lower criminal courts within a state court system, augmented by substantial state funding. Further hope lies in a more widespread employment of trial court administrators. During the past five years, a number of court managers have made marked progress in improving the administration of justice in their courts. Upgrading the skills of court clerks should be a further priority.

Part of the problem in achieving a more equal status for the lower courts is a certain jealousy and opposition from higher level trial court judges.[32] These judges are used to looking down upon the lower court judges, with their lower salaries, lesser legal qualifications, shabbier quarters, and heavier caseloads. But the administration of justice is weakened by any weak link. And most felony defendants were once defendants in the lower criminal courts. The lower criminal court and the upper criminal court should be one court, and the sooner this is accomplished, the better.

There are examples of good bail and pretrial release programs,[33] but implementation of these reforms remains scattered. And while the American Bar Association has recommended the abolition of the private commercial bail bondsman, his office can still be seen across the street from the courthouse in most American cities. The economics of reduced jail and bail use has been demonstrated repeatedly, but still our local jails are filled.

We are doing a better job of training prosecution and defense counsel, and judges of this level and all levels have been attending an increasing number of judicial education programs to increase their skills and knowledge.

But the lower court system is a systematically bad system, and requires comprehensive as well as structural change. Bar associations have neglected this court in their work to improve justice. Supreme courts, with administrative responsibility for state court systems, have also neglected these settings. Like the juvenile courts, the lower criminal courts have been largely isolated from the centers of judicial power.

We are getting about what we pay for in the lower courts. The quality of justice is inadequate. Funding is inadequate. But just doubling the manpower will not double the quality of justice. We have demeaned the misdemeanor court, and the result is more business for the felony courts. We have an undernourished probation-rehabilitation system in the lower courts,[34] and this has influenced the development of more costly correctional services for misdemeanant offenders turned felons. The citizen has been disinterested in this court, to the detriment of his own self interest.

Questions for Discussion

1. Should there be a right to a jury trial for petty offenses subject to jail sentences for not more than six months?
2. Why have legislatures which repealed public drunkenness as a crime, not also repealed criminal liability for crimes committed while intoxicated?
3. Why must prosecutors prove a criminal charge beyond a reasonable doubt?
4. In an approach to priorities, should misdemeanor courts be allocated more, fewer, or the same equivalent resources as the felony courts?
5. What approach to bail is prevalent in your community?
6. Should any judge who has power to sentence an offender to jail be required to be a lawyer?
7. Should the police exercise discretion, with a provable offense, in referring an offender for prosecution?
8. Are there any formal adult diversion programs in your community? If so, who is the sponsoring agency: Prosecutor? Probation? Court? Private nonprofit corporation? For the previous year, what percentage of cases diverted to the program were felonies? Misdemeanors?
9. Is there a public defender system in your community? An assigned private counsel system? Both Systems?
10. Ideally, what alternatives should a lower criminal court judge have available at sentencing?
11. Does wearing a white shirt and tie improve a convicted defendant's chances for probation? Is bail or jail status of a convicted defendant an influencing factor in a judge's sentencing decision?

References

1. President's Commission on Law Enforcement and Administration of Justice, *Task Force Report: The Courts* (Washington, D.C.: Government Printing Office, 1967), p. 29. For a useful reader on these courts, see John A. Robertson, *Rough Justice: Perspectives on Lower Criminal Courts* (Boston: Little, Brown & Co., 1974).
2. Raymond Moley, *Our Criminal Courts* (New York: Minton, 1930).
3. Address to the New York State Bar Association, 1919. Proceedings of the New York State Bar Association, pp. 240–41, as quoted in President's Commission, *Task Force: Courts,* p. 29.
4. See *Report on Criminal Procedure:* National Commission on Law Observance and Enforcement (Wickersham Commission), (Washington, D.C.: Government Printing Office, 1931); reprinted (Montclair, N.J.: Patterson Smith Publishing Corp., 1968).
5. Robert C. Underwood, "The Illinois Judicial System," *Notre Dame Lawyer* 47 (December 1971): 247–66.
6. American Bar Association Commission on Standards of Judicial Administration, *Standards Relating to Court Organization,* Standards 1.10, 1.12 (Chicago: American Bar Association, Approved Draft, 1974).
7. National Advisory Commision, *Courts,* Standard 8.1.
8. President's Commission, *Task Force: Courts,* pp. 34–36. *The Justice of the Peace Today* (New York: Institute of Judicial Administration, 1965). For an authoritative history of the development of different courts see Roscoe Pound, *Organization of Courts* (Boston: Little, Brown & Co., 1940).
9. See *Modernizing Louisiana's Courts of Limited Jurisdiction,* (Chicago: American Judicature Society, 1973).
10. La. Rev. Stat. Ann. Const. Art. VII, Sect. 47.
11. Ward v. Village of Monroeville, 409 U.S. 57, 93 S.Ct. 80 (1972).
12. Gideon v. Wainwright, 372 U.S. 335, 83 S.Ct. 792 (1963).
13. In re Gault, 387 U.S. 1, 87 S.Ct. 1428 (1967).
14. Argersinger v. Hamlin, 407 U.S. 25, 92 S.Ct. 2006 (1972).
15. See *Criminal Justice in Cleveland:* Report of the Cleveland Foundation Survey of the Administration of Criminal Justice in Cleveland, Ohio, directed and edited by Roscoe Pound and Felix Frankfurter, 1922; reprinted (Montclair, N.J.: Patterson Smith Publishing Corp., 1968).
16. Ted Rubin, *The Felony Processing System, Cuyahoga County, Ohio* (Denver: Institute for Court Management, 1971), pp. 16–17.
17. President's Commission, *Task Force: Courts,* p. 31.
18. Ibid., p. 32.
19. Ibid., p. 121.
20. Charles E. Ares, Anne Rankin, and Herbert Sturz, "The Manhattan Bail Project: An Interim Report on the Use of Pretrial Parole," *New York University Law Review,* 38 (1963): 67.
21. National Advisory Commission on Criminal Justice Standards and Goals, *Corrections,* Chapter 4 (Washington, D.C.: Government Printing Office, 1973) pp. 98–110.
22. *1974 Annual Report* (Seattle: City of Seattle Municipal Court, 1974), p. 22.
23. Paul Wice and Rita J. Simon, "Pretrial Release: A Survey of Alternative Practices," *Federal Probation* 34 (December 1970): 60–63.

24. "While enthusiasm for diversion in concept may not be inappropriate, it should not obscure the complex evaluative questions that have been left untouched in research up to this point," Raymond T. Nimmer, *Diversion: The Search for Alternative Forms of Prosecution* (Chicago: American Bar Foundation, 1974), p. 108.
25. National Advisory Commission, *Courts,* Standard 13.15.
26. *Hennepin County Municipal Court* (Minneapolis: Hennepin County Municipal Court, 1974), p. 13.
27. Duncan v. Louisiana, 391 U.S. 145, 88 S.Ct. 1444 (1968).
28. Williams v. Illinois, 399 U.S. 235, 90 S.Ct. 2018 (1970).
29. Tate v. Short, 401 U.S. 395, 91 S.Ct. 668 (1970).
30. President's Commission, *Challenge,* p. 128.
31. Ibid., p. 129.
32. Warren P. Marsden, "The California Effort at Trial Court Reorganization, 1970–1972," *Judicature* 56 (1972): 206.
33. Paul B. Wice, *Freedom for Sale* (Lexington, Mass: D. C. Heath & Co., 1974).
34. Tully L. McCrea and Don M. Gottfredson, *A Guide to Improved Handling of Misdemeanant Offenders,* National Institute of Law Enforcement and Criminal Justice (Washington, D.C.: Government Printing Office, 1974).

4 The Juvenile Courts

The juvenile court is a special institution in American society. It receives considerable attention from the general public, and its efforts in behalf of children, families, and the community involve a wide web of collaborating agencies and citizens. It touches the lives of many of the poor. Teachers and school personnel are intensely aware of its presence. The middle and upper class citizens who work to improve social services for children and families learn to solicit the juvenile court judge's support for their efforts. Police officials and the juvenile court staff maintain an ambivalent working relationship—they approach their functions differently, although they share certain common objectives. The judge of this court is far more active, generally, than other judges in exploiting his status to secure the expansion of needed health and welfare services. Serious crimes committed by youth disturb our image that this is the court of the lesser violation.

This court is a far more complex instrument than outsiders imagine. It is law, and it is social work; it is control, and it is help; it is the good parent and, also, the stern parent; it is both formal and informal. It is concerned not only with the delinquent, but also with the battered child, the runaway, and many others. It is undergoing substantial change, possibly more change than any other court. Criminal courts have projected a more predictable role to the public. The juvenile court has been all things to all people. It should probably narrow its scope and more carefully define its purpose.

One starting point for beginning to comprehend the juvenile court is to focus on the question of what the role of the juvenile court should be in this society. To project this role into the future requires an examination of the present and the past. And the examination of the present should focus initially on the structure and jurisdiction of this court. By structure is meant the place of the juvenile court in relation to other courts. By jurisdiction is meant the legislative provision as to those matters which can lawfully be considered by this court. The structure and the jurisdiction of the juvenile court vary from state to state.

The Structure of Juvenile Courts

Factors useful in understanding the structure of the juvenile court, and in ascertaining its relative status among the various courts, include whether it is organized as a higher, lower, or separate court; the comparative pay of its judges; and whether appeals from its decisions are taken to the general trial court or to the state's appellate court system.

In California the juvenile court is really the juvenile division of the Superior Court. The Superior Court is the highest court of general trial jurisdiction. A presiding judge of the Superior Court typically assigns one or more judges to serve in the juvenile division. These judges were appointed as Superior Court judges. They frequently serve a year in the juvenile division and are then reassigned to a different division. Appeals taken from any division of the Superior Court go to an appellate court. The juvenile division, however, does not always have a status which is really equal to the other divisions, and better judges are not always willing to be assigned to the juvenile bench.

In Utah the juvenile court is a separate, statewide juvenile court system. Its judges are appointed by the governor, and throughout their term hear only juvenile cases. A term of office in this juvenile court is six years. The Utah equivalent of the California Superior Court is called the District Court. Utah juvenile court judges receive the same pay as the District Court judges. Appeals from both Utah juvenile courts and District Courts are taken to the Utah Supreme Court.

In Colorado, until 1965, there was one separate juvenile court in Denver; in the other sixty-two counties of that state, juvenile matters were heard in the county court. It was not required that the county court judge be a lawyer except in about ten of the largest counties. The great percentage of judges hearing juvenile cases were not lawyers, though probably the majority of juvenile cases were considered by lawyer judges. The Colorado equivalent to the California Superior Court is the District Court. While a Denver juvenile court judge received the same pay as a District Court judge before 1965, a county court judge was paid less. Further, appeals from the county court were taken to the next court up, the District Court, rather than directly to a state appellate court. The county court was ranked as an inferior court. A 1962 constitutional amendment, followed by implementing legislation in 1964, removed this structural inferiority and placed the juvenile function in the District Court throughout the state except in Denver, where a separate court has been retained.

The Juvenile Court for the District of Columbia, a separate court for many decades, was abolished in 1970 and its functions were transferred to a family division of the new Superior Court for the District of Columbia. In 1972 Delaware created a statewide family court, somewhat similar to Utah, but with a jurisdiction handling a wider array of family-related matters. The District of Columbia and the State of Delaware illustrate the two major structural directions in juvenile court reorganization. The first is the movement to place the juvenile jurisdiction within the highest court of general trial jurisdiction, and to retain its specialness, either as a juvenile or a family division, but within the larger court organization. The latter is the movement to extend the separateness of a juvenile or family court as an independent structure. Massachusetts and Kansas are other states where new and separate juvenile courts have been approved in several communities in recent years. These two directions are in conflict. They may be termed the "Unified Trial Court Movement," and the "Specialized Trial Court Movement." Nationally, there seems to be more support for the former.

There are a variety of other structures for courts of juvenile jurisdiction. One is Maine, where a juvenile court is part of the lower district court in each of the districts of that state. Another includes states like Michigan, where a probate judge (the probate court is responsible for the administration of the estates of deceased and mentally incompetent persons and has jurisdiction over mental illness and retardation commitment procedures), also presides over the juvenile jurisdiction. In a number of states there are separate juvenile or family courts in larger counties, but in the remainder of the state the juvenile function is either in the court of highest general trial jurisdiction (Georgia) with the requirement of lawyer judges, or in a county-level court (Alabama, Mississippi) which does not require a lawyer judge, and where appeals go not to the state appellate court system but to the highest court of general trial jurisdiction.

Figures 4 through 10 illustrate different models of juvenile court and probation organization.

The Jurisdiction of Juvenile Courts

There is enormous variation in the types of matters which can be brought before juvenile courts. In California, four major types of

ORGANIZATION OF COURT OF JUVENILE JURISDICTION AND OF JUVENILE PROBATION AND RELATED SERVICES

Figure 4. Alaska Model

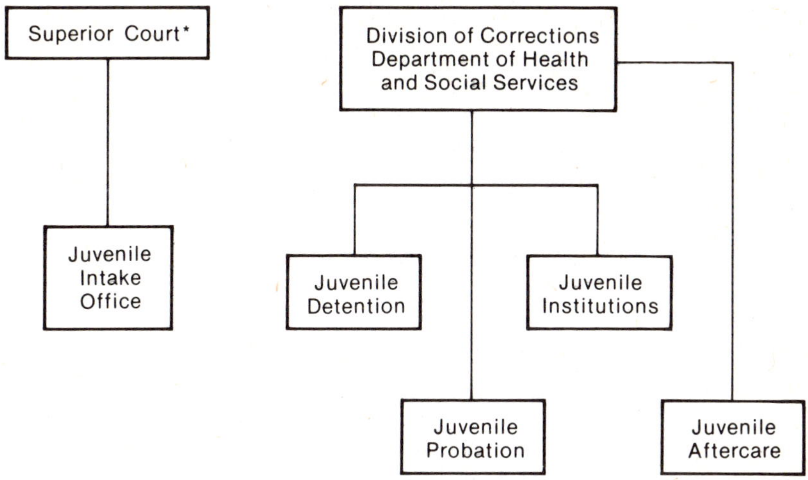

*Highest court of general trial jurisdiction.

Figure 5. California Model

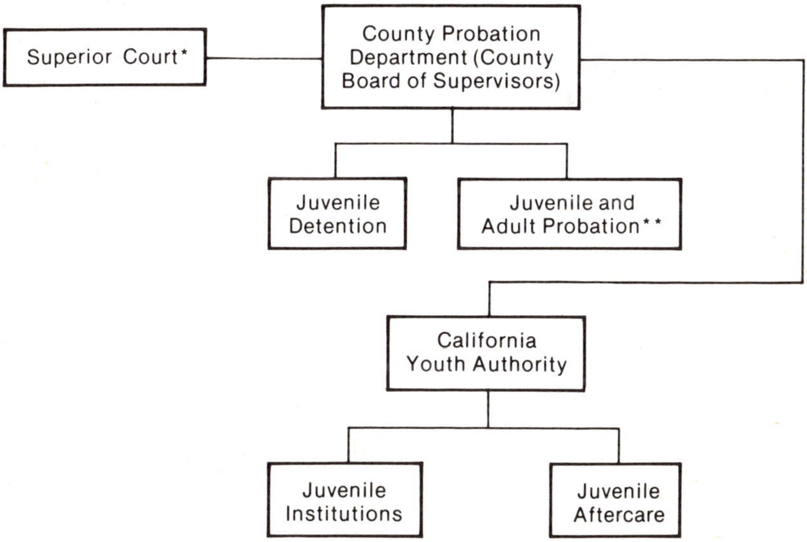

*Highest court of general trial jurisdiction.

**Two counties have separate juvenile probation departments.

Figure 6. Colorado Model

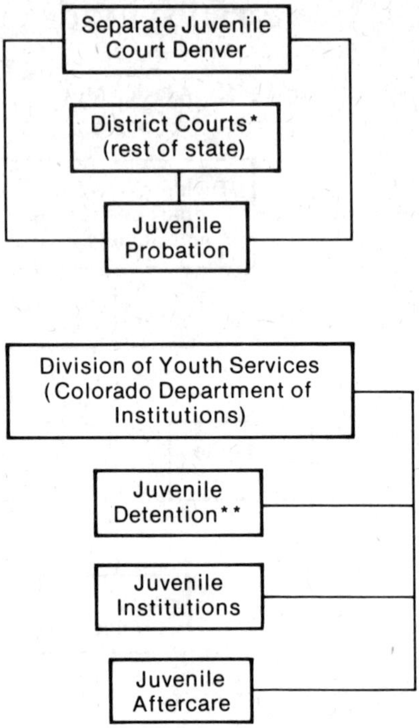

*Highest court of general trial jurisdiction. These courts and all juvenile probation are funded by the state judicial system.

**Detention administration was transferred from the judicial system to the Division of Youth Services on July 1, 1973.

Figure 7. Florida Model

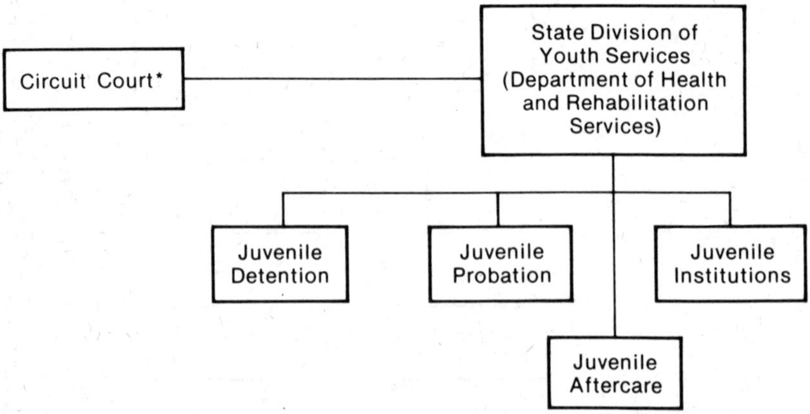

*Highest court of general trial jurisdiction.

Figure 8. Massachusetts Model

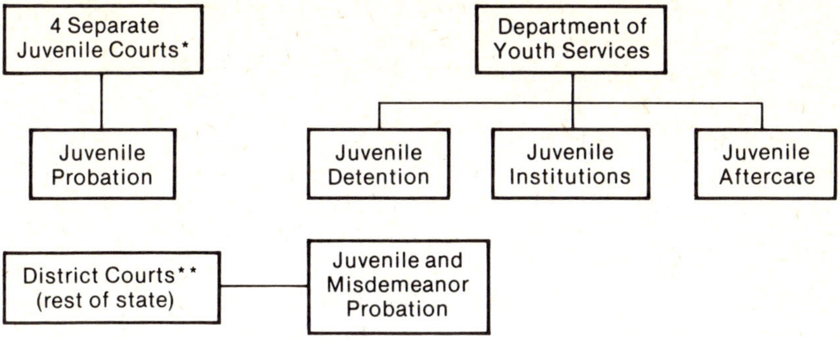

*Boston, Worcester, Springfield, Bristol.

**The Lower Court.

Note: Juvenile probation services are frequently organized into a regional probation district to serve up to five or six district courts within the same county.

Figure 9. North Carolina Model

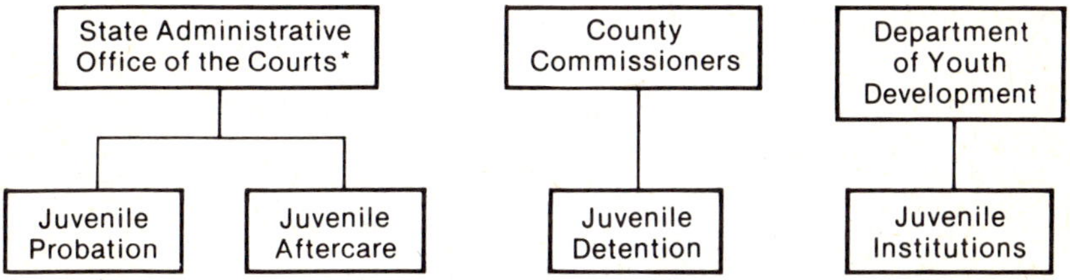

*Juvenile jurisdiction is within the District Court, the lower court. Chief District Court Counselors are appointed by the Administrative Director of Juvenile Services (Administrative Office of the Courts), with the concurrence of the Chief District Court Judge. Court Counselors are appointed by the Chief District Court Counselors, with the concurrence of the Administrative Director of Juvenile Services. The state funds the salaries and expenses of all court counselors (juvenile probation and aftercare workers).

Figure 10. Utah Model

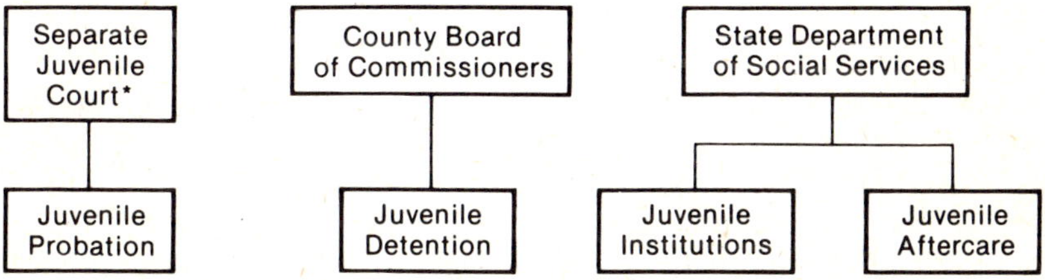

*This is a separately organized, statewide juvenile court. Its judges receive the same pay as judges of the highest court of general trial jurisdiction.

cases are heard by juvenile courts: the delinquent child (Section 602 of the Welfare and Institutions Code), the child in need of supervision (Section 601), the dependent or neglected child (Section 600), and the juvenile traffic offender. All juvenile courts handle the first three types of children and youth. Slightly more than one-third of our juvenile courts deal with the juvenile traffic offender. In the other states, this child is handled as an adult in the basic traffic court.

Utah juvenile courts also have jurisdiction over these four types of matters, although juvenile traffic offenders may be heard either in juvenile court or in the basic traffic court. However, the Utah Juvenile Court Act defines in-need-of-supervision types of offenses as juvenile delinquency. In Utah an habitual truant, or one who is beyond the control of his parents, is labeled delinquent and is subject to commitment to the same delinquency institution to which a child who steals or robs may be sent. California appears to have been the first state to have legislatively separated from juvenile delinquency (Section 602), the juvenile status offenses of runaway, incorrigibility, and habitual truancy, to have categorized these separately (Section 601), and curtailed the power of the juvenile court judge to commit these youngsters to the California Youth Authority.

In 1962, the New York legislature adopted a similar reclassification, calling these children "persons in need of supervision" (PINS). While that legislature also restricted what a judge could do with this child, the absence of community service alternatives to receive or work with these children resulted in a subsequent amendment permitting New York family court judges to place these children in delinquency institutions. In 1965 Illinois adopted a similar provision, titled "minor in need of supervision" (MINS), and in 1967 Colorado established the category "child in need of supervision" (CHINS). During the past fourteen or fifteen years more than half the states have created such a new category,[1] and concurrently have sought to restrict, if not prohibit, the capability of a judge to commit such a child to a state delinquency institution. Until this movement began, these children were known as delinquent children. Whether the child committed an armed robbery or simply ran away from home, the juvenile court judge had the power to place this child in a state delinquency institution. The creation of the "in need of supervision" category reflects the criticism that children are discriminated against by juvenile court legislation. Adults who run away, are incorrigible, or are habitually truant from their vocational or college training programs, are not subject to court intervention or restriction.

A major issue today is whether legislatures should take the next step and remove this type of offense from any sanction by the juvenile court. In the meantime, a child who runs away in Wyoming is a "delinquent child," but his cousin who runs away in New Mexico is a "child in need of supervision." In states such as New Mexico, juvenile delinquency is limited to a violation of a law which when committed by an adult would subject that adult to the jurisdiction of a criminal court.

The "dependent and neglected" category, also known in states such as Georgia as "deprived child," generally refers to the child who is abandoned, who has been subjected to abuse, who lacks proper parental care, or who is failing to receive necessary medical care. The battered child falls into this category. The child whose parents have died, are hospitalized, or are imprisoned, and for whom no suitable private care plan has been provided, is within this category. These children cannot be committed to delinquency institutions, and the judge is restricted to ordering social services, foster home or group home care, or medical or mental health services. Most juvenile courts hold the power to terminate parental rights to this child, involuntarily and permanently under circumstances of severe or ongoing neglect or abuse. Such termination of rights frees the child for adoption, and permits a subsequent application to adopt this child by other parties. However, only about one-fifth of juvenile courts have jurisdiction to hear adoption proceedings.[2] In the other states, the adoption proceeding is heard in a different court. Many states provide that juvenile courts may entertain the petition of a parent or parents who voluntarily seek to terminate their rights to their child. This proceeding is often referred to as "relinquishment." All states permit this proceeding, but generally it is not held in the juvenile court. Relinquishment also frees the child for adoption.

About one-fourth of juvenile courts have been granted jurisdiction to determine the paternity of a child;[3] and to issue support orders for the children. Further, some juvenile courts have jurisdiction over proceedings in connection with a child who is mentally ill or mentally retarded, and subject to commitment to mental health or retardation facilities. Many juvenile courts also hold jurisdiction over adults who may induce, aid, or encourage a child to violate a law. This is frequently known as "contributing to delinquency." Some juvenile courts may also be the center for proceedings against parents who may neglect or abuse their children, and the court may take punitive action against such parents. This is different from the dependency or neglect jurisdiction referred to earlier, where the court's concern is whether or not the child has been neglected rather than whether the parents have neglected this child.

The Utah Juvenile Court Act grants juvenile court jurisdiction over juvenile violations of fish and game laws, but the Colorado statute places such juvenile violators in another court.

Family Courts

The concept of a family court embraces the juvenile jurisdiction plus a range of adult matters which relate to the family. The 1970 District of Columbia law sets forth perhaps the broadest range of family and juvenile matters subject to the jurisdiction of a single family court division. This court has jurisdiction over divorce and the range of divorce related matters such as custody, visitation, property settlement, alimony, and support of children. This court also has jurisdiction over intrafamily misdemeanor offenses, for example when a husband or wife injure each other or another family member. Its jurisdiction also includes paternity, child support (where there has been no divorce), mental illness and retardation as to children and adults, relinquishment and adoption, and delinquency, in-need-of-supervision, neglect, and additional miscellaneous matters. However, the Family Court for Jefferson County, Alabama (Birmingham), the Family Court in New York, and the Family Court in Delaware, are all entitled family courts, but their jurisdiction is less broad, and excludes divorce, for example. It is necessary to go beyond the title of a court to determine its jurisdiction.

The movement to unify courts and place juvenile courts within the court of highest general trial jurisdiction raises the question whether the new juvenile division of this court should really become a family court division. If so, what range of family-related matters should be tied together into one court division?

Jurisdictional Age

The question of what a juvenile court is also requires definition in terms of the age range for the court's original jurisdiction. Approximately thirty-four states including the District of Columbia assert jurisdiction over juvenile offenses until the eighteenth birthday.[4] Five states terminate this jurisdiction on the sixteenth birthday, and all other states on the seventeenth birthday. Until recently, three states had differing sex-age jurisdictional provisions. In Oklahoma juvenile court age went to the eighteenth birthday for girls, but to the sixteenth birthday for boys. Illinois and Texas juvenile courts went to the eighteenth birthday for girls, but to the seventeenth birthday for boys. Appellate court decisions in Oklahoma and Texas voided this age difference as unconstitutional. Illinois, in 1972, made a similar change by legislation. Subsequent legislation equalized the maximum jurisdictional age for boys and girls at seventeen years in Illinois and Texas, and at eighteen years in Oklahoma.

In New York State, where delinquency jurisdiction stops on the sixteenth birthday, but PINS jurisdiction continued until the eighteenth birthday for girls, an appellate court ruled that girls may no longer be subject to court sanctions for status offense behavior at age sixteen or seventeen years, since boys were not similarly subject to PINS jurisdiction after their sixteenth birthday.[5]

In recent years, a number of legislative efforts have attempted to drop the basic delinquency age by one or two years. Such attempts have generally been defeated, although some states have made changes so that within juvenile court age, but above a certain age, those who may have committed certain more serious offenses may be filed on directly in the criminal court and treated as an adult. While the criminal court judge, generally, has more severe sentences available to his disposition, this is not always true. Certain adult offenses are subject to maximum sentences of, for example, two years, whereas the same offense may subject a twelve-year-old youth to a statutory maximum of nine years probation or institutionalization. This is because many states place no restriction on the extent of juvenile probation or institutionalization other than, "to the twenty-first birthday unless sooner discharged." In reality, few youths serve such lengthy sentences, although they frequently serve more time on probation or in institutions and on parole than their adult counterparts.

Six states set minimum ages under which no child may be considered for a delinquency petition. Four states set such minimum age at ten years, two other at seven years.[6] One other age factor requires comment. Many juvenile court acts include provisions for what is known as a transfer or waiver hearing. These provide, generally, that if a child is over a certain age, such as sixteen years (although in some states this is either fourteen or fifteen years) and commits what would be a felony offense if committed by an adult (although some states fail to restrict these offenses to felonies), a special hearing may be held in the juvenile court where the judge considers whether to transfer this youth to the criminal court for consideration as an adult. Whether or not the youth is transferred hinges, usually, on the seriousness of the present offense, the past delinquency record, attempts to rehabilitate the youth, and the capability of the juvenile system to arrange rehabilitative programs which may be expected to achieve rehabilitation without further violation.

A decision to transfer a child to the criminal court should be seen as the most serious decision a juvenile court judge may make. While studies of what happens to transferred youngsters have shown that some are found innocent in criminal court and others are placed on probation, nonetheless the likelihood of an extensive sentence of penal incarceration looms for every youth transferred.[7] The next most serious decision a juvenile court judge makes is the commitment of a youth to a state delinquency institution, symbolic of a failure to achieve rehabilitation at the local level.

In Colorado, where the minimum delinquency age is ten years, Denver police have joked about holding a birthday party for certain children who are about to become ten years of age. The police, who have known these youngsters well from a variety of offenses, can then ask the court to file a delinquency petition. While the behavior of certain of these youngsters could have been categorized as a status offense (CHINS) by court intake, legislative strategy had preferred noncourt assistance for such youthful law violators. Who comes within today's and tomorrow's juvenile court jurisdiction is strongly influenced by our inheritance of early philosophy and practices relating to juveniles and the law.

Juvenile Offenses and the Law Prior to 1899

Early American law descended from English law. On both sides of the Atlantic and for hundreds of years, there was little difference in the application of law between children and adults. The basic criminal law, as set forth initially by the common law of England and then America, expressed the "law of the land," the basic consensus as to what actions should be subject to punishment by the designated instruments of the state we now call courts. Juveniles as well as adults were punished in the criminal courts for a wide variety of actions, from vagrancy to murder, and juveniles were sentenced along with adults to jails and workhouses. One difference was that children under seven years of age were held to be incapable of committing a crime. Further, from seven to fourteen years of age children were presumed incapable of committing a crime, but this presumption could be overcome by evidence supporting the contention the child was capable of criminal intent. Few lawyers accompanied children to court in those days, and the legal and constitutional safeguards which attach to youngsters brought before today's bar of justice were relatively unknown in those times. The jails and workhouses were grim and desolate facilities where limited nourishment, long hours of work, and overcrowded conditions did little to reform juvenile or adult inmates. Possibly the severity of these conditions influenced certain judges and magistrates to accept alternatives to this experience for certain juvenile offenders.

Criminal laws relating to adults and juveniles were strongly influenced by the concerns of those who drafted the Elizabethan Poor Laws hundreds of years ago in England. Vagrancy and idleness were subject to sanction, as were theft and assault. The death or illness of parents, and poverty or tenuous family life conditions, often led children to the streets and toward ultimate arrest. The reach of the law was broad. While it has been speculated that the underpinning of such legislation was to force youth and adults into low pay farm and factory jobs and other underpaid work settings to facilitate entrepreneurial profits, others assessed this coerced encouragement to fulfill the work ethic as good for the individual and good for society.[8]

Begging on the streets was distasteful to the middle-upper class establishment of late eighteenth and early nineteenth century America. Poverty was seen as related to intemperance, and newer immigrants to the eastern United States were judged harshly when their life styles were at variance with those of that day's power elite. In 1824 the New York Legislature authorized that juveniles who committed a variety of crimes, including such lesser offenses as vagrancy and begging, should be confined to a newly established private institution, the House of Refuge in New York City, and to county poor houses in the remainder of the state. Mixed motives apparently accompanied this "reform." While there was concern that the adult prison system was harmful to society's interest in children, there was also a puritan motivation in taking the indolent children of the poor, restraining their liberty and training them in rigorous and monotonous work habits.[9] It was undoubtedly hoped that the funds from the sale of the products of these institutions would come close to the cost of maintaining the facilities. Similar houses of refuge followed in Philadelphia and Boston, and in the 1850s Chicago created a "Reform School" where youngsters were committed by courts for a wide variety of acts.

Beginning in 1853 an alternative to the court system was developed for juvenile paupers and vagrants in New York City, "the placing-out system." Countless juveniles were swept off New York streets onto boats which carried them through New York State and out into the Western Reserve. Families, frequently recruited by religious organizations, would select a youth from the available group, under an indenture arrangement whereby the youth was required to fulfill a rather long-term work requirement in exchange for housing and food. This system was subject to abuse and failure, as well as to some success. But family home placements, as well as the private congregal institutions structured for such youth, were not always effective, and in addition the urban courts continued to handle thousands of juveniles through their normal criminal procedures. However, in the second half of the century, several rudiments of separate processing of juvenile offenders developed in Massachusetts and Illinois, where juveniles were considered in a separate court session, where separate records were maintained and where, in Massachusetts, the use of probation officers was initiated.

The Establishment of the First Juvenile Courts

Reform efforts led by social workers, interested lay citizens, and the Chicago Bar Association, resulted in the 1899 Illinois legislation creating the juvenile court division of the Circuit Court for Cook County (Chicago). This act, "A Law for the Care of Dependent,

Neglected, and Delinquent Children," provided a specialized court with a specialized law relating to children, a restriction on the jailing of children under a certain age, a statement of legislative purpose to reform rather than punish, and among other provisions allowed for the appointment of probation officers. As an omen of the future, the law provided that children under twelve years could not be detained in a jail or police station, but "were to be confined in a 'suitable place,' although no money was provided to lease, build, or otherwise find such a place. A provision to pay for such special detention was deleted by the Legislature."[10]

This act had extended a concept from English law under which the King of England protected the property interests of fatherless children. Known as *parens patriae,* or "the parent of the nation," this doctrine was used to authorize the juvenile court judge to use sentencing alternatives other than those typically practiced in the criminal court, and to provide supervision of these youths in their own homes, to place them in foster homes and private group facilities administered generally by sectarian religious agencies, or to institutionalize them in state facilities. The undergirding philosophy of parens patriae has over the years been both the greatest strength, and perhaps the greatest weakness of juvenile courts. While benevolent intentions have helped many youngsters and families, "helping efforts" resulted in a basic unconcern with legal procedures, and combined with the general inadequacy of available rehabilitative services caused the scarring of countless young people and families.

By improvisation and by legislation, juvenile courts developed rapidly in the larger cities during the first decade of the twentieth century. Historians usually assign the second juvenile court to Denver, whose ebullient and crusading judge Ben B. Lindsey traveled throughout the land and into many European countries advocating this new way of dealing with children.[11]

Juvenile court acts had a delinquency prevention goal: to intervene with children demonstrating predelinquent activities to avert their later delinquencies. Broad jurisdictional clauses subjected virtually any activity by children to the juvenile court's rather awesome powers. A provision of the South Dakota act, finally repealed in 1968, defined a delinquent child as:

> Any child who, while under the age of 18 years, violates any law of this state or any ordinance of any city or town of this state; who is incorrigible, or intractable by parents, guardian, or custodian; who knowingly associates with thieves, vicious, or immoral persons; who, without cause and without the consent of its parents, guardian, or custodian, absents itself from its home or place of abode; who is growing up in idleness or crime; who fails to attend school regularly without proper reason therefor, if of compulsory school

> age; who repeatedly plays truant from school; who does not regularly attend school and is not otherwise engaged in any regular occupation or employment but loiters and idles away its time; who knowingly frequents or visits a house of ill repute; who knowingly frequents or visits any policy shop or place where any gaming device is operated; who patronizes, visits or frequents any saloon or dram shop where intoxicating liquors are sold; who patronizes or visits any public poolroom where the game of billiards or pool is being carried on for pay or hire; who frequents or patronizes any wine-room or dance hall run in connection with or adjacent to any house of ill-fame or saloon; who visits, frequents, or patronizes, with one of the opposite sex, any restaurant or other place where liquors may be purchased at night after the hours of nine o'clock; who is found alone with one of the opposite sex in a private apartment or room of any restaurant, lodging house, hotel, or other place at nighttime or who goes to any secluded place or is found alone in such place, with one of the opposite sex, at nighttime with the evident purpose of concealing their acts; who wanders about the streets in the nighttime without being on any lawful business or lawful occupation, or habitually wanders about any railroad yards or tracks, or jumps or attempts to jump onto any moving train, or enters any car or engine without lawful authority; who writes or uses vile, obscene, vulgar, profane, or indecent language, or smokes cigarettes or uses tobacco in any form; who drinks intoxicating liquors on any street, in any public place, or about any school house, or at anyplace other than its own home; or who is guilty of indecent, immoral, or lascivious conduct.[12]

It was more often the children of the poor who were brought to this court and subjected to its helpful and hurtful intervention. The misbehaving children of the well-to-do were shuttled off to military schools and private educational facilities, psychiatrists, and other resources. Further, the law had taken a remote second place to the interest in rehabilitation.

While the original strategy had been to develop a partnership between the court and the developing professions of social work, psychology, psychiatry, sociology, and education—and indeed the first child guidance clinics, the antecedents of today's community mental health clinics, were developed in conjunction with juvenile courts in Chicago and Boston—the probation staffs and the related community agency services were never enough to meet the high goals of juvenile court enthusiasts. While juvenile courts obtained certain remedial assistance that many families could not obtain through their own resources, state industrial and training schools began filling up with children, juvenile processing became somewhat mechanical, and scores of thousands of children were detained in jails despite general legislative prohibitions to the contrary. One commentator refers to the "long history of financial starvation of correctional systems. Current interactionist sociological theory would have it that the legislature acted so as to ensure an adequate supply of deviant youth."[13]

Mr. Justice Douglas observed in 1969:

> Many things happened which prevented this dream from becoming a widespread reality. First, municipal budgets were not equal to the task of enticing experts to enter this field in large numbers. Second, such experts as we had, notably the psychiatrists and analysts, were drawn away by the handsome fees they could receive for rehabilitating the rich. Third, the love and tenderness alone, possessed by the white-coated judge and attendants, were not sufficient to untangle the web of subconscious influences that possessed the troubled youngster. Fourth, correctional institutions designed to care for these delinquents often became miniature prisons with many of the same vicious aspects as the adult models. Fifth, the secrecy of the juvenile proceedings led to some overreaching and arbitrary actions.[14]

The initial burst of momentum had waned, and comparatively limited commentary on juvenile court practice and legal developments was evident until more modern times.

The Reexamination of Juvenile Justice

Then certain developments led to a renewed interest and concern for juvenile courts. The civil rights movement of the early 1960s, and a series of adult criminal cases appealed to the Warren court, led to U.S. Supreme Court proclamations expanding constitutional protections to minority citizens and criminal defendants. The growing decay of large American cities and our inability to effectively integrate newer urban immigrants and the poor, led to spiraling delinquency rates. The weakening American family, a troubled educational system, the loosening of traditional American values, and growing violence, also accompanied this era. Social scientists directed increasing research interest to juvenile courts and institutions, and reached numerous conclusions critical of the juvenile justice system.[15] Lawyers became more available to juvenile court clients, and began to challenge the adequacy of these hearings and the constitutionality of statutes and procedures. The significance of labeling theory was beginning to be understood. Once the child had been brought into the court, he often saw himself more negatively, and his parents, peer group, and teachers saw him differently. With the broad range of juvenile court jurisdiction, and the limited rehabilitative resources available to the court, there was question whether the court was hurting more children than it was helping.

From 1899 until 1966, no juvenile delinquency case was formally decided by the U.S. Supreme Court. But in 1966, 1967, 1970, and 1971, the court promulgated four decisions which significantly affected American juvenile justice. The most famous of these decisions, *In re Gault,* decided May 15, 1967, signaled that the juvenile court must become a real court, and its procedures must be regularized in accordance with constitutional requirements.[16] The justices were critical of the chronic failures of informal juvenile justice and ordained that children must be provided constitutional protections. The Supreme Court cited studies showing chronic failures in achieving rehabilitation, determined that the real issue was the threat of a deprivation of freedom, pointed out that juvenile institutions were little more than junior prisons, and, among other provisions, extended the right of counsel and free counsel to the child whose freedom was endangered.

Emerging Issues in Juvenile Justice

Juvenile court statutes set forth two major criteria which should govern decisions whether a child is detained, whether a child is handled formally, and the disposition a judge should make once he finds a delinquent act has been committed. These standards are: the best interests of the child, and the best interests of the community.

Obviously, these criteria are not clearly defined. Critics of the court have charged further that the court has been preoccupied with the best interests of the child and has slighted the best interests of the community. They point to the sometimes serious offenses committed by youths and the court's preference to retain youths in the community under probation status, or in conjunction with services provided by noncourt agencies. They point further to frequent repeat offenses by youths placed on probation or returned to their parents pending court consideration. In reality, we are only now beginning to gather reliable data as to recidivism and as to the effect of various interventive strategies in facilitating a juvenile's adjustment.

In part, our society has very mixed feelings about its children. Many recognize that adolescence is a period of experimentation, of searching to find out who one is, of emerging from a more dependent status into greater independence. On the other hand, we still wish to punish our children, or at least maintain a vehicle, such as a juvenile court, to threaten punishment when our children fail to conform to our expectations as to how they should behave. Schools still dump their "troublemakers" on the court. Parents turn to the court when their children rebel against parental expectations. And many believe the police more readily refer a child to court when his attitude is contentious than when he is subservient.[17]

Candidates and other politicians, in trumpeting their concern for mounting delinquency and crime rates, berate processing inadequacies as well as the policies of "soft headed judges." Prominent media attention to such utterances may result in a decision by a judge to detain a juvenile rather than not to detain him, or a decision to institutionalize rather than to continue with probation. While it is true that institutional alternatives remain underdeveloped, and that rehabilitative services are often ineffective, it is also true that many juvenile institutions contribute more to the destruction than the enhancement of the individual. It is important to recognize, however, that to urge improved rehabilitative services, and to veer away from unnecessary institutionalization, is not necessarily to ignore the principle of holding a youth responsible for his misdeeds. It can be said that both critics and friends of the court are dissatisfied with the rehabilitation services provided by or through the court.

Four major directions for juvenile justice now seem clear:

1. That the juvenile court is a court, and law and lawyers will play an increasingly more powerful role in the juvenile court of the future.
2. The movement to narrow the court's jurisdiction will continue. Concern for such victimless offenses as runaway, incorrigibility, and habitual truancy will lessen, while concern will focus more on youths who violate laws which if committed by adults would constitute crimes.
3. The court will rely even more on community-based alternatives to standard delinquency institutions.
4. The court will be increasingly professionalized, with better trained personnel, and with greater research and knowledge about the system utilized more extensively than ever before.

The Juvenile Court as a Court of Law

The Supreme Court's rulings have had marked effect upon the juvenile court. The 1967 *Gault* decision ruled not only that a child had the right to a lawyer and to a free lawyer if indigent, but also that written notice of the specifics of the offense must be provided the child and his parents, that the child must be advised by police officers of his right to silence and of his right to counsel during police interrogation, and finally that hearsay evidence was not admissible in the hearing which adjudicates whether or not an offense was committed. A year earlier, the *Kent* decision ruled that in procedures concerning transfer from juvenile to criminal court due process fairness must attach, a hearing is required, counsel should represent the child at this hearing, and probation officer reports should be made available to the child's lawyer.[18] In 1970, the *Winship* decision ruled that the measure of proof in a delinquency trial must be beyond a reasonable doubt. The court reasoned that since one's freedom was at stake, due process required that the amount of testimony necessary for conviction be as high as the standard used in an adult criminal case.[19]

In 1971, in the *McKeiver* case, the court reverted to an early rationale in ruling that the federal constitution did not compel that states provide the right of jury trial to an accused juvenile. The court majority stated that since the juvenile proceeding was not a criminal proceeding, and since the federal constitution compelled jury trials only in criminal proceedings, juveniles were not constitutionally entitled to jury trials, although a state may legislate this option, or a state appellate court might determine that its state constitution compels a jury trial right within the state.[20] Eleven states allow jury trials for children charged with delinquency, either by statute or by case decision.[21] In many states which allow jury trials for juveniles, this right is infrequently invoked. The court opinion ruling against the right to a jury trial was also based in part on the majority's concern that jury trials might enormously expand court delays and confusion, increase formality and an adversary quality, and further disrupt this troubled institution.

The court resolved a further issue in 1975, deciding in *Breed* v. *Jones* that the double jeopardy clause of the Fifth Amendment applies, through the Fourteenth Amendment, to juveniles. In that case, a juvenile in California had been adjudicated on an armed robbery charge. Rather than receiving "sentence" on this offense, the juvenile court judge transferred his case to a criminal court where he was tried again and sentenced to an institution. The court held that it is the risk of duplicate trial and conviction, rather than the risk of duplicate punishment, which underpins the double jeopardy provision. This decision, then, announced an added constitutional protection for juvenile offenders.[22]

State appellate courts have been far busier than the U.S. Supreme Court in considering questions of juvenile law and procedure during recent years. It is probable that more appeals have been considered during the past five years than in the approximate seven decade prior history of the juvenile court. Legislatures have also been extremely busy in modernizing juvenile codes. Many juvenile codes had not received major revamping for forty years or more. A few states—California, New York, Illinois, Colorado, and several others—had approved major revisions prior to the *Gault* decision, but since then South and North Dakota, Texas, Georgia and Ohio, New Mexico and New Jersey and many other states have recast their juvenile court acts.

The defense lawyer is probably more central to the legal renaissance in the juvenile court than is the judge. Also, the prosecuting attorney will play a far stronger role in this forum in the future than in the past. While annual reports of contemporary juvenile courts still show a limited number of contested juvenile trials, not unlike the criminal courts, lawyer activity in juvenile courts is quantitatively and qualitatively far stronger than in 1967. Law is a clearer priority.

The prosecutor's role is directed toward the community's interest. The defense attorney's objective is the child's interest. But these attorneys have broader concerns. Juvenile prosecutors regularly insist that police officers perform more skillful investigations, or that the practices of probation officers comply with legal requirements. Defense attorneys challenge the constitutionality of various juvenile code provisions and juvenile court practices, and ferret out community resources useful to their clients which may have escaped court attention. They have the adversary role at trial, but perform many other useful services. Yet acceptance and encouragement of attorneys is far from uniform among juvenile court judges, and the assignment of adequate numbers of prosecution staff is frequently of low priority to district attorneys.

A judge's interest in strengthening the legal component of his court depends on certain variables: the state juvenile code; the "cultural environment" of his court and community which encourages formalization or discourages legal representation; his relationship to the funding authority and whether he wishes to jeopardize this relationship by authorizing increased payments for expanded lawyer representation of indigent juveniles; the judge's own convictions, orientation, and background; his tolerance of legal challenges to his procedures and decisions.

Representation of juveniles by defense lawyers varies among the courts from perhaps 5 percent to 100 percent. Certainly the trend is toward greater representation, and there is increasing support for the view that no child should come before a juvenile court judge without legal counsel.

Narrowing the Jurisdiction of the Juvenile Court

The President's Commission on Law Enforcement and the Administration of Justice recommended in 1967 that "The conduct-illegal-only-for-children category of the court's jurisdiction, should be substantially circumscribed so that it ceases to include such acts as smoking, swearing, and disobedience to parents and comprehends only acts that entail a real risk of long-range harm to the child. . . . Serious consideration, at the least, should be given to complete elimination of the court's power over children for noncriminal conduct."[23]

While no state has thus far excised this conduct from juvenile court purview, legislatures have unsuccessfully tried to do this, at least in California and Massachusetts. In 1972 Pennsylvania shifted habitual truancy away from delinquency and into its "deprived child" (dependent/neglected) category, and in 1971 Utah removed the single act of runaway from its delinquency definition, permitting jurisdiction to apply only when this child may be beyond control of his or her parents. Consensus has developed that these children should be more substantially handled away from court, and countless communities have developed a variety of service alternatives to court.

Such a trend is not universal. This author studied one hundred youths referred for delinquency violations and ninety-seven youths referred for juvenile noncriminal conduct (status offenses) between April 1, 1971, and January 31, 1972, to the King County Juvenile Court in Seattle, Washington. Only nine of the former cases were formally filed, while nineteen of the ninety-seven status offenses were filed. Eighteen of nineteen youngsters referred for "ungovernability" were formally filed, although none of the fourteen auto theft referrals and only two of nineteen burglary referrals were formally filed. Interestingly, and this is seen as a common pattern, girls are more commonly represented than boys among status offense referrals, and status offenses are not infrequently detained for longer periods of time in juvenile detention facilities than regular delinquency referrals.

A significant number of legal challenges have sought to invalidate court jurisdiction over status offenses on a number of grounds: as being "void for vagueness" (the statutory description of the banned behavior is not specific enough); as being punishment of a status rather than a criminal law violation; as unequal protection of the law (adults are not brought to court for similar activity). In general, these appeals have been denied by state appellate courts to date. Yet concern for elimination of this jurisdiction is gaining momentum. The National Council on Crime and Delinquency, in 1975, issued a policy statement, "Jurisdiction over Status Offenses Should Be Removed from the Juvenile Court." NCCD has launched a major national program to remove such offenses from juvenile codes in all fifty states and the District of Columbia. A contra position was taken earlier by the National Council of Juvenile Court Judges, however.

The Juvenile Justice and Delinquency Prevention Act of 1974, enacted by the U.S. Congress, stipulates that eligibility for federal funding under this act requires a state plan within two years providing (1) that status offenders should no longer be held in locked pretrial detention centers, and (2) that status offenders should no longer be committed to state juvenile delinquency institutions. This latter provision will strengthen the implementation of Standard 14.1, *Courts,* National Advisory Commission on Criminal Justice Standards and Goals, which recommended a similar concept, and also urged that the definition of delinquency be limited to the violation of an act which would constitute a criminal offense if committed by an adult. The President's Crime Commission had also recommended, "Traffic violations by juveniles should be dealt with by traffic courts, except for serious offenses such as vehicular homicide and driving while under the influence of alcohol or drugs."[24] However, few of the eighteen states which included the basic juvenile traffic offenses within juvenile court jurisdiction have subsequently transferred this jurisdiction to the basic traffic court.[25]

The Increasing Reliance on Community Alternatives to Institutionalization

Despite the pressure from law and order advocates to mete out harsher sentences to juvenile offenders, a number of states in recent years have closed down juvenile institutions or significantly reduced institutional populations. California, through its probation subsidy law, has provided a financial incentive to county probation departments to intensify local probation services, provided commitments to both juvenile and adult state institutions are reduced. The consequence has been a number of closings of both juvenile and adult institutions, with significant cost savings.[26] Massachusetts has taken major steps in shutting down delinquency institutions and offering alternatives through small group home care and intensified community delinquency services. Washington state has shut down a delinquency institution, and Colorado has sharply reduced institutional populations. Monies made available to states and communities through funds from the Law Enforcement Assistance Administration and the U.S. Department of Health, Education, and Welfare have in recent years encouraged the development of a wide variety of community correctional alternatives, notably group homes and halfway houses, youth services bureaus, volunteer programs, decentralized probation services, and the addition of paraprofessional and ex-offender staff aides.

There has been recognition of the high cost of institutional care, the difficulties in effectively administering delinquency institutions, and the relatively high recidivism rate of institutional graduates. Such recognition supports the development of community alternatives. Further, the recognition of the stigma which attaches more significantly to youth the further they go in the juvenile justice system, is increasing the diversion of youth from police and court intake to alternative community services. Also, the increasing presence of defense counsel has placed added checks on the system. Lawyer advocates for children generally advocate against institutionalization and for reduced penetration.

A Heightened Professionalization of Juvenile Justice

Recent years have seen a dramatic expansion of training opportunities for the functionaries of the system. Judges, probation and detention staffs, prosecution and defense counsel, and staff members of a wide variety of related agencies, have taken advantage of increased in-service and out-service training programs to improve their knowledge, skills, and perceptions. Research has expanded, along with the development of more adequate information systems to provide more complete information on what is happening in juvenile courts and related agencies. A number of larger juvenile courts now have computer capability, and regular printouts permit managerial analysis of the system, and allow for greater utilization of this information to change and shift the ways courts and related agencies function. While many juvenile courts lack the managerial capability to utilize the information they gather, court management skills are improving.

The Juvenile Justice Caseflow Process

Juvenile processing is best understood by examining the decisions made at the different discretion points in the caseflow system: the offenses reported and not reported to the police; the juveniles apprehended by police officers, referred or not referred to the court; of juveniles taken by police officers to pretrial detention facilities, those detained and those released; of those detained, which are released one to three days later, following a "detention hearing"; which referred juveniles become the subject of formal court petition; for formal cases, where an offense is admitted to or found to be true, what dispositional alternatives are used by the judge, with which youth, for what reasons?

This process can be seen in the form of an inverted pyramid. At the top of the pyramid, somewhere between two and three million youngsters have police contacts during a year (this is not an unduplicated count: a given youngster may have five or ten police contacts in a year). At the bottom of the pyramid is the number of youths committed to state delinquency institutions. This number has been approximated as 100,000 annually.[27]

Initial Discretion: The Police-Public Interface

Law enforcement agencies are the most frequent referral agents forwarding juveniles to juvenile courts. This is as it should be. Juvenile actions which have come to the attention of police officials should be the major focal point of society's concern for juvenile law violations. While remembering that juvenile arrest provisions are very broad in many states, and that not all offenses of juveniles, or of adults for that matter, can be proven at trial, annual reports of juvenile courts reflect that police referrals predominate, although there are differences in referral patterns. In 1973, in the Cook County Juvenile Court, Chicago, law enforcement agencies referred

99 percent of delinquency cases and 71 percent of status offense cases. In 1970 in Ft. Wayne, Indiana, law enforcement referrals constituted 79 percent of all juvenile court referrals. Interestingly, the probation department made 17 percent of these referrals, which suggests that probation officers enforced quite strictly violations of the terms of probation. In 1974, Tulsa, Oklahoma, police referred 88 percent of all delinquency and status offense referrals. During 1970, in the Juvenile Court of Memphis and Shelby County, Tennessee, law enforcement officials referred only 74 percent of all delinquency and in-need-of-supervision cases. Schools referred 14 percent, reflecting a substantial reliance by Memphis area schools on the authority of the court. Probation officers referred but 3 percent of such offenses, and parents referred 7 percent.

Many juvenile courts have urged that schools handle truancy matters and juvenile discipline problems without referral to the courts. Such a position has often irritated school officials who grew up with an earlier juvenile court model where courts were more receptive to school referrals. Courts in one southeastern state frequently committed habitual truants to state delinquency institutions, even though institutional school programs were often only one and one-half hours a day.

Major educational reform and the development of a wide array of educational alternatives is preferred to the ego destruction which may well be suffered by the truant child who finds that school is too difficult or conflictful, and also has a new problem, a court label.

Police decisions whether or not to refer to the court vary considerably from city to city. The chief of the Atlanta Police Department's detective division told this author during summer 1971, "Our policy has been to take everything to juvenile court."[28] The captain of the Salt Lake County Sheriff's Office, Juvenile Division, a month later, estimated that 75 percent of contacts with youngsters are referred to the court.[29] And a few days later the head of the Seattle Police Department Juvenile Bureau estimated that 45 to 50 percent of its juvenile cases were referred to the court. He added, "We know about how many the court can handle. If we referred a thousand more cases each year, probation would come unglued."[30]

Different factors seem to affect suburban and urban police decision-making. Suburban police seem more sensitive to cooperating with the parents of their community, who may well have the resources to obtain private programs to assist their children. Further, if a policeman has to make a 40-mile round trip to deliver a child to a detention center, he may well prefer to release the child to the parents and avoid such a drive. In urban centers, heavy court caseloads almost require extensive release by police officials. While such discretion may well favor the white middle class youth and disadvantage the urban minority youth, this is not universally true.

The more objective criteria utilized in police decision-making include the seriousness of the offense, the past record of the juvenile, the age of the juvenile. More subjective factors include the attitude of a juvenile, and possibly his color, ethnic background, and economic status. Parental availability and apparent parental resourcefulness are other factors assessed.

Growing concern over irregular exercise of discretion by police officials (as well as by probation intake officers, prosecutors, judges, and parole officials) has precipitated the recommendation for official guidelines to direct discretionary practices. The National Advisory Commission on Criminal Justice Standards and Goals recommended in 1973 that "Every police agency should establish in cooperation with courts written policies and procedures governing agency action in juvenile matters. These policies and procedures should stipulate at least . . . (c) the procedures for release of juveniles into parental custody; (d) the procedures for the detention of juveniles."[31]

Detention Admission

In some communities such as Houston and Wilmington, Delaware, an apprehended juvenile is taken before a local magistrate, advised of his rights, and then remanded to detention or released to his family. In Boston police officers bring the youth before the juvenile court judge during court hours. At other times a designated probation officer is contacted who, following telephone discussion with the policeman, decides whether or not the child should be taken to the detention facility. The more common approach, however, is for police officials who consider that detention is indicated to take the child directly to the detention center. Historically, most youngsters brought to the detention center have been admitted.

Few states provide a bail system for juveniles. Most statutes provide that a child should be released by police or by detention admitting officers unless his detention is necessary for his welfare or that of others. In 1972 a Pennsylvania statute set out additional admission criteria, such as that the child may abscond or be removed from the jurisdiction of the court, or that he has no parent or custodian able to provide supervision and care and return him to court when required.

Many statutes provide that children should not be detained in jail, except that above a certain age they may be detained separately from adults. But mounting evidence suggests that neither statutory constraints nor juvenile justice rhetoric has stanched the flow of youths into local jails. A 1970 survey of 4,037 locally administered jails discovered 7,800 juveniles detained on a single day.[32] Two years later a comparable study of 3,921 jails found 12,744 juvenile inmates under eighteen years of age.[33] A more recent assessment stated, ". . . it is probable that up to 500,000 juveniles are processed through local adult jails each year in the United States,"[34] Most of these youths were awaiting trial.

Most jails fall far below national standards of space, supervision, and medical care. While some children in recent years have hanged themselves in jails, and four youths perished in 1965 in a small jail in Arizona due to asphyxiation from a defective gas heater when the jail was left untended, two youths also hanged themselves in the Denver Juvenile Hall, one in 1970 and one in 1971. Such grim events need to be measured against the statutory instruction to the juvenile court, when it must remove a child from his family, to provide him with the care, guidance, and rehabilitative services he may need.

While a number of communities have developed quite effective juvenile detention facilities, frequently known as juvenile halls, detention centers in many urban communities are overcrowded and underprogrammed, and in more rural areas frequently do not even exist. In California juvenile halls are administered by county probation departments. In Tulsa, Oklahoma, as in many cities, the detention facility is administered by the juvenile court. In New Orleans, Louisiana, the welfare department adminsters this center. In Salt Lake County, Utah, the county commissioners have administered this program. In states such as Georgia, a regional detention structure has been created whereby, throughout the state, there is a designated facility in each region. This contrasts with other states where some areas are covered by detention facilities and other areas are not. A movement to a statewide detention administration is believed necessary to assure more uniform provision of facilities throughout a state.

It may be generalized that we have taken too many youngsters into our detention centers and we have kept them too long. In too many communities the police, in effect, determine detention admission. This author, in 1972, asked the superintendent of the Ft. Wayne, Indiana, detention facility how well he got along with the police department. He responded there were no problems at all. He was then asked whether he ever rejected for admission a child brought to the center by police officers. He answered to the negative.

More and more juvenile courts and probation departments are interposing screening staff to interview the child and his parents as immediately as possible, and to return home, without entry into the detention center, a substantially increased number of juvenile referrals. Improved communication between juvenile justice component agencies, together with increased agreement as to what types of youths should be detained, will reduce "overdetention," and result in more appropriate police referrals for detention.

The juvenile court in Salt Lake City maintains an eighteen-hour screening staff at the detention center, a staff member being "on call" the other six hours a day. Seattle and Atlanta provide screening staff twenty-four hours a day. Still, many courts do not provide such a service, and "overdetain," while others screen eight hours a day.

Overdetention may also be reduced by "detention alternatives." The Juvenile Court in the City of St. Louis maintains a corps of paraprofessional community workers, each to work daily with five youths who otherwise would be in detention pending court proceedings. Salt Lake County maintains more than fifty foster homes, and an open-group shelter adjacent to the detention center, to temporarily house youths who in the past had been detained in locked detention. The probation department in Sacramento, California, provides intensive crisis intervention counseling to referred youths and their families, and has significantly reduced detention admissions and the length of stay in detention.[35]

Detention Hearings

Many courts hold daily detention hearings, generally presided over by a judge or referee, to provide judicial review of probation officer screening decisions at detention, and/or as a further check against overdetention or unnecessary detention, and for what may be a due process concern since few states provide bail procedures for juveniles. Parents are asked to attend these hearings, and some courts have legal counsel available for the child. The basic issue is whether or not this youngster needs to be detained further.

Statutes providing for detention hearings generally require them within forty-eight to seventy-two hours after admission. Many courts hold these the day after admission, and it is likely that more courts will begin to hold Saturday detention hearings as well. A representative from the probation department is generally present to set forth his reasons in support of detention or release. Parental willingness to assume responsibility for the child is often a factor in whether a judge or referee releases the child to his parents.

The Court Intake Process

Whether or not a referred youth should become the subject of a formal petition, should have no further action taken against him, or should be handled through some informal procedure, is the next decision to be made. In most courts, this is made by the probation staff, particularly, the intake division of this department. There has been a decided move in the last decade to divide probation into an intake unit and a field supervision unit. In a number of California probation departments there is an in-between unit, the investigation division, which largely conducts social history studies of youths for use by the judge at the time of disposition. Variations in the delinquency intake process are illustrated in Figures 11 through 14.

DELINQUENCY INTAKE PROCESS

Figure 11. California

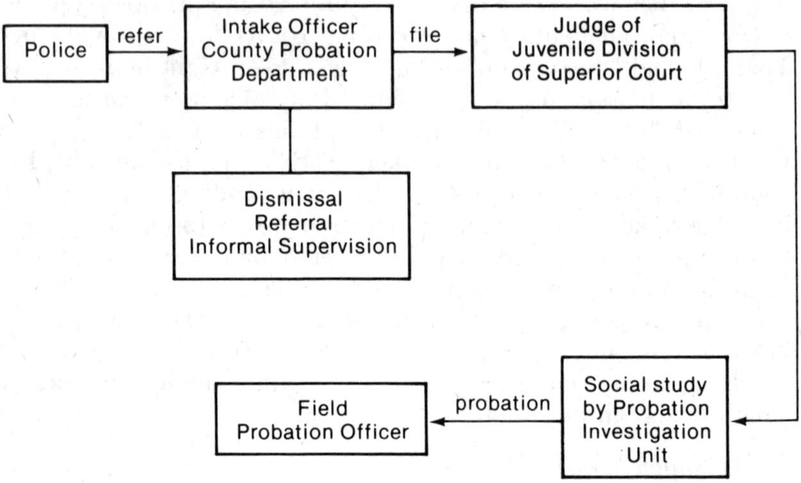

Note: County probation department administers juvenile detention, probation, ranches, special schools, and related community programs. Juvenile jurisdiction is in the Superior Court, the highest court of general trial jurisdiction.

Figure 12. Denver, Colorado

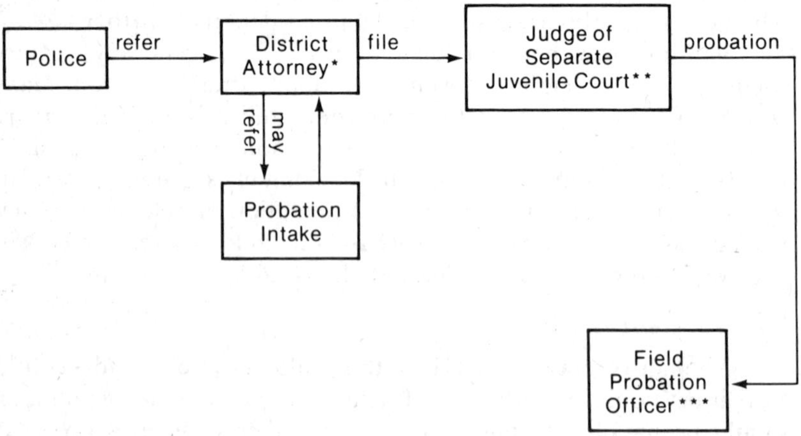

*A 1973 statute granted the prosecutor a decision-making role on delinquency referrals, and provided that the prosecutor *may* ask for intake investigation where further information is needed to make a final decision.

**Judges receive the same pay as judges of the highest court of general trial jurisdiction.

***Approximately sixteen paraprofessionals carry limited probation caseloads.

Figure 13. Florida

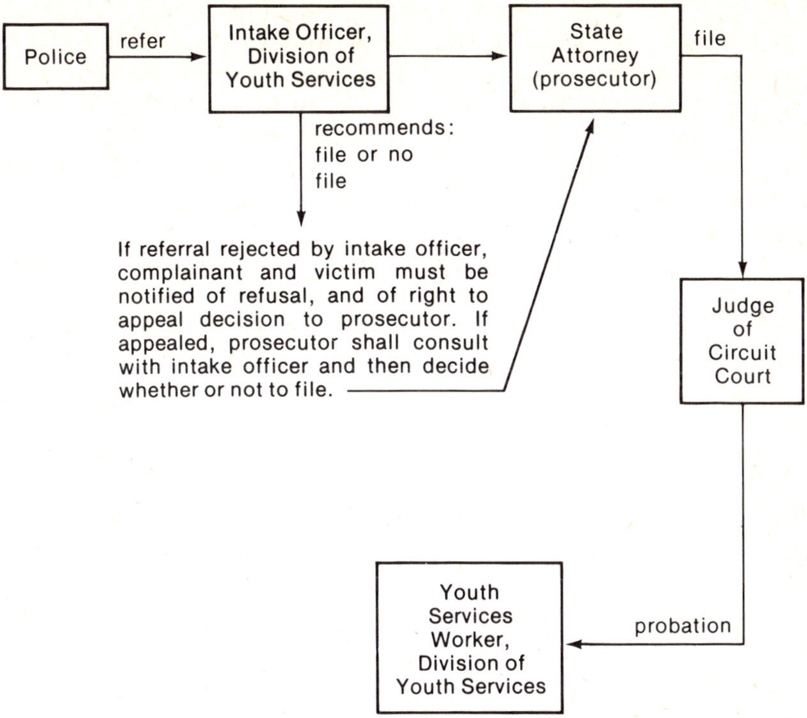

Note: The Division of Youth Services, Florida Department of Health and Rehabilitation Services, administers all juvenile intake, probation supervision, detention, institutions, and aftercare. Juvenile jurisdiction is in the Circuit Court, the highest court of general trial jurisdiction.

Figure 14. Massachusetts

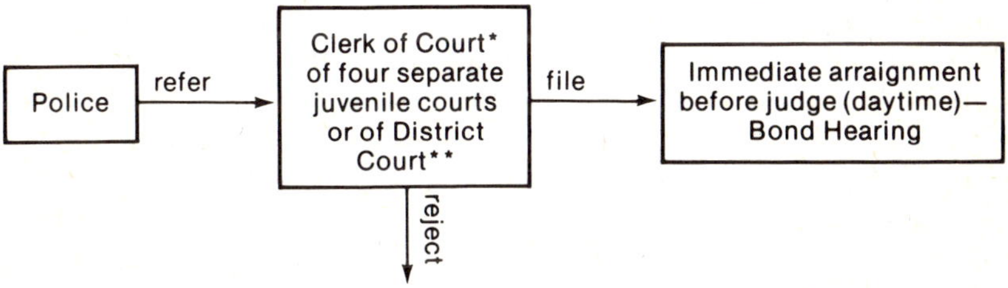

*Clerk of court is an independent, appointive officer.

**Lower court.

Note: On nights and weekends, police contact an on-call probation officer, who advises whether a child should be released or placed in detention. If detained, he is arraigned before a judge the next judicial morning. There is no probation intake and detention is administered by the Department of Youth Services; probation is a local or regional judicial function. The Clerk of Court prepares the petition.

However, a number of courts still maintain probation staff who make intake decisions, conduct social studies, and provide field supervision for the same youth as he wends his way through the process. An advantage of the separate division system is greater attention to each function. The disadvantage is that the child and parents must adjust to two or three different probation staff members. The trend is, however, toward the former, a specialization of function.

There are other approaches to intake decision-making. In the Boston Juvenile Court the complaint is referred to the clerk of the court who scrutinizes the police report as to legal sufficiency. If the complaint is found sufficient a hearing is held with a judge or referee, who decides whether or not the case should go further. In some states or communities the district attorney is the decision-maker, and he may or may not have the advantage of a preliminary investigation by the probation department. In Seattle the case first goes to the probation intake division. By agreement with the Seattle prosecutor's office, the intake probation officer may adjust in-need-of-supervision cases, misdemeanors, and certain felonies, but may not dismiss or adjust other specified felonies without the concurrence of the prosecutor. If there is disagreement, a hearing is held before a judge or referee to determine whether or not the case shall be filed. In Florida intake officers who decide against filing a referred case must advise complaining witnesses that they may appeal this decision to the prosecutor.

One national statistical source reports that for 1973, 1,143,700 delinquency and status offense cases were referred to American juvenile courts.[36] Of this number, 54 percent were handled "nonjudicially," 46 percent judicially. This means that somewhat more than four of each ten cases referred to juvenile courts were handled by formal petition. The remaining cases were handled by dismissal or informal adjustment. This report makes the following comment: "Even though it may be appropriate to handle as many cases as possible in this manner, it raises the question as to why so many that do not require judicial determination should even be referred to court."[37] A further breakdown on these figures reveals that 50 percent of juveniles referred to urban courts were handled nonjudicially, compared with 67 percent of those referred to semi-urban courts, and 44 percent to rural courts.[38]

What is emerging is that the intake process has two major investigative areas: legal and social. Until recent years, intake departments had largely ignored careful scrutiny of the legal case against the child. Further, district attorneys were not particularly interested in assigning manpower to this court. The social investigation was stressed, although even this was often cursory.

Legal screening is best done by a prosecutor. Social screening is best done by an intake probation officer. If the legal foundation is sufficiently strong, and the social reasons justify a formal petition, then the petition should be filed. Factors influencing intake decision-making include the seriousness of the present offense, the past offense record, age, family resourcefulness, school adjustment, peer group associations, existing community alternatives to be used in lieu of the court, and, probably, attitude. Here, too, decision-making is irregular. The spirit of individualized justice is stronger than that of equal justice. The future should see more courts and intake officers develop written criteria as to what cases shall, might, or should not receive formal judicial consideration. Good administration suggests that these criteria be periodically reviewed in the light of experience and research, and adjustments made as indicated.

The case may be dismissed at this point. Or by legislation, court rule, or historical practice, the child may be placed under informal adjustment or supervision. For three to six months he is to counsel with a probation officer or work with a community agency, or just "keep out of trouble." If no further offense has occurred, and the youth has complied with basic requirements, the offense is permanently dismissed.

Since 1967 some states have legislated a "consent decree" provision. This occurs, generally, subsequent to filing. In Pennsylvania and Tennessee, for example, an informal consent agreement is taken to a judge or referee to ratify. Upon successful completion of the approved requirements, the case is dismissed.

Disposition Hearings

When a case is filed, the child formally appears before a judge or referee, along with his parents. A probation officer generally attends. Defense and prosecution counsel may be present. The youth enters a plea to the complaints alleged in the petition. The general plea is an admission or denial to the allegations, juvenile court euphemisms for guilty and not guilty. While trials occur far more frequently today than ten or even five years ago, most juveniles still admit to the charges.

This author's study of referrals to three juvenile courts between April 1, 1971, and January 31, 1972, included 205 cases in Atlanta, 293 cases in Salt Lake City, and 197 cases in Seattle.[39] Approximately half of each sample were violations of the law, and the other half, juvenile status offenses. Atlanta formally filed 20 percent (42 cases), Salt Lake City 47 percent (138 cases), and Seattle 14 percent (28 cases). In Atlanta, 28 of these 42 cases went to trial, with the charge proven in 22 cases, and not proven in 6 cases. In Salt Lake

City there were 13 trials among the 138 formal petitions, 6 resulting in the charge being proven, while 7 were not proven. In Seattle there were 5 trials among the 28 formal cases, 3 resulting in the charge being proven, 2 resulting in the charge not being proven. The number of innocent judgments suggests that the legal screening mechanisms in these courts may need to be tightened.

When a child admits to a petition or is found at trial to have committed an offense, a disposition hearing is held to determine what orders the judge should enter. In criminal court this is called a sentencing hearing, in juvenile court a disposition hearing. The disposition hearing may be held immediately following the plea or trial, or at a later date. A minority of juvenile courts calendar a two or three week delay between the adjudication and the disposition hearing. This affords more time for probation staff to complete a social investigation of the child's background and present adjustment, and to propose recommendations for judicial orders. The judge reviews this report prior to or at the time of the disposition hearing. Most states now permit defense counsel to review this report and question the probation officer at the hearing.

Many juvenile courts have achieved a certain distinction through broad-based disposition hearings, very careful deliberation, and strongly developed treatment plans. In general, juvenile court judges prefer to use community alternatives to institutionalization, and indeed this is what most juvenile court acts compel judges to favor. Close working relationships with mental health services, private and public community agencies, volunteer programs, and educational agencies, have frequently fulfilled a court's responsibility to enhance the future of a given child.

Violations of Probation

Probation is the most common disposition ordered by juvenile court judges. However, the extent of court utilization of probation depends upon the severity of delinquency offenses, the availability of alternative community services, public attitudes toward judicial use of probation and community services, judge and probation officer preferences, and other factors. The Cook County Juvenile Court, Chicago, during 1973, placed 2,416 youths on probation while committing 1,648 to state correctional centers. By contrast, Utah juvenile court judges in 1974 ordered probation status for 1,251 youths while committing but 75 to the state industrial school.

Trends in the delivery of probation services include more assistance from volunteers and from paraprofessional workers who are sometime ex-offenders; a greater use of group counseling and group activities programs; greater involvement of parents, including parent groups; a move to decentralize to branch probation offices in neighborhoods within a city or region; and growing evaluation of the effectiveness of probation services.

Youths on probation are required to follow certain rules prescribed by the judge. Certain of these rules are technical, such as reporting regularly to the probation officer, or being home at a given hour. Other rules broadly prohibit the youth from violating any further laws. When a violation of technical rules occurs the probation officer must decide whether to handle the matter informally, or bring it formally before a judge. When law violations are referred by the police they may be received by the youth's probation officer, or go through the court intake process with the decision to file either retained by intake staff or delegated to the youth's field probation officer. Here too, certain discretion is involved. While some courts expressly prohibit other than a formal consideration of a repeat offense, other courts leave this discretion to a probation officer without a clear directive. More than likely a technical violation is ignored or adjusted informally. A law violation is more often formally petitioned.

For youth institutionalized in state delinquency facilities, supervision may be assigned to a juvenile parole or aftercare worker upon release. This parole agent generally has discretion to adjust technical violations and minor repeat offenses. However, in some states, the repeat offense by a youth on parole goes back into the juvenile court intake process, and the decision whether formal action should be taken is made by juvenile court personnel rather than parole or aftercare workers.

The Juvenile Court—Internal Issues and Structural Relationships

It is essential that the juvenile court become a well-coordinated, well-administered legal mechanism in which the more serious and more repeated juvenile offenders are processed and assisted. Its importance as a court has increased, due to the renaissance of law in this area, and to the enormous public attention riveted onto the court as a result of media publication of the extent of juvenile offenses, and, in certain cases, their seriousness.

While more states are structurally reorganizing the juvenile court into the court of highest general trial jurisdiction, the juvenile court division frequently retains a lower status than other divisions of the court. This is an historical inheritance, but it is also due to the fact that few cases are considered in other divisions where there are not lawyers on each side. Further, the stakes in a criminal trial or a civil suit often appear to be higher and of greater impact than the disposition of a juvenile offense. Yet, is this really valid?

One can obtain support for the proposition that it is better to more generously assign probation and community resources to juveniles, since they are often more pliable than adult offenders and their characters are less rigidly fixed. We can all agree that juvenile cases should be processed speedily, that the right decision should be made at the discretion points so that those who require it are moved along further into the system, while others are handled alternatively.

Juvenile court judges have been far too involved in administration, though they lack basic skills and training. But increased litigation in this court is keeping judges on the bench for longer periods, forcing them to rely more on their top staff. And this, in general, is good.

The current reform movement to organize all trial courts into a statewide court system, with a statewide court management relating to the local court management, and the new questions asked of the courts by state executive and legislative branches, is causing a positive discomfort to traditional juvenile courts.

Should juvenile courts continue to administer juvenile probation departments as they do in many states and localities? If so, what is the judge's role in hiring and firing? Is it rational that probation programs in some parts of a state approach adequacy, but are grossly inadequate elsewhere? Is it tolerable that some communities have pretrial detention centers for juveniles, but other areas of the state do not? What should be done when Court A takes 40 days from referral to disposition, but Court B takes 113 days? And what about Judge A. who committed 50 youths to the state last year, while Judge G. committed 200, and they both sit in the same juvenile court? While our goal remains individualized justice, there should be some uniformity of procedure and service throughout a state.

Juveniles are not afforded all the legal protections provided adults. Juveniles generally do get better probation and community rehabilitative service than adults. Yet many are made worse by the system. One of the most interesting legal challenge theories is called "right to treatment." Lawyers are arguing that if the court removes a child's freedom, effective treatment and rehabilitation must be added to the equation. Where juveniles have been institutionalized under custodial rather than rehabilitative conditions, then, it is argued, the state has failed in its obligation and the rationale for continuing institutionalization has been removed. Based on this theory a boys' delinquency school in Indiana has been ordered to significantly upgrade its program, two Texas juvenile institutions have been ordered to close, the detention center in Chicago was ordered to take a deaf child daily from the center to a special school for the deaf, the juvenile section of the Baltimore jail was shut down, and a District of Columbia court ordered that a detention center must provide psychiatric assistance if one of its residents is in need of this assistance.[40]

A different argument is also developing, one which is less in contrast to the right to treatment than initially appears. Emanating from liberal sources, this view is termed the "right not to be treated," or the "right to punishment." It believes that rehabilitative efforts have been punitive, discriminatory, and ineffective. It urges that judges abandon treatment as a dispositional strategy, and argues that treatment services should be strictly voluntary. It contends there should be no discretion exercised by functionaries of the system, that humane punishment is an acceptable disposition, that institutional commitments should be for short and definite rather than for indeterminate terms, and that an institutionalized offender should be permitted to reject all service offerings without delaying his release date.[41]

Juvenile justice observers are carefully watching certain developments in states such as Florida, where juvenile probation and detention services have been transferred to the State Division of Youth Services, which also administers juvenile institutions, aftercare, and certain community services for juveniles. Will this state level executive branch agency be the model for the future, reducing the judge's powers over those social service workers who work with youngsters within or who have come through his jurisdiction?

Another significant issue is whether the movement to family courts, combining juvenile jurisdiction with divorce related matters, mental illness/retardation procedures, and criminal offenses within a family, will prove advantageous or whether the family will continue to be fragmented in these consolidated courts.

There is also the increased role of the prosecuting attorney, who has begun to challenge the intake powers traditionally held by probation staff. Concomitantly, some district attorneys have begun to ask for more repressive juvenile code amendments. A further development is the increased organization of probation and court staffs into unions, and the impact this may have on court processes and services.

Despite its certain chaos and conflicts, the juvenile court is now an improved and stronger court than a decade ago, somewhat better prepared to grapple with the complex issues and with the excessive demands and expectations which we have given it.

Questions for Discussion

1. In the face of greatly extended constitutional rights for juvenile offenders, why should delinquent youth continue to be handled in specialized courts rather than in criminal courts?

2. How might the role of a juvenile defense lawyer differ from that of a criminal defense lawyer? Who is his client? Should he seek to have a charge dismissed on a technicality?
3. What are the arguments for and against a court's administering juvenile probation and detention services?
4. Would it be a wise policy to repeal juvenile court jurisdiction over runaway, incorrigibility, and truancy offenses?
5. Should juveniles have a right to bail?
6. What might be the best age span for juvenile court jurisdiction over juvenile offenders?
7. What juvenile court practices could be advantageously utilized in criminal courts?
8. How should a juvenile court judge balance the best interests of the child and the best interests of the community?
9. What is a juvenile court's responsibility for the prevention of delinquency?
10. What court in your community has jurisdiction over juvenile delinquency? Is this the higher or lower court, a separate juvenile or family court? How are its judges elected or appointed, and for what term do they serve in the juvenile court?
11. What are the advantages and disadvantages of the typical juvenile court practice of conducting hearings in private?
12. How are police, school, and parent referrals of juveniles screened and evaluated, prior to judicial consideration, in your local juvenile court?

References

1. Mark M. Levin and Rosemary C. Sarri, *Juvenile Delinquency: A Comparative Analysis of Legal Codes in the United States* (Ann Arbor: National Assessment of Juvenile Corrections, The University of Michigan, 1974), p. 12. This survey analyzed juvenile statutes through 1971, and reported twenty-five states had enacted such a separate legal category. Additional states subsequently created this legal category.
2. Ted Rubin, "The Structure and Jurisdiction of the Juvenile Court," preliminary report submitted to the Juvenile Justice Standards Project, Institute of Judicial Administration, New York, 1972 (mimeographed).
3. Ibid.
4. Levin and Sarri, *Juvenile Delinquency,* p. 13.
5. A. v. City of New York, 286 N.E.2d 432 (1972).
6. Rubin, "Structure and Jurisdiction."
7. Ted Rubin, *Three Juvenile Courts: A Comparative Study* (Denver: Institute for Court Management, 1972) pp. 331–52.
8. William J. Chambliss, "A Sociological Analysis of the Law of Vagrancy," *Social Problems* 12 (1964): 67–77.
9. Sanford J. Fox, "Juvenile Justice Reform: An Historical Perspective," *Stanford Law Review* 22 (1970) 1187.

10. Ibid., as reprinted in Fox, *Modern Juvenile Justice, Cases and Materials* (St. Paul, Minn.: West Publishing Co., 1972), p. 42. Also see Anthony Platt, *The Child Savers* (Chicago: University of Chicago Press, 1969).
11. See Charles Larsen, *The Good Fight: The Life and Times of Ben B. Lindsey* (Chicago: Quadrangle Books, 1972).
12. South Dakota Revised Code, Section 43.0301 (Repealed 1968).
13. Fox, *Modern Juvenile Justice,* p. 42.
14. DeBacker v. Brainard, 396 U.S. 28, 90 S.Ct. 163 (1969).
15. Edwin M. Lemert, *The Juvenile Court—Quest and Realities,* and Stanton Wheeler, Leonard S. Cottrell, Jr., and Anne Romasco, *Juvenile Delinquency—Its Prevention and Control,* President's Commission on Law Enforcement and Administration of Justice, *Task Force Report: Juvenile Delinquency and Youth Crime* (Washington, D.C.: Government Printing Office, 1967) pp. 91–106, 409–28.
16. In re Gault, 387 U.S. 1, 87 S.Ct. 1428 (1967).
17. See Irving Piliavin and Scott Briar, "Police Encounters with Juveniles," *American Journal of Sociology* 70 (September 1964): 206–14.
18. Kent v. U.S., 383 U.S. 541, 86 S.Ct. 1045 (1966).
19. In re Winship, 397 U.S. 358, 90 S.Ct. 1068 (1970).
20. McKeiver v. Pennsylvania, 402 U.S. 528, 91 S.Ct. 1976 (1971).
21. Levin and Sarri, *Juvenile Delinquency,* p. 49.
22. Breed v. Jones, 95 S.Ct. 1779 (1975).
23. President's Commission on Law Enforcement and Administration of Justice, *The Challenge of Crime in a Free Society* (Washington, D.C.: Government Printing Office, 1967), p. 85.
24. Ibid.
25. Levin and Sarri, *Juvenile Delinquency,* pp. 23–24.
26. *California's Probation Subsidy Program: A Progress Report to the Legislature 1966–1973* (Sacramento: California Department of the Youth Authority, 1974).
27. U.S. Department of Health, Education, and Welfare, Social and Rehabilitation Service, *Statistics on Public Institutions for Delinquent Children, 1970,* National Center for Social Statistics (Washington, D.C.: Government Printing Office, 1971).
28. Rubin, *Three Juvenile Courts,* p. 233.
29. Ibid., p. 262.
30. Ibid., p. 284.
31. National Advisory Commission on Criminal Justice Standards and Goals, *Police,* Standard 1.3.2. (Washington, D.C.: Government Printing Office, 1973).
32. U.S. Department of Justice, *National Jail Census, 1970,* Law Enforcement Assistance Administration, National Criminal Justice Information and Statistics Service (Washington, D.C.: Government Printing Office, 1973), pp. 10–15.
33. U.S. Department of Justice, *Survey of Inmates of Local Jails, 1972,* Law Enforcement Assistance Administration, National Criminal Justice Information and Statistics Service (Washington, D.C.: Government Printing Office, 1973).
34. Rosemary C. Sarri, *Under Lock and Key: Juveniles in Jail and Detention* (Ann Arbor: National Assessment of Juvenile Corrections, The University of Michigan, 1974), p. 5.
35. Roger Baron and Floyd Feeney, *Preventing Delinquency Through Diver-*

sion. The Sacramento County Probation Department 601 Diversion Project. A Second Year Report (Davis: University of California, 1973).

36. U.S. Department of Health, Education, and Welfare, Social and Rehabilitation Service, *Juvenile Court Statistics, 1973,* Office of Human Development, Office of Youth Development, p. 7.
37. Ibid., p. 4.
38. Ibid., p. 7.
39. Rubin, *Three Juvenile Courts,* pp. 457–96.
40. See Donna E. Rehn, "The Right to Treatment and the Juvenile," *Crime and Delinquency* 19 (October 1973): 477; James D. Silbert and Alan Sussman, "The Rights of Juveniles Confined in Training Schools," *Crime and Delinquency* 20 (October 1974): 373; Peter B. Sandmann, "The Juvenile's Right to Treatment," in *Proceedings of the Second Annual Management Seminar of State Juvenile Delinquency Program Administrators* (College Park, Md.: American Correctional Association, 1975), p. 77; Ted Rubin, "The Expectations of Juvenile Courts," in *Proceedings of Program Administrators,* p. 124.
41. Sanford J. Fox, "The Reform of Juvenile Justice: The Child's Right to Punishment," *Juvenile Justice* 25 (August 1974): 2; John Irwin, "The Right Not to Be Treated," in *Proceedings of Program Administrators,* p. 91.

5 The Civil Courts

Jurisdiction and Organization

Civil courts are less well known to the public than the criminal courts. They are less well covered in the daily press except for the announcement of multimillion-dollar judgments. A citizen has contact with these legal forums particularly in connection with a divorce proceeding, the administration of a relative's estate, or as a party to a broken contract. These courts review enormously complex litigation and also the simplest of small claims actions. The civil courts are the civil divisions of the lower and upper trial courts; frequently they constitute a separate and specialized court such as a probate court.

A civil action may result from an unsettled dispute between two or more parties where a civil wrong, as contrasted with a criminal wrong, is alleged. For example, an apartment dweller has failed to pay his monthly rent and the landlord brings suit to enforce his right of collection. Civil courts also deal with the adjudication of a status, matters which do not require a dispute between parties. The adoption of a child or a determination of how a deceased person's estate should be distributed would be among such cases. These matters are regulatory in nature. The legislature has provided that a court should supervise proceedings in connection with subject areas such as these. A will may clearly specify who shall receive what from a deceased person's estate. Relatives do not challenge the will or the distribution. The dollars and property are divided and proof of the distribution is filed with the court. In another example, a disinherited relative may challenge the mental capacity of the deceased when he signed his will, seeking to void the designated distribution.

Other civil actions may involve citizen challenges to governmental actions, and the reverse of this coin, governmental actions to enforce its grant of authority in relation to citizens. A businessman sues to challenge the ruling of a zoning commission which denies him the opportunity to open a certain business in a particular neighborhood. Or, by contrast, a governmental entity asks a court to determine a fair price for land it claims is necessary to purchase under its power of eminent domain—it seeks to extend a highway and the landowner disagrees with the price offered for his property.

Civil actions comprise the bulk of the legal business of the upper trial courts. In the lower trial courts civil case filings are voluminous, but they are overwhelmed by the number of traffic cases, criminal ordinance violations, and misdemeanor filings.

For example, in fiscal year 1972–73 the California Superior Courts (highest court of general trial jurisdiction) recorded 393,478 civil case filings compared with 61,605 criminal felony informations and 64,217 juvenile jurisdiction matters.[1] The breakdown of the civil cases included: probate and guardianship, 62,406 cases; family law, 149,062 cases; personal injury, death and property damage, 62,865 cases; other civil, 112,432 cases; insanity and other infirmities, 6,713 cases. California Municipal Courts, the lower court in districts of more than 40,000 residents, recorded 600,350 civil filings that year as compared with 478,072 lesser criminal cases and 3,753,503 traffic violations.[2]

As an illustration of the litigation explosion which has occurred in recent years, California's reported comparisons between fiscal year 1972–73 and fiscal year 1962–63 are instructive. Superior Court filings over this decade reflected: probate and guardianship cases, 17 percent increase; family law cases, 60.2 percent increase; personal injury, death and property damage cases, 49.8 percent increase; insanity and other infirmities cases, 73.7 percent decrease.

The decrease in involuntary mental illness/retardation commitment cases demonstrates the impact of changes in public opinion upon legislative actions, and in turn upon the role of the courts. Until perhaps two decades ago the only way a person could become a patient in a state mental hospital was through a court proceeding which reviewed medical evidence as to mental illness and adjudicated one as mentally ill, depriving the person of all civil rights while under this status and ordering him hospitalized. But as mental health treatment approaches modernized, greater attention was given to early interventive strategies in the community to avoid hospitalization, and there was recognition that court adjudicative processes were stigmatizing, severe, and far less necessary than earlier thought. Statutes were changed to permit voluntary admission to psychiatric facilities; short-term involuntary admission by way of physician certification was also authorized. Judicial proceedings were to be reserved for persons, dangerous to themselves or others, who were resistant to noncourt avenues of admission. Involuntary commitment no longer resulted in an automatic loss of civil rights. Statutory definitions of mental illness were tightened. The reduced filing rate, as in California, is deceptive, however, in assessing the amount of judicial time required for this type of case. An increased number of states have strengthened due process safeguards for the involuntary patient, requiring appointment of an attorney or guardian for the patient, along with periodic court review of the necessity to keep such persons confined against their will. Too frequently, however, the development of community mental health services has fallen short of goal; and state mental hospitals have remained the "snakepits" of yesteryear. One federal court was forced to place the entire Alabama state hospital/retardation system under its supervision, and to order comprehensive improvements under threat of an order releasing large numbers of civilly committed patients who were receiving little or no treatment for their condition. Hundreds of requirements were set forth as "minimum constitutional standards for mental institutions."[3]

There has been challenge to the capability of psychiatrists to predict that a person will be dangerous, a requisite for involuntary hospitalization in certain states. Further changes in the interface between mental illness and the law appear imminent in the light of a major U.S. Supreme Court decision in June, 1975.[4] The Court ruled that the harmless mentally ill, capable of surviving safely in freedom with the assistance of others, may not constitutionally be confined against their will. This ruling should result in a narrowing of statutory definitions of eligibility for mental illness commitment. A still larger issue raised in this case was avoided by the court, but undoubtedly will rise again: whether the compulsorily confined mentally ill have a constitutional right to treatment.

Lower court civil proceedings are often simple in nature and purposely so. Legislation defines the nature of these actions and the dollar limits of the claims that may be requested in these courts of "limited jurisdiction." This upper dollar limit varies from state to state, as shown in Table 3. By design, money demands in the highest court of general trial jurisdiction begin with $1.00 above the limit of the lower court, and are otherwise unlimited. The simplified legal procedures of the limited jurisdiction courts are intended to provide a quick and easy remedy. Court filing fees are inexpensive. The reality is that these courts are heavily utilized by collection agencies and businesses to collect payment defaults on loans and credit purchases, or by landlords seeking collection and eviction orders for nonpayment of rent.

Table 3. Dollar Limits of Lower Civil Court Claims
January 1, 1972

State	*Name of Court*	*Dollar Limit*
California	Municipal Court	$ 5,000
	Justice Court	1,000
Colorado	County Court	500
Florida	County Court	2,500
Maine	District Court	20,000
Maryland	District Court	5,000
Michigan	District Court	10,000
Oregon	District Court	2,500
South Dakota	District County Court	1,000
Washington	District (Justice) Court	1,000

SOURCE: *National Survey of Court Organization,* National Criminal Justice Information and Statistical Service, U.S. Department of Justice, 1973.

Garnishment cases are another bill of fare in these courts. Garnishment procedures are especially difficult for working class people. Statutes permit a bill collector to obtain a judgment garnisheeing the wages of a debtor. The debtor's employer is ordered by the court to hold back a certain amount of money from the regular paycheck of the debtor, and to forward this to the court for reimbursement to the collector until the debt is extinguished. Employers resent the extra work which this occasions, and have commonly terminated the employment of their employee—following the first or second garnishment order. Statutory reforms in recent years have sought to prohibit firings on this basis.

Limited claim suits under tort or negligence grounds are also heard in these courts. For example, a man slips on the ice as he is about to enter a department store, breaks his glasses, and sustains mild injuries as a consequence of the fall. He contends the store was negligent in not removing the ice and should compensate him several hundred dollars for injuries sustained. Or a driver, stopped at a red light, is rear-ended by a second driver who has failed to notice the red light. The driver of the first vehicle is not injured but his auto has sustained $500 damage. The second driver is uninsured. Suit is filed. Larger claims, and the amount varies from state to state, would be filed in the upper trial court.

The number of lower court civil case filings grows as a result of increased population, and, predictably, with more difficult economic conditions. More people out of work mean more defaults on monies owed to creditors. Such cases in Colorado jumped 21.8 percent in fiscal year 1973–74 over the prior twelve-month period.[5] Real estate foreclosures also increase during difficult times; bankruptcies, handled in the federal courts, likewise accelerate.

In certain states there are separate probate courts which process wills and estates, appoint guardians and conservators, and, as in Connecticut, handle mental illness commitment procedures and process adoptions. Probate courts in Michigan and Kansas also deal with juvenile delinquency and neglect of children. Attorney services for probating estates are well compensated. Young attorneys in the early, struggling years of their practice joke among themselves that things will become better if they only outlive the clients for whom they have written wills or trusts. In reaction, at least one well-purchased paperback has been published describing the legal procedures for one to process necessary probate documents without employing an attorney. But the court fees cannot be avoided, and probate courts, like traffic courts, may show an annual profit. Connecticut has reported, "In Calendar Year 1969, the 125 probate courts reported total receipts of $3,078,397, against which $1,285,770 in wages and other expenses were charged, resulting in gross earnings for these courts of $1,792,627."[6]

Most courts, however, reflect a substantial net loss each year, particularly the civil courts which schedule a substantial number of jury trials, the criminal courts, and the juvenile courts. Observers consider that the net profits which accrue to so many town and city traffic courts result in strong local resistance to proposals to merge these courts into a state court system, where both court expense and court income would be allocated and accrued by the state.

Divorce jurisdiction, with few exceptions, is vested in the general trial court. One exception is Rhode Island, where a separate statewide family court with specialist judges hears domestic relations, juvenile, and other family-related actions. There are also separate family courts throughout the states of New York and Delaware, but, despite their names they have not been authorized to review divorce applications. In Boston there is a separate housing court which hears only housing-related matters, from landlord-tenant disputes to actions to enforce building and fire-and-safety codes.

Civil Case Processing

A criminal case is entitled, for example, "The People of the State of Minnesota vs. John Jones, Defendant." A juvenile delinquency case is entitled, for example, "State of Utah in the interest of James Jones, a person under eighteen years of age." A typical civil action is entitled, "James Smith, Plaintiff vs. John Jones, Defendant." The civil case caption reflects the private dispute between the parties; the state is not a party to the action.

With exceptions, such as certain small claims actions and dissolution of marriage suits, civil actions are usually initiated by an attorney for the plaintiff. This attorney may have consulted earlier with the person or business organization which will become the defendant in this action, or with the attorney for the potential defendant. Negotiations may have been entered into, but a mutually satisfactory solution had not been obtained. This attorney prepares the complaint which outlines the basic facts of the case, sets forth the civil wrong which he alleges his client has suffered, and ends with a request for a court-ordered remedy such as money damages. The complaint is filed with the clerk of the local court and the required docket fee is paid. Typically, the complaint is appended to a summons, issued by the clerk, and these are both served upon the defendant either by a public official, such as a deputy sheriff, or by an individual, such as one who has established a company which serves legal proceedings. The summons is the court form which directs the defendant to file an answer to the complaint within a defined number of days, usually twenty or thirty, otherwise, default judgment may be taken against the defendant. By implication, failure to file a contest of the action is equated with acceptance of the basis of the complaint and agreement that the remedy plaintiff seeks is a just one.

All states have promulgated rules of civil procedure, which augment statutes and specify the detailed procedures regulating how civil cases are initiated and processed. Certain provisions are quite technical, as for example the procedures to be undertaken when, after judgment is entered and the defendant defaults, a "writ of execution" is requested, and the sheriff is ordered to seize the property of the defendant and to sell this in satisfaction of judgment. States have also enunciated procedures for legal service on a defendant who is no longer present in the state in which an action arose and suit was initiated. Civil actions involving larger sums of money are typically contested, at least at the early stages of pleadings, although settlements are often reached prior to trial.

Probate cases proceed differently. Notice is provided to the heirs of an estate as to the content of the will, if there is one, and opportunity is provided to contest the capability of the deceased to have "drawn" this will, or to challenge the particular assets which are to be divided with court approval. Separate laws but similar procedures govern the administration of estates where there is no will or where a will has been improperly executed.

Limited claims for tort or negligence matters, filed in the lower courts, generally proceed to trial quite speedily even if contested. The trial is where it "all hangs out." But civil suits seeking larger money sums often have several years intervening between the filing of the answer by the defendant and the date of trial. This space is often filled with a series of intermediate procedures known under the general term of "discovery." Commonly, there is attorney delay and court scheduling delay as well. The large-scale use of discovery prior to trial, a development of the past three or four decades, replaced the earlier "sporting theory of justice." Formerly, other than the legal proceedings filed by the parties to an action, each side sallied into trial knowing very little about the content of the evidence to be presented by the opponent. The complaint and the answer, in themselves, are only rather skeletal outlines. How the trial would develop was rather unpredictable except to know that the plaintiff had the burden of proof to show that each element of each particular ground sued upon had been proved by the weight of the evidence. In civil actions the burden of proof is a preponderance of the evidence, or 50.1 percent. This is a substantially more modest measure than the criminal trial requirement of proof beyond a reasonable doubt.

The introduction of state rules of civil procedure, modeled after the federal rules which had been initially promulgated in 1938, changed the civil case process and opened up discovery procedures. Broad civil case discovery later led to broadened criminal case discovery, although the particular methods used in civil and criminal discovery are quite different.

A basic civil approach is the deposition. The parties and their witnesses are placed under oath and must answer questions concerning any matter not privileged which relates to the subject matter of the pending suit.[7] Deposition processes also require any party or witness, upon request, to produce such documents as contracts, leases, and financial records. Upon application of opposing counsel the physician for a party claiming physical injury must undergo a deposition, and the plaintiff must undertake examination by a physician selected by the other party or by the court. Deposition interviews may well take hours and sometimes days, and skillful attorneys frequently are able to elicit important information which leads to either a satisfactory settlement or a better prepared trial. Interrogatories are a second form of pretrial discovery. These are a series of written questions directed at the opposing party and his witnesses, which must be answered in writing.

With the completion of discovery many courts then schedule pretrial conferences where both sides meet with a judge to narrow the issues of fact and law, obtain rulings upon the admissibility of certain answers to deposition questions or interrogatories which have been challenged, review the exhibits which will be offered at the trial, consider anticipated evidentiary problems, and explore possibilities of settlement. Other courts avoid a routine pretrial conference, and set the trial date once both attorneys have filed a "certificate of readiness."

The trial may be before either a judge or a jury, and in the latter event the jury determines the amount of the money award if the case is proven. This practice differs from the general criminal court procedure where, except for capital cases, a jury determines the issue of guilt and a judge determines the sentence. Different rules govern jury selection in civil cases and in criminal cases, and there are certain other differences in trial procedures as well. The number of jurors in civil cases frequently differs from criminal juries, and civil jurors are not locked up overnight during the course of a civil trial. The civil trial, however, is nonetheless fundamentally similar to the criminal trial.

Civil courts are beginning to set guidelines as to the maximum length of time which should elapse from when different types of cases are at issue until their trial, influenced by criminal court speedy trial rules.

Major Issues in the Civil Courts

The Changing Role of the Courts

Not all disputes between disagreeing parties go to court. Not all such disputes should go to court. Attorney and court costs should not limit the use of the courts to the well-to-do. What cases should come to court? Can further alternatives to court be developed to resolve the disputes of dissatisfied parties? What is the role of the courts as an arbiter?

Whether or not to go to court with a complaint is more than a decision by a party or parties to a dispute. It is, in a more general sense, a decision made by legislative bodies. For a number of decades legislatures have seen fit to establish a variety of administrative commissions authorized to hold fact-finding hearings and to rule on civil disputes. Workmen's compensation legislation is an outstanding example of such a direction. Earlier, an injured employee brought suit seeking damages for injuries he suffered because of the alleged negligence of his employer. Beginning in the 1930s state executive agencies were authorized to appoint hearing commissioners to rule on whether the injury was job-sustained, and if so, the amount of money damages which should be paid to the complainant. Statutes guidelined the amounts of the awards for various types of injuries. A right of appeal to the courts was available to dissatisfied parties.

State civil rights complaints are a more recent example. A complaint is brought before a state commission which authorizes investigation by a staff member. If investigation and negotiation fail to resolve the complaint, an administrative hearing may be held and a ruling entered on the issue of discrimination. Again, a dissatisfied party may appeal to the courts.

An applicant for welfare assistance may bring a complaint to the public welfare department alleging he was wrongly denied benefits to which he is entitled by law. Administrative mechanisms are authorized to formally consider these matters, as well as the concerns of welfare recipients who believe they are receiving less than they are entitled to or that their payments were terminated improperly. Still more recently, laws directed that alleged violations of air pollution standards or requests for a variance from these regulations initiate with public administrative agencies.

Court litigation volume is influenced by legislative action. Statutory provisions concerning divorce further illustrate this point. Early divorce legislation severely restricted the legal grounds for divorce, thereby determining the nature of the court proceeding and, basically, the volume of the case filings. Adultery was an early ground along with "incurable insanity," impotency, desertion, and physical cruelty. For many years courts did not have to assign substantial judge time to hear divorces. American mores through the first three decades of this century militated against divorce. Legal evidence requirements were overbearing, and both the divorce process and divorce status were seen negatively. A changing society subsequently brought changing personal relationships and revised divorce legislation. The ground of mental cruelty was enacted and became the fundamental basis on which most divorces were initiated. Such a charge was difficult to defend. Recurrent complaints and argumentation causing any material upset of the other party were satisfactory proof of mental cruelty. Partnerships were dissolved readily by the courts; divorce hearings became five minute affairs; marriage became a more temporary thing in a more temporary society.

The quest to harmonize law with evolving mores continued. Realities were more honestly faced. A few states added a more realistic divorce ground, incompatibility. Growing recognition of the falseness of the court proceeding, with its requirement of proof that one party had wronged the other when in reality both parties had contributed substantially to the marital failure, brought a new wave of reform legislation. "No-fault divorce" was enacted in state after state, a procedure which neither party could defend if desired since the only requirement was one party's allegation of an irretrievable breakdown of the marriage. Many of these enactments cast out the term "divorce," and retitled the procedure "dissolution of marriage." The role of the court as a controlling force restricting divorce had now dissolved. Voluntary efforts at marital counseling remained an option, but the court role was narrowed to resolving child custody disputes, determining support amounts, enforcing support orders, and regulating visitation rights.

Simplified divorce procedures achieved another result. Attorney fees no longer had to handicap the formal dissolution of marriage, at least with the short-lived marriage where there were no children and little property to divide. Courts began to supply simple forms which parties could fill out without counsel. Guidebooks were published on how to obtain a divorce without an attorney, and court calendar clerks could reduce the amount of judge time scheduled for what earlier had been called the noncontested divorce. Some divorce judges have found, however, that nonattorney divorces frequently take more time in that parties enter into their own agreements which contradict the law or common sense.

This legislation has tended to increase the number of dissolution filings. Easy divorce has brought to court many parties, previously separated, who had deferred the legal surgery. Also, it may encourage disagreeing parties to opt for an earlier exit. Some states have shown a case filings jump of 20 percent or more per year following this legislative change. The issuance of the dissolution decree is now a simple process. The recurrent hearings to review nonpayment of support, to determine or modify support and visitation provisions, and to decide whether child custody should be transferred from one parent to another parent are often more frustrating "no win" experiences for the judge and the parties.[8]

No-Fault and Personal Injury Litigation

The primary objective of no-fault automobile legislation was to reduce automobile insurance costs to the insured. This has happened in those states which followed the lead of Massachusetts, whose pathfinding legislation took effect January 1, 1971. A further benefit, speedy settlement of accident claims and a substantial reduction in court litigation of these claims, has also occurred. This reform eliminated the basic need to ascertain that one driver negligently caused injury to a second vehicle and its occupants. Instead, the company insuring the injured party accepted the responsibility to pay designated benefits to its own insured regardless of who was at fault. This company, however, would request reimbursement from the other party's insurance company where negligence otherwise could have been proven. Whether such recovery is appropriate is determined by agreement or by arbitration within the insurance industry. "In practical effect, then, the Massachusetts plan is a 'no-fault' plan in its treatment of injured persons, but a fault plan in its final allocation of costs."[9] Personal injury suit may still be brought in no-fault states where more serious injury or death is sustained and the damage claim at issue exceeds a legislatively determined minimum. This legislation has substantially reduced case filings of tort complaints growing out of automobile accidents. Accordingly, judges can be more attentive to other demands of their workload.

In California, where no-fault insurance is yet to be legislated, auto accident suits move slowly, often requiring two to four years; severe hardship may be occasioned and some plaintiffs may accept a money settlement less than they could obtain at trial in order to ease pressing financial burdens. "... Personal injury cases comprise approximately 80 percent of the civil trial backlog and require a high proportion of total jury trials."[10]

Congestion and Delay

Legislators, bar associations, consumer organizations, and others are searching for ways to make the law more responsive to the citizen, to examine whether additional court matters might be handled outside the court, in whole or in part, and to simplify court procedures.

Compulsory and noncompulsory arbitration of disputes is one approach which is increasingly utilized. It is common to employer-employee contract provisions concerning pay, employment conditions, and grievances. It is provided by rule of the Michigan Supreme Court in auto negligence cases, and in Philadelphia arbitration by a three-lawyer panel is mandatory for such suits under $10,000. Another reform making its way through legislative halls is modernization of probate codes. Certain procedures which have long required probate judge hearing or approval have been modified or repealed, and other procedures have been simplified.

Processing delay depends upon the volume and types of cases coming into court, as well as how courts are organized and administered. The experience in no-fault auto insurance states appears to be that despite the elimination of a vast number of auto accident cases, civil court calendars continue to grow. There are many reasons for this. One is the sharp expansion in product liability suits. These are negligence actions charging manufacturers with selling defective and dangerous products. These suits reflect an enlarged consumer awareness, and a shift in the law to ease the process of holding manufacturers responsible for injuries caused by defective products. These cases involve automobiles and power saws, fireworks, lawnmowers, and countless manufactured items. Reportedly, these cases increased from 100,000 in 1966 to more than half a million in 1971, and may well reach one million lawsuits by 1980.[11]

Suits alleging malpractice against the medical profession have grown in number and—rather spectacularly—in the size of damage awards. A health care crisis flared during 1975 when physicians, angered with the steep rise in malpractice insurance rates, went on strike, refusing to perform other than emergency operations in several states and threatening like action in others. "We know there is a problem when the cost of malpractice premiums rises 950 percent for surgeons and 540 percent for other doctors in ten years, and when less than a dozen firms now write 90 percent of the malpractice business."[12] The malpractice issues spilling over into state legislatures are economically dominated, but underneath they may represent a collision between two of our principal professions. Doctors have resented lawyer challenges on the medical turf. Lawyers contend these actions benefit their clients as well as the public, and cite improved medical safety procedures which have resulted from successful suits.[13]

Lawyer fees in such actions are "contingent": no payment is made unless the complainant has received monies via settlement or trial. If the suit fails, the attorney receives no payment. If successful, contingent fees range from perhaps 25 percent to 50 percent, the latter percentage more typically occurring where an appeal follows the trial. The doctors contend that contingent fees are unconscionable, and that lawyers are overly rewarded, especially where settlements or trial awards are in six or seven figures. The attorneys argue that an hourly fee for service charge would dissuade clients from pursuing just actions, and that unjust actions are discouraged, since lawyers are hesitant to invest their time when the potential of a favorable award is slight. Insurance companies and legislative bodies are now parties to this problem and to the solution. Binding arbitration in lieu of court remedies appears to be one likely direction for smaller claims. The reorganization of insurance programs, possibly aided by state reinsurance or catastrophe loss fund, may also develop.

Increased civil filings arise in additional areas as well. Suits for false arrest by law enforcement officers are becoming more common. Actions for personal injury suffered other than through auto accidents are growing also. Suits against home builders have become more frequent, as have actions brought against auto repair shops. Eminent domain actions, suits by a governmental unit to acquire privately owned property for necessary governmental use, increased by 1,240 cases in Los Angeles County in one year.[14] New legislation concerned with environmental control and conservation of resources has produced a strong demand for judicial policy determination. Controversies which concern the public schools increasingly result in judicial review.

Judges and court administrators are casting sharp eyes on ways to improve the flow of cases through their courts. The introduction of automated data processing to the courts is enabling court management to better determine where jam-ups occur and to take steps to alleviate these problems. It needs to be borne in mind, however, that computers are tools and not remedies in themselves. But court record systems from an early day are still found in certain jurisdictions, as shown, for example, in one study from 1971: "Massachusetts is one of the few remaining states not yet using flat filing. Its present filing system is characterized as follows:

> "the files are cumbersome;
> "they are time consuming to use, requiring unfolding of papers and removal of rubber bands;
> "the life of the file envelope is shortened by frequent foldings and use;
> "papers easily get out of order;
> "there are limitations on the maximum size of a file;
> "there is no room on the file for recordkeeping or a case chronology, and it is impossible to place some routinely filed documents, such as transcribed depositions, in the file.

"A related problem is the standardization of forms and papers. Some documents are backed, some are mere cards, and there is no standardization among them."[15]

The improvement of civil caseflow requires approaches similar to those used in addressing the criminal caseflow problem, yet there are differences. There is no need to make sure the sheriff has brought the defendant in from jail for the hearing, or that a probation officer has completed a presentence investigation prior to hearing. Instead, private attorneys have the task of coordinating the presence of their parties and witnesses. There is a basic consensus around the following:

1. The court should control its calendar, and this should commence with the filing of the complaint.
2. The court should administer a strict policy prohibiting a continuance of a scheduled hearing except under emergency conditions.
3. Processing time standards, guidelines as to how long particular cases should require in moving from stage to stage, should be determined and monitored for compliance.
4. The chief judge of the trial court should be chosen because of administrative skills rather than seniority. He should assert the type of leadership and have available the type of information needed to facilitate efficient caseflow.
5. The court administration, including court clerks and other nonjudicial employees, should eliminate duplicative, inefficient procedures, and regularly review ways to improve caseflow and streamline clerical tasks.
6. The most economical use of juror time should be made.
7. The most economical use of judge time should be made.

Adding more judges may be helpful, but in most courts we do not make optimum use of the judges we now have. California, using weighted caseload measures, has developed a promising tool for assessing judicial manpower needs. This index measures the workload capacity of a court in terms of numbers of cases, types of cases, and judge time required for different cases. Based on the recorded experience of the judges of a given court, a weight is determined which is the average amount of time required for a particular type of case. When each weight is multiplied by the number of filings of each type of case, these sums are totaled, and the number of hours a judge is available annually to hear cases is factored in, the annual amount of judge time needed in a court can be estimated. It can project how many more judges may be needed in a given court or, through comparisons between different counties or districts in a state, can suggest that certain courts are not keeping up with other courts in case disposition. It can also be useful in predicting the impact of legislative change upon the number of judges necessary to a court, as with a no-fault insurance bill.

In this discussion it needs to be reiterated that efficiency is not an end in itself. It is rather a means to the end of effective justice. Theoretically, a court may be so efficient that justice suffers when sufficient time for the preparation and trial of a case is not allowed. Immediate case processing would threaten the goals of justice. Court congestion is one matter. Court delay is another. "A distinction exists between delay that is desirable, that is tolerable, and delay that is destructive or dysfunctional. If degrees of delay are pictured as a continuum, the extremes are clear. The point at which delay jeopardizes justice is destructive or dysfunctional. The point at which delay expedites justice is desirable."[16]

A different observer suggests that a number of the proposed cures for destructive delay "are much worse than the disease itself," that "Slow justice is bad, but speedy injustice is not an admissible substitute", and ". . . the vital neglected problem is the quality, not the speed, of the processes."[17] The relationship of the criminal courts to the civil courts must be cited: ". . . along with fairness, impartiality, and openness, celerity is a fourth dimension of quality criminal justice. For reasons of humaneness as well as efficacy, criminal prosecutions must enjoy an absolute priority. . . . What is perfectly clear is that we cannot and must not use our court facilities to deal with civil law suits if the consequence is to force persons criminally accused to languish behind bars awaiting trial."[18]

While we work on the problem of delay in both civil and criminal jurisdictions, we must continue to address structures for out-of-court resolution of disputes and even the handling of quite routine matters that have occupied court time in the past.

Small Claims Courts

These legal settings are in severe need of re-evaluation. They were initiated years ago as subunits of limited-jurisdiction civil courts, to provide a simplified and ready resource to the wide public to resolve small grievances. They were legislated in response to challenges such as: "If a way can be found for administering justice in small causes which is ideally prompt and inexpensive, we must adopt it or stand convicted as a people who are less concerned with justice than with litigiousness."[19] Typically lawyers were barred from these courts. Claims were limited to $50.00. Hearings were often held in the evening. But "reforms" frequently integrated these courts into the regular jurisdiction of limited jurisdiction courts.

Regretfully, the contemporary hallmark of these courts is not of the citizen as plaintiff but rather of the citizen as defendant, "brought there at the behest of the retailers, utilities, and finance companies which have come to monopolize use of the forum's cheap, simple procedures."[20] A survey in Denver, Colorado revealed that individuals filed only 5 percent of the 15,000 cases filed annually in the lower civil court; 70 percent were filed by collection agencies and 25 percent by landlords.

The usual scenario is for a lawyer for a collection agency, loan company, or retailer to bring forward 25, 50 or 100 small-claims actions, and to pre-empt the court's time for an hour or more. One fourth to one third of defendants fail to appear; this paves the way for entry of a default judgment. Further, many such cases are continued to another date for failure of the plaintiff to accomplish legal service upon the defendant. Few trials occur. Few defendants are represented by counsel. When they are, the hearings are often hurried, or the judge may push for a settlement to speed up calendar movement. Certain provisions of law have placed defendants at a serious disadvantage in these actions. For example, someone buys a television set and finances it through a loan company. The set is unsatisfactory and the seller refuses to repair it. The buyer stops payment. The finance company sues. Historically, the buyer had no defense against the finance company. His remedy was to employ an attorney to sue the retailer or perhaps the manufacturer. Recent consumer legislation has now changed this procedure in a number of states to provide protective rights to the defendant against the loan company.

Poverty organizations, legal services agencies, and consumer groups have tried to increase the awareness by the general public and, more particularly, the poor that these courts also exist to assist them. These efforts have not been enormously fruitful. But it seems clear their lack of use by individuals symbolizes the alienation of lower income people from the court system. It may be inappropriate to suggest that these courts advertise in community newspapers their availability for small suits, but it is appropriate to suggest they employ clerks and paralegals to assist parties in completing legal forms. These courts, in conjunction with a variety of community groups, could hold informational meetings and provide informational brochures to pass the word to a wider public.

The Provision of Legal Services in Civil Matters

Legal services, like medical services, are under searching public inquiry. Lawyers, like physicians, have become increasingly entrepreneurial and often function more remedially than preventively. The poor have long lacked ready access to private attorneys. Legal aid societies were formed in a number of cities decades ago to serve those unable to afford private counsel. Frequently funded by United Way agencies, these societies' overworked attorneys provided representation in legal proceedings and assisted their clients in resolving disputes. Legal aid programs were substantially expanded through Office of Economic Opportunity funds during the 1960s, attracting very bright and assertive young law graduates who, in the spirit of the times, preferred this work to a traditional career with prominent downtown law firms. Frequently working through decentralized offices, they were deluged with tenant complaints, matrimonial cases, garnishment victims, welfare recipients claiming they had been denied their legal entitlements, workers beset by problems with employers, and families and juveniles who sought their representation in juvenile court proceedings. These attorneys increasingly litigated actions which sought rulings affecting larger numbers of persons. This often involved challenges to corporations, public agencies, and courts. This did not sit well with governors and other prominent public officials who constantly sought to narrow this representation to individual case services. These attorneys and agencies rejected such an approach believing the overall welfare of the poor would regress further unless they continued to hurl legal challenges at the political, governmental, and social establishments. "In 1969 the total annual budget for all civil legal aid operations was approximately $55,000,000, as compared to a pre-OEO, 1964 figure of $4,300,000. That growth also reflects a marked increase in the number of legal aid agencies serving the poor (from 241 to 645) and in the number of clients served (from 413,638 to 1,024,492)."[21] Despite its staunch political critics, this program was seen as perhaps the most important of OEO programs. In 1974 Congress gave it a new home authorizing the Legal Services Corporation as the federal funding mechanism for local legal services programs.

Concern over the availability of legal services is not limited to those in or near poverty. A prepaid legal services program which offered members of the program, in this case a labor union, a variety of legal services from an open panel of lawyers, was launched in Shreveport, Louisiana in 1971. This program had the blessings of the American Bar Association. Carefully researched, the Shreveport project was the antecedent of similar programs in a number of states. It alleviated the threat of extensive legal fees and provided basic legal services, many of them of a preventive nature, to its insured clients.

A revolution has begun in the delivery of legal services. Employer-financed group legal plans are becoming an important objective of labor union collective bargaining. A congressional act, in 1973, approved bargaining for such benefits, but prohibited payments to attorneys to bring actions against an employer except in workmen's compensation cases. The legal establishment, sensing this overall change in direction, evolved support for prepaid legal services plans, but opted quite strongly for the open panel as against the closed panel. Under the former plan the insured could select his own lawyer from a participating panel. With the latter, groups of attorneys formed group practices stressing effectiveness and efficiency of services; the insured had no real choice as to the particular lawyer's office into which he was ushered. Bar associations' efforts to find attorney participation in closed panels an unethical practice ended with the U.S. Supreme Court decision prohibiting actions which denied "associations of workers or others the means of enabling their members to meet the costs of legal representation."[22] The court held that efforts to achieve or develop such programs were protected by the First Amendment privilege of free speech and the right to petition and assemble.

Certain consumer groups have also developed prepaid legal services programs. In reality these programs are not comprehensive as yet, and provide only limited services without fee, with the cost of additional services performed at a predetermined cost. Legal ethics bar lawyer advertising much as medical ethics bar physician advertising. But prepaid medical plans have advertised for years, and the same is expected to follow for legal service plans which can be tailored within ethics requirements.

The field is now open; both open and closed panels are "legal." Group legal services will probably forge ahead with an expanded use of paraprofessional employees and the creation of legal form banks and other time and money savings approaches to service delivery. Consumer groups may soon sit down with group practice attorneys to bargain about their fees and services. New law firms are forming with a specific interest in affiliating with a group services contract. Traditional bar associations view closed legal practice as a threat to traditional lawyer independence and quite possibly a competitive threat to their income. They are working rather vigorously through their associations to develop open panel programs. Concurrently, labor unions and consumer groups, which traditionally have preferred group medical practice programs to open physician panels, are opting for closed panel services.

A president-elect of the American Bar Association faced his bias pragmatically:

> The real issue, as I see it, is how to provide quality legal services economically and efficiently. A sophisticated public simply will not buy open panel plans unless they are more efficient and less costly. Instead they will turn to closed panel plans because of their economy. It is thus apparent that a bar association desiring to preserve "freedom of choice" of attorney in prepaid plans must deal with the problems of upgrading the service and of improving each lawyer's capacity to provide quality representation at lower cost.[23]

Questions for Discussion

1. Need a civil trial be a public trial?
2. Consider the merits of the public policy to subsidize civil court cases so that filing fees in general do not nearly approximate actual case costs to the judicial system.
3. Must a court waive civil filing fees for poverty litigants?
4. Should all legal aspects of the divorce process, including property division, child custody, support, and visitation, be handled by administrative agencies, with an appellate right to the courts for dissatisfied parties?
5. What steps should a state court system take to learn of pending legislation and to present information to the legislature on the potential impact of these measures upon the courts?
6. Civil division judges in larger courts may be assigned criminal cases to facilitate court adherence to criminal speedy trial rules. Discuss the implications of this practice upon the administration of justice.
7. Since comparatively few civil cases as well as criminal cases end up with a trial, should law schools deemphasize training in trial skills and increase coursework in negotiation skills?
8. Consider the effects of making efficiency the primary modus operandi of the courts.
9. Should civil courts require that a copy of an attorney's motion to postpone a hearing, or a notice of his failure to file pleadings on time, be mailed to his client? If so, how should the courts monitor that this is done?
10. Analyze the viewpoint that legal aid services should be prohibited from suing governmental agencies.

11. What are the implications of prepaid group legal services contracts upon the traditional independence of the legal profession?

References

1. *Annual Report of the Administration Office of the California Courts* (Sacramento: Judicial Council of California, 1974), p. 107.
2. Ibid., p. 136.
3. Wyatt v. Stickney, 325 F.Supp. 781, 334 F.Supp. 1341, and 344 F.Supp. 373 (M.D. Ala., 1971 and 1972). Also see New York State Association for Retarded Children v. Rockefeller, 357 F.Supp. 752 (E.D. N.Y., 1973).
4. O'Connor v. Donaldson, 95 S.Ct. 2486 (1975).
5. *Annual Statistical Report of the Colorado Judiciary, July 1, 1973 to June 30, 1974* (Denver: Office of the State Court Administrator, 1974), p. 106.
6. *State of Connecticut Report of the Chief Court Administrator 1969–1970* (Hartford: Chief Court Administrator, 1971), p. 31.
7. Milton D. Green, "The Business of the Trial Courts," The American Assembly, *The Courts, The Public, and The Law Explosion,* ed. Harry W. Jones (Englewood Cliffs, N.J.: Prentice-Hall, 1965), pp. 20–28.
8. Denver District Court Judge Edward J. Byrne advised the author in a conversation in February, 1975, that 90 percent of the original support orders he entered were unrealistic in the light of the father's income and the mother's needs for the children. Many such orders would later require court review due to nonpayment or upon motion to decrease or increase.
9. John G. Ryan, "Massachusetts Tries No-Fault," *American Bar Association Journal* 57 (1971): 433.
10. *California Courts, 1974,* p. 108.
11. Jonathan E. Maslow, "Products Liability Comes of Age," *Juris Doctor* 5 (1975): 26–27.
12. Senator Gaylord Nelson, "Mushrooming Malpractice: A Federal R_X," *Trial* 11 (1975): 19.
13. Robert E. Cartwright, "The Cure and the Prevention," *Trial* 11 (1975): 2.
14. *California Courts, 1974,* p. 108.
15. *Study of the Civil Calendar Management System in the Massachusetts Superior Court of Suffolk County (Boston)* (Denver, Colo.: Institute for Court Management, 1971), p. 76.
16. Ernest C. Freisen, Jr., Edward C. Gallas, and Nesta M. Gallas, *Managing the Courts* (Indianapolis, Ind.: The Bobbs-Merrill Co., 1971), p. 61.
17. Maurice Rosenberg, "Court Congestion: Status, Causes, and Proposed Remedies," The American Assembly, *The Courts, The Public and The Law Explosion,* ed. Harry W. Jones (Englewood Cliffs, N. J.: Prentice-Hall, 1965), pp. 57–58.
18. Maurice Rosenberg, "Devising Procedures that are Civil to Promote Justice that is Civilized," *Michigan Law Review* 69 (1971): 809.
19. Herbert L. Harley, "Justice or Litigation," *Virginia Law Review* 6 (1919): 144.

20. Michael Minton and John Steffenson, "Small Claims Courts: A Survey and Analysis," *Judicature* 55 (1972): 324.
21. Theodore Voorhees, "Legal Aid: Past, Present and Future," *American Bar Association Journal* 56 (1970): 767.
22. United Transportation Union v. State Bar of Michigan, 401 U.S. 576 (1971).
23. James D. Fellers, "The Challenges of Supplying Legal Services," *American Bar Association Journal* 60 (1974): 46.

6 The Appellate Courts

The principle of one trial and one appeal is imbedded in the American public mind and the judicial system. The concept of an appellate remedy had been present in English jurisprudence, and Anglo-Saxon law and procedure dominated the development of the American legal system. Article III of the United States Constitution vested the judicial power in a Supreme Court and in such inferior courts as the Congress might establish. State constitutions also provided structures for appellate review.

The United States Supreme Court pronounces the supreme law of the land. Certain decisions spark raging debates across the land. The call to impeach one or more of the justices has been heard from time to time, accompanied by congressional efforts to initiate amendments to the Constitution to overcome Supreme Court interpretation of present provisions. The nine justices in Washington, and their colleagues on the U.S. Circuit Courts of Appeal and District Courts, all hold lifetime tenure following their nomination by the president and confirmation by the Senate. Indefinite tenure may provide the independence to decide cases more freely and with less concern for political parameters. Antagonists of the court who react severely to a particular decision score the indefinite appointment of these jurists and urge their tenure be revised to provide for periodic electoral affirmation or rejection.

During the early years of the Republic, most state and local judges secured their positions through appointment, another practice borrowed from England. The subsequent era of Jacksonian

Democracy and the early rise of Populism revised this practice to provide for popular judicial election in many states. Only in the last ten or fifteen years has there been a decided swing back to a greater use of the appointive process in judicial selection, but even then many states which provide for gubernatorial appointment of judges tend to require that the judiciary return to the people periodically for a yes/no, unopposed contest, "running on their record."

This chapter will focus on the state appellate courts, their organization and processes, and the particular problems they face in accomplishing their critical functions. The jurists of these courts are far fewer in number than their trial court colleagues. Their prestige is high, their task a rather enormous one. Judges of state supreme courts are usually referred to as justices. Judges of state intermediate courts of appeal are usually titled judges. The salaries of appellate court jurists typically are substantially higher than those of trial court judges; salaries parallel the judicial system hierarchy. For example in Missouri, in 1974, Supreme Court justices were paid $31,500; Court of Appeals judges, $30,000; general trial court judges, $28,000; and judges of courts of limited or special jurisdiction from $16,200 to $28,000.[1]

During 1974, New York was top ranking among salaries paid to appellate jurists, its Court of Appeals (highest court) judges receiving $60,575. Utah was at the bottom of the scale paying its Supreme Court justices $24,000. New Hampshire is an exception to the hierarchical pay system, valuing its general trial court judges only $104 less than its Supreme Court justices. In many states, a chief justice receives a slightly greater annual salary than other justices of the court, in compensation for the additional responsibilities he must fulfill. In New Jersey this differential is $2,500. In New Hampshire it is $208.[2]

Purposes of the Appellate Courts

The decisions of the appellate courts are the more important in terms of the development of the law, but the decisions of the trial courts are more important to the individual parties whose lives are affected by court decisions. The plain fact is that the overwhelming mass of court cases are finalized in the first trial court in which a matter is considered. The appellate route is always present but is sparingly utilized. New Mexico court statistics for 1974 reflect this reality:[3]

Magistrate Courts	73,057 cases filed
District Courts	40,118 cases filed
Court of Appeals	470 cases filed
Supreme Court	392 cases filed

The sparse use of the appellate remedy is still more clearly illustrated by 1972 Illinois court statistics.[4] In that state there is but one trial court, the Circuit Court, with nearly 600 circuit judges and associate circuit judges; the Appellate Court is organized on a district basis with 30 appellate court judges serving the state's five districts, and with more than half of these judges concentrated in the appellate court district for Cook County; the Supreme Court of Illinois has seven justices. Case filing statistics reveal:

Circuit Court	2,912,958 cases filed
Appellate Court	3,020 cases filed
Supreme Court	447 cases filed

The purpose of appellate review may be distilled into two basic functions, "To do justice to the litigants, and to provide for the development and growth in the law." Elaboration of this view suggests:

> In the individual case, an appellate court corrects the mistakes made at the lower level so as to prevent miscarriages of justice between the litigants. This action also tends to provide an effective way of encouraging modesty among the trial judges which is important to creating confidence in the system.
>
> . . . The appellate court, by its opinions, teaches other judges, lawyers and all citizens something about the law, what premises are acceptable, what interpretations are proper. In a sense, the litigation of some individuals has a larger public purpose, particularly at the appellate level. Private litigation provides the vehicle for development and direction of growth in the law, for unifying different interpretations, etc.[5]

Certain appellate cases combine these functions: the decision corrects an error to achieve justice between the parties, and provides a legal or constitutional opinion which "teaches the law," or "settles the law" for the present.

In general, a trial court opinion is not a published opinion which appears in law libraries. A trial court judge may issue his opinion orally at the conclusion of a trial; it is then transferred to a written order which he signs, and the order is placed into the case file with copies provided to the parties. However, the trial court judge may issue a written opinion, or the attorneys may embody the oral decision in a written order for the judge's signature; copies go to the file and to the parties. Trial court opinions are not binding on other judges, not even on the judges of the same trial court. These decisions "make law" only in a very restricted sense.

An appellate court decision, however, is binding upon all trial courts in that state. It is "precedent." Legal precedent is necessary to give stability to a legal system. Otherwise a state supreme court might speak one day, a trial court judge a week later could ignore the decision and reach his own, and judges, lawyers, and the general and litigating public would have no standard from which to understand the meaning of the law.

Precedent decisions can be overturned when distinctions can be drawn between the facts or the law on which the first decision was based and different facts or changed social circumstances which permit a later, different interpretation of the same law. Particularly the Constitution, but also statutory law possesses a certain flexibility which permits distinguishing interpretations under distinct conditions. From a sociopolitical and psychological reference, the appellate process provides a defusing opportunity to try to convince a higher court of the rightness of one's viewpoint. The supreme court may also disagree with this point of view, but one has had the opportunity to take his case to a higher authority.

Structure and Jurisdiction of the Appellate Courts

There are at least five models of state appellate court organization.[6] Included in the first model would be states such as Utah and Idaho, where the only appellate court is the supreme court. In 1974 there were twenty-six states in this group, many of them among the less populous states. (Table 4 is a convenient reference for this section.) The highest appellate court, except in a few states, is known as the supreme court. New York and Maryland, not in this group of states, title their highest court the Court of Appeals, and Massachusetts and Maine, also not in this grouping, title their highest court the Supreme Judicial Court. This highest state appellate court will be referred to generically as the supreme court.

State supreme courts typically have five, seven, or nine justices, although there are only three justices in Delaware, four in Wyoming, and six in Connecticut.

The second approach to appellate organization interposes an intermediate court of appeals between the highest general trial court and the supreme court. This is the structure in New Mexico and Colorado, and in a number of other states. This intermediate court is known generally as the court of appeals, and usually comprises from five to ten judges. Historically, states created trial courts and a supreme court, but as the workload of the supreme court became more onerous, legislatures or constitutional amendments interposed a court of appeals to deflect a certain amount of the workload from the highest court.

The jurisdiction of the New Mexico Court of Appeals includes civil appeals, criminal appeals except where there has been a sentence of death or life imprisonment, and appeals from decisions of state administrative agencies. The New Mexico Supreme Court reviews all criminal sentences of death or life imprisonment, all other cases where appellate jurisdiction is not vested in the Court of Appeals, habeas corpus petitions, certain original actions which seek to force public officials to carry out apparent mandates or question the way mandates were executed, and finally, the Supreme Court has the discretion to accept for review cases earlier determined by the Court of Appeals. In 1974 the New Mexico Supreme Court agreed to hear fifteen petitions for writ of certiorari (a request for a supreme court to grant review of an appeal) while denying fifty-three such petitions. This discretionary provision characterizes the supreme court in many states which have an intermediate appellate court.

The Colorado Court of Appeals, created in 1970, was not authorized originally to hear criminal appeals. These matters were reserved for the state Supreme Court. During 1974, however, the legislature granted the Court of Appeals primary jurisdiction over criminal appeals and four additional judges were added to enable that court to administer its expanded jurisdiction. The Colorado Supreme Court reserves exclusive appellate jurisdiction over questions concerning the constitutionality of any statute, ordinance, or municipal charter provision, and exclusively determines appeals from the Public Utilities Commission, water cases, and proceedings under the election code. It also maintains certiorari review over appeals which lie initially to the Court of Appeals.

A third appellate structure creates district courts of appeal rather than a single, central court of appeals for a state. Illinois, with a five-district Appellate Court employing overall thirty judges in 1975, and California, with five District Courts of Appeal utilizing fifty judges in 1975, illustrate this approach. District courts of appeal are physically located in different parts of a state, and hear appeals from trial courts within that district.

It appears unwise to proliferate more and more appellate court districts if this can be avoided. The decision of one district court of appeals is not binding on the judges of another district court of appeals in the same state. It may be instructive, but it need not be followed. The consequence is that a supreme court in such a state is more likely to accept discretionary writ of certiorari petitions to resolve the differing opinions between various district courts of appeal.

The fourth approach to appellate structure is to authorize one court of appeal to hear civil appeals and a separate court of appeal to hear criminal appeals. This is the form in Alabama, and a modification of this occurs in Texas. In the latter state, the Court of Civil Appeals is an intermediate court, but the Court of Criminal Appeals ranks side by side with the Supreme Court of that state. The Texas

Table 4. Courts of Appellate Jurisdiction,

State	Courts of Last Resort: Name of Court	Courts of Last Resort: Number of Judges as of July 1, 1971	Courts of Intermediate Appeals: Name of Court	Courts of Intermediate Appeals: Number of Judges as of July 1, 1971
Alabama	Supreme Court	9	Court of Civil Appeals	3
			Court of Criminal Appeals	3
Alaska	Supreme Court	5	None	
Arizona	Supreme Court	5	Court of Appeals (2 Departments)	9
Arkansas	Supreme Court	7	None	
California	Supreme Court	7	Courts of Appeal (5 Districts)	48
Colorado	Supreme Court	7	Court of Appeals	6
Connecticut	Supreme Court	6	None	
Delaware	Supreme Court	3	None	
District of Columbia	Court of Appeals	9	None	
Florida	Supreme Court	7	Courts of Appeal (4 Districts)	20
Georgia	Supreme Court	7	Court of Appeals	9
Hawaii	Supreme Court	5	None	
Idaho	Supreme Court	5	None	
Illinois	Supreme Court	7	Appellate Court (5 Districts)	27
Indiana	Supreme Court	5	Court of Appeals	9
Iowa	Supreme Court	9	None	
Kansas	Supreme Court	7	None	
Kentucky	Court of Appeals	7	None	
Louisiana	Supreme Court	7	Court of Appeals (4 Circuits)	26
Maine	Supreme Judicial Court	6	None	
Maryland	Court of Appeals	7	Court of Special Appeals	10
Massachusetts	Supreme Judicial Court	7	None	
Michigan	Supreme Court	7	Court of Appeals	12
Minnesota	Supreme Court	7	None	
Mississippi	Supreme Court	9	None	
Missouri	Supreme Court	7	Court of Appeals (3 Districts)	9
Montana	Supreme Court	5	None	
Nebraska	Supreme Court	7	None	

SOURCE: *National Survey of Court Organization*, National Criminal Justice

with Number of Judges, by State, January 1, 1972

State	*Courts of Last Resort*		*Courts of Intermediate Appeals*	
	Name of Court	*Number of Judges as of July 1, 1971*	*Name of Court*	*Number of Judges as of July 1, 1971*
Nevada	Supreme Court	5	None	
New Hampshire	Supreme Court	5	None	
New Jersey	Supreme Court	7	Appellate Division of Superior Court	15
New Mexico	Supreme Court	5	Court of Appeals	4
New York	Court of Appeals	7	Appellate Division of Supreme Court (4 Departments)	24
			Appellate Terms of Supreme Court (3 Terms)	15
North Carolina	Supreme Court	7	Court of Appeals	9
North Dakota	Supreme Court	5	None	
Ohio	Supreme Court	7	Court of Appeals (11 Districts)	38
Oklahoma	Supreme Court	9	Court of Appeals	6
	Court of Criminal Appeals (3 Districts)	3		
Oregon	Supreme Court	7	Court of Appeals	5
Pennsylvania	Supreme Court	7	Superior Court	7
			Commonwealth Court	7
Rhode Island	Supreme Court	5	None	
South Carolina	Supreme Court	5	None	
South Dakota	Supreme Court	5	None	
Tennessee	Supreme Court	5	Court of Appeals	9
			Court of Criminal Appeals	7
Texas	Supreme Court	9	Court of Civil Appeals (14 Districts)	42
	Court of Criminal Appeals	5		
Utah	Supreme Court	5	None	
Vermont	Supreme Court	5	None	
Virginia	Supreme Court of Virginia	7	None	
Washington	Supreme Court	9	Court of Appeals (3 Divisions)	12
West Virginia	Supreme Court of Appeals	5	None	
Wisconsin	Supreme Court	7	None	
Wyoming	Supreme Court	4	None	

Information & Statistics Service, U.S. Department of Justice, 1973.

Court of Criminal Appeals is the court of last resort for criminal matters: they cannot be reviewed further by the Texas Supreme Court. Salaries paid the jurists of these two highest courts of Texas are the same, while judges of the Court of Civil Appeals receive $5,000 less annually.

The fifth approach to appellate organization occurs in New York and New Jersey. In those states, appellate divisions have been created in the general trial courts rather than as separate intermediate courts of appeal.

Staffing Assistance in the Appellate Courts

Historically, staff assistance was provided an appellate court by the clerk of the supreme court. This person was responsible for receiving the legal pleading and briefs filed by the attorneys, maintaining court files, and scheduling the oral argument calendar. Secretarial assistance was also provided to facilitate correspondence with attorneys and to prepare the written opinions of the court for distribution and publication. In time each jurist had his own secretary, and a new aide position was developed, the law clerk. The justices needed help in the conduct of their legal research and in the preparation of their opinions. The use of law clerks is best known in the United States Supreme Court which for many years tapped the brightest law school graduates to serve as their assistants for twelve months. A number of distinguished judges, law school professors, and attorneys initiated their legal careers in this fashion.

State appellate courts have followed this approach, and while the pattern is for a single year's clerkship, some justices have retained their law clerks for many years. The preferred former approach brings to the justices the infusion of the views of contemporary legal training, and provides this new law graduate with a strong opportunity to further his legal knowledge and skills before entering legal practice. It is increasingly common for at least the chief justice to have more than one law clerk, but case volume rises in the appellate courts have created the need for other helpers for beleaguered justices.

The Michigan Court of Appeals which had added a second law clerk for each judge, decided in 1968 to pool all second law clerks into a central research unit into which other attorneys were also added. "There a staff attorney prepares a substantial memorandum of the case, summarizing the facts and the contentions of the parties and analyzing the issues in light of the pertinent legal principles. A copy of this memorandum, along with the record and the briefs, goes to each judge on the three-judge panel to which the case has been assigned. . . . The judges use the staff memorandum in preparation for oral argument and in writing opinions later."[7] Staff lawyers also prepare preliminary drafts which the court utilizes in routine cases where a full opinion is not written. The court may then adopt or edit the draft and issue it as the court's opinion.

In California's First District Court of Appeals, in San Francisco, five attorneys have performed a central research function, and the senior attorney has also conducted a screening function: ". . . he examines the briefs quickly to determine whether the appeal is routine, with the outcome readily predictable. . . . If in his judgment the case appears to be of that type he retains it for staff treatment . . . a staff lawyer prepares a memorandum of the Michigan type and a draft of a recommended per curiam opinion. . . . If all three judges concur . . . the case will be decided without argument and without conference."[8] The judges may then adopt or edit the memorandum and then issue it.

Staff approaches to screening and central research assistance are being replicated in a growing number of appellate courts. The justices retain the full power of decision and determine whether or not cases shall receive full treatment or briefer consideration. Programs such as these are considered to increase judicial productivity and reduce delay while maintaining or even improving quality. Cases which present no novel or difficult issues can be separated out and, with judicial approval, brief court opinions can be drafted by attorney staff. Supreme courts which must determine whether to issue a writ of certiorari can benefit from preliminary screening staff assessments.

Several other assistance efforts should be cited. The rules of many state court systems permit the assignment of a trial court judge to sit temporarily on a court of appeals or supreme court, often for a week at a time, and to hear cases with the regular jurists and then draft opinions for their approval. This approach has the mutual benefit of facilitating the appellate court's work product and providing the trial judge with firsthand knowledge of the appellate process. It does not offer the promise of larger scale assistance which results from a screening and research attorney project. Further, the absence of the trial judge from his trial court slows caseflow at the local level.

The use of "appellate court commissioners" as judicial assistants, which characterized a number of state supreme courts in the early decades of this century, has now disappeared. Statutes had authorized the appointment of these attorneys to perform record and legal research, in some states to hear appellate cases, and to submit written opinions to the court for its review.[9] Today's appellate courts appear sensitive to constraining the role of assistants and to maintaining judicial integrity by directly supervising research conducted under their aegis and retaining responsibility for all decisions and work products which they issue.

The Process of Appeal

A trial court judge, unsure as to his ruling, cannot initiate an appeal. Nor can an interested organization which is not a party to a suit but would like to have an issue decided at the appellate court level. Appeals must be brought by a party to the trial court proceeding. An interested organization may obtain permission from an appellate court to join in an appeal when it was not one of the parties at trial. Through this method, known as *amicus curiae,* "friend of the court," a number of civil liberties and civil rights organizations have participated in appellate court review.

A second accompanying principle is that appeals may be taken only from final judgments. For example, a judge makes a ruling on a preliminary motion at the beginning of the trial, and one party considers the judgment incorrect. The trial cannot be stopped to permit this party to appeal this ruling. He must wait for the completion of trial and the entry of final judgment. Then he holds the prerogative to appeal. A further requirement is timeliness. A party may not indefinitely delay initiating the appeal process. States have rules defining the steps of an appeal and the time requirements for each step. The first step, filing the notice of appeal, is the most critical one. If notice is not lodged within the deadline it is very difficult to obtain consent to initiate appeal. Conversely, rules guidelining time frames between the subsequent steps receive frequent waiver, permitting late completion.

When a party files a notice of appeal a typewritten transcript of the verbatim record of the trial must be prepared by the court reporter and reviewed and certified by the trial court judge. This is a major delay point. Reporters are busy taking care of other trials, and often cannot find time to complete the typed transcript speedily. Transcript delays are occasioned also when payment for reporter services is not made promptly, and further transcription is held back pending payment.

With completion of the transcript the moving party, the appellant, must prepare an opening brief citing the issues of fact and law, including relevant prior appellate decisions, together with written argumentation as to why the case should be reversed. The other party, the appellee, upon receipt of the opening brief, is provided a certain number of days to complete and file an answer brief, his side of the case. The case becomes "at issue" when the appellant next completes the reply brief, his written response to the appellee's answer brief. The case is then scheduled for oral argument unless the parties have agreed to have this matter determined without live presentations of their viewpoints.

Oral argument, before a division of the bench or the entire bench, is frequently scheduled for one hour. The lawyer for the appellant opens, presenting major arguments in twenty to twenty-five minutes, interspersed with questioning from the justices. Appellee's counsel rebuts these statements and argues his own position for up to one half hour, again with judicial questioning interruptions. Appellant's attorney then returns for a final five minute statement. Prior to the argument the justices have individually reviewed the cases or staff summaries, and have conferenced on the major issues they expect to consider in each case. Either on the day of the argument or soon thereafter the justices again conference and seek to reach their tentative opinions. Responsibility is assigned to one justice to prepare a draft opinion. The draft opinion is circulated among the other jurists prior to a subsequent conference where final decision may be reached and the draft opinion amended and approved. Dissenting opinions may be issued as well.

The entire court may hear the oral argument and join in the opinion, or, by rule, panels of three jurists may hear a case and issue the ruling. In a state with an intermediate court of appeals, the supreme court more typically hears all cases "en banc," with all justices sitting on the bench.

Supreme courts, as in Illinois, schedule terms, or blocks of time, where they will hear cases, interspersed by time periods where they are living at home, and working daily from an office provided them in their home community. In that state, there must be one justice from each of four districts and three justices from the Cook County district. These justices conduct frequent conference telephone calls from local offices to review cases they have heard during term and for which written opinions are being prepared and final decisions made.

A state supreme court is the final arbiter for decisions concerning the laws of that state. Decisions from that court which rule, for example, on whether a state statute or court procedure contravenes the federal constitution, may be appealed to the United States Supreme Court. This is done by a petition for writ of certiorari, and that forum, with the immense number of cases presented it, must cull out the great majority of petitions and accept comparatively few of those filed. The Supreme Court also receives a vast number of cases arising from the federal court system. It selects cases for review whose consequences are considered most significant. It must accept jurisdiction over a limited number of cases such as conflicts between two or more states. Within the two major functions of appellate review, to do justice to litigants and to teach the law, this court must favor the latter purpose as its prime selection strategy.

The Effect of Appellate Court Decisions

Appellate courts, of course, determine both civil and criminal appeals. In 1972, the Appellate Court in Illinois disposed of 1,310 civil cases and 1,216 criminal appeals.[10] It reversed more of its civil appeals than its criminal appeals. Thirty-nine percent of civil appeals were reversed compared with 23 percent of criminal appeals. The New Mexico Court of Appeals, in 1974, showed a somewhat different pattern, reversing 23 percent of civil appeals and 22 percent of criminal appeals.

While an intermediate appellate court decision may be considered for further review by a state supreme court, and a state supreme court decision which deals with a federal issue may be submitted for review consideration to the U.S. Supreme Court, an initial appeal is more typically the final appeal. The substantial majority of appellate efforts stop there.

The effect of an appellate court appeal which is not appealed further takes several forms. The reversal of a civil case may find the appellate court instructing the trial court to hold a new trial, or to take additional evidence in a defined area pursuant to the decision; the appellate decision could result in the dismissal of a claim with no further action to be taken by the trial court; an appellate decision may affirm in part and reverse in part the issues raised on appeal. For example, evidence of negligence may have been sufficient, but restraints placed by the trial judge upon the money damage claim phase of the initial trial may have been incorrect. Further, an appellate decision might find error was committed by the trial court judge but not "prejudicial error." The initial judgment is therefore affirmed since there was sufficient evidence to have justified the original finding.

Appellate court judges are sensitive to the fact that they had not heard the original trial and that, as to certain types of cases such as child custody disputes, the trial judge was in a better position to evaluate the parties' claims for the custody of a child. Accordingly, appellate courts do not disturb such trial court findings except for "an abuse of discretion."

Criminal court appeals are typically initiated by a defendant who was convicted in the original trial. His victory in an appellate court frequently sends the matter down for a new trial. This is not double jeopardy since this constitutional precept protects against a second prosecution for the same crime for which a defendant has earlier been found innocent. With another criminal appeal, an appellate court may find that the evidence submitted against a defendant at the initial trial was insufficient, that the case should have been dismissed, and that to correct this error the appellate court will dismiss the case without retrial. Another decision may find that the trial judge should have suppressed certain evidence; the case is remanded for new trial, but the prosecutor determines this evidence was so critical to his case that because of its inadmissibility he will be unable to prove the charge, and decides not to bring the case to trial again.

Appellate determination that a criminal statute is so vague as to be unconstitutional does not allow for retrial in the original court. It sometimes happens that following the conduct of the retrial, as ordered by an appellate court, the case is again appealed and a new appellate review conducted.

Major Issues Related to Appellate Processing

Not unlike trial court problems, the major issues at the appellate level relate to case volume and case delay.

Case Volume

Total cases filed in the California Courts of Appeal increased from 3,577 during fiscal year 1962–63 to 9,186 a decade later, an increase of 157 percent. The total of criminal appeals during this span increased by 209 percent, overwhelming the number of civil appeals which a decade earlier had been more frequent than their criminal counterpart. During the same decade petitions filed for review of Courts of Appeal decisions in the California Supreme Court jumped from 907 to 2,386. Whereas 121, or 13.3 percent of these were granted during fiscal year 1962–63, only 181, or 7.6 percent, were authorized a decade later.[11] Statistical volume data from appellate courts in other states show increases, frequently in substantially greater proportion than population expansions. This is not always true. Appellate case filings in less populous states may not reflect an explosive gain.

The heightened volume of appeals threatens the quality of appellate court opinions and jeopardizes the already overextended amount of time required for a case to complete the appellate process. There are various proposed remedies to the case volume crisis. The creation of an intermediate court of appeal has been a major one. Expanding the jurisdiction of the intermediate court and reducing the cases eligible for supreme court review is an approach favored by harried supreme court justices, but frowned upon by jurists of intermediate courts of appeal.[12] The addition of screening and central research attorneys has earlier been addressed. More jurists, restrictions on the appellate right, and elimination of the oral argument, are others. But today's average case in the appellate courts of any state is far more complicated and has more legal considerations than the average case of a decade or two decades ago. These complexities and ramifications take time and energy to unravel. "Then, too," one writer has commented, "the qualities that we would hope to find in 'better' appellate judges—greater circumspection, greater technical proficiency, greater social wisdom—are not necessarily qualities that lead to the production of a greater number of decisions. On the contrary, something might even be said for reducing the quality of judges if all we want to do is increase their quantitative production."[13]

The expansion of the right of free counsel on appeal for indigent defendants has been a substantial factor in volume increase. Concern has been expressed that many of these appeals are frivolous, and would not have been entertained if the appellant had to pay the lawyer and the costs of appeal. This may be true for some of these appeals, but it is alien to the concept of a fair judicial system to require, for example, a public defender appellate unit to screen out all but the most meritorious appeals when their indigent clients, facing long term incarceration, instruct their counsel to prepare the case for appellate review.

Certain civil appeals and criminal appeals, even where the appellant pays for counsel, may be clearly destined for appellate affirmation of the trial court ruling. One U.S. Supreme Court justice suggested in 1924 that perhaps 90 percent of appealed cases could be decided only one way. A more contemporary federal jurist has suggested that one third of all appeals have little merit and can be decided quickly. A legal scholar has estimated that 80 percent of appeals are easily determinable. Another jurist has suggested that at least one half of the appellate caseload was subject to almost immediate decision.[14] A common strategy which appellate courts have applied to this problem is to differentiate between cases which can be disposed of briefly with an opinion of only a paragraph or two, and those which merit full treatment, including oral argument and an extensive written opinion. To a certain extent, this is the difference between the functions of providing justice to litigants and teaching the law.

Delay

The problem of delay in completing the appellate process relates to the issue of volume, but it is connected as well to the complexities of this process and to how an appellate court organizes itself to expedite court business. We can expect that most appellate courts will distinguish between the more routine case which can be decided by a brief "per curiam" or memorandum opinion, and the less routine case requiring comprehensive consideration by the court together with an extensive, handcrafted opinion. The latter approach has been recommended when a case ". . . establishes a new rule of law or alters or modifies an existing rule . . . involves a legal issue of continuing public interest . . . criticizes existing law . . . represents a significantly new contribution to the legal literature through historical review or through resolution of apparent conflict . . . is an appeal from a judgment in the court below in which there has been a published opinion."[15]

Screening and research attorneys to examine the case record and provide a written analysis to the judges prior to their consideration of a case, and law clerks to justices to provide additional research and editorial assistance, represent strategies aimed at coping with volume and reducing delay, while improving the quality of the work of a court.

Court control of the timeliness with which notices, transcripts, and briefs are filed is becoming more common. A busy appellate court which does not worry about a case until all prerequisites have been completed will have a longer processing time than the court which makes rigorous efforts to enforce the timely completion of these requirements from the date the notice of appeal is filed. A prominent delay factor is the slowness with which the verbatim transcript of the trial is transcribed. Trials are recorded on stenotype machines, electronic tape recordings, and by "voice writing." The former method is still the dominant approach for trials which are appealed to the appellate court system. Extensive research is underway to develop new approaches to both recording a trial and transcribing the record. It is expected that someday some form of recording-computer process will enable an automated printout of the trial record to be completed almost instantly. Whenever this is accomplished we can expect the enactment of appellate court rules requiring the completion of an appeal within a shortened period of time.

Another delay factor occurs when the original trial attorney is replaced by a second attorney who brings the appeal. This discontinuity compels additional time for the new lawyer to wait for the recorded transcript, examine it thoroughly, and conduct the necessary research prior to writing the opening brief. One federal circuit court of appeals has published a rule providing that unless good cause is shown, trial counsel appointed and paid through public funds shall be automatically continued as counsel on appeal.[16]

New Mexico, in 1974, reported the average elapsed time for cases that the Supreme Court closed by written opinion:[17]

From notice of appeal to filing of transcript in Supreme Court	108 days
From transcript to issue	94 days
From issue to submission	87 days
From submission to opinion	138 days

That court and most appellate courts search for ways to maintain quality, cope with volume, and reduce delay. Meanwhile, litigants shove recordbreaking numbers of cases into the funnel of the appellate courts.

Further Functions and Responsibilities of Supreme Courts

The justices of the highest state courts are increasingly performing responsibilities over and above deciding cases.

Rule-Making Function

Most supreme courts adopt rules governing procedure in the various courts of their state although some states require that these rules be concurred in by the legislature prior to official promulgation.

In 1974 the New Mexico Supreme Court "... adopted a new Code of Judicial Conduct, new Criminal and Civil Rules for Magistrate Proceedings and new Rules of Appellate Procedure. Rule work in progress includes preparation of uniform jury instructions for use in criminal cases, new rules of criminal appellate procedure and rules for proceedings under the Children's Code, all of which are expected to be completed during 1975."[18] Procedural rules do need updating and changing from time to time. Adherence to these rules facilitates a more orderly and more uniform system of justice. Attorneys, law professor consultants, and representatives of agencies related to the justice system frequently participate with the judiciary in the development of these rules. This process requires extensive time commitments by the justices.

Administrative Responsibility for the State Court System

While procedural rules appear to have been the first adopted, supreme courts are now adopting administrative rules, and a variety of other guides for the conduct of the court system. Constitutional amendments, particularly in the past decade, have empowered many chief justices to act as the administrative head of the state court system. "General administrative and supervisory authority over all courts is vested in the Supreme Court and shall be exercised by the Chief Justice in accordance with its rules."[19]

Although some states have created a judicial council or judicial conference, comprised of judiciary representatives, attorneys, and, in California, legislators, to perform certain administrative functions, the dominant trend is to grant overall administrative authority to the chief justice. The chief justice, in concert with the state court administrator, increasingly takes an active role in superintending the administration of justice in his state. Such responsibilities may well pre-empt 30 to 40 percent of the time of a chief justice. He becomes responsible for the interim assignment of judges to courts other than their own to assist with heavy caseloads or judicial absences, for the administration of state-funded expenditures by state and local courts, for the primary liaison role with legislative and executive branches, for the issuance of policy directives, and for innumerable additional matters that arise daily and which concern the administration of a judicial system. Many now address their state legislatures biennially with a "State of the Judiciary" presentation.

One writer has made the following observations:

> When a chief justice is called upon to be the executive who is responsible for the operation of such a system, his administrative responsibility is indeed awesome. But the successful administration of something as complex as a state judicial system obviously requires the cooperative efforts of many people on many levels and cannot nor should not be a one-man autocracy, regardless of constitutional authority. . . . I say to you that the people will have proper and efficient management of the court system and if the chief justice is not willing to assume this role in this time of great public concern for law and justice and of great public criticism of courts, the people or the legislature may very well place or try to place this responsibility elsewhere, perhaps with some official or somebody outside the judicial system and responsible to the executive or legislative branch of government. This can only lead to the diminution of the prized independence of the judicial branch of the government, an independence that must ever be preserved if the American constitutional scheme is to be maintained. The authority of the judiciary over its own operations has already been significantly diminished by attrition in some jurisdictions.[20]

Additional Functions

In some states, the supreme court is the disciplinary board which reviews grievances filed against attorneys and determines whether formal action shall be taken. Complaints are often initially screened through a committee of lawyers appointed by the supreme court or the bar association. The supreme court may censure attorneys, suspend them for a defined period of time, or disbar them. The supreme court, under recent constitutional provisions in a number of states, is the disciplinary board which ultimately reviews alleged judicial misconduct. Again, there is typically a separate officially designated investigative body, known as the Judicial Inquiry Board in Illinois and the Judicial Qualifications Commission in Georgia, composed of judges, lawyers, and lay persons, which may recommend removal or suspension from judicial office, or the censure or reprimand of a judge. The Illinois Courts Commission, composed of one supreme court justice, two appellate court judges, and two circuit court judges, reviews the complaints against judges which are presented by the Judicial Inquiry Board, and determines whether and what disciplinary action shall be taken. In other states the supreme court itself serves this function.

In states which utilize judicial nominating commissions to recommend candidates for judicial appointment to the governor, supreme court justices may serve as nonvoting chairpersons for the nominating commissions.[21]

In most if not all states there is an annual conference of judges convened as an educational workshop and to consider suggestions for the improvement of the administration of justice. Frequently the chief justice presides over this conference.

Illinois designates one justice as Supreme Court liaison to the monthly meetings of the Conference of Circuit Court Judges.

Appellate judges participate in training seminars which are conducted on a national level by the Institute of Judicial Administration at the New York University School of Law, and at Louisiana State University.

Supreme courts and chief justices are authorized in certain states to make certain appointments. The Illinois Supreme Court appoints that state's Appellate Defender. The Connecticut Supreme Court appoints certain prosecution officials. The chief justice in Kansas appoints the chief judges of the general trial courts of that state. The supreme court or the chief justice determine the appointment of the state court administrator, the clerk of the supreme court, and the supreme court librarian, and frequently their staffs as well.

Relationship of the Chief Justice and the State Court Administration with the Judicial System

The chief justice is becoming the focal point in providing leadership and supervisory direction to a state's overall administration of justice. This duty goes well beyond a chief justice's traditional responsibility to preside over the court's decision-making and rule-making duties. Many chief justices now superintend the widespread functions of the state court administrator, intersect more actively with legislative and executive branches, spearhead court reform efforts, search out ways to reduce backlogs and speed caseflow in the various courts, approve or disapprove grant requests sought by the courts for U.S. Law Enforcement Assistance Administration monies, convene judges and related criminal justice agencies to hammer out disputes and seek approaches to better interagency cooperation, enter administrative directives for the trial courts, and chart priorities for court system improvement. This is no easy task. To accomplish it, the term of a chief justice may be lengthened, his selection is based increasingly on his administrative and leadership skills rather than his seniority, and a new role definition is being applied to this position.

The strong chief justice model may cause problems at the trial court level. We ask that judges be quite independent and be willing to enforce the law even against hostile public opinion. With these characteristics, and particularly in states where judges are elected, their interest in complying with chief justice directives is not always impressive. They may prefer to run their court or their docket as they see fit, and not face the superintending oversight of the chief justice. An issue which focuses this present or latent conflict deals with the power to select a chief trial court judge. A chief justice may well contend that he should hold this power, for through the appointment of the judge he considers best able to steer a trial court he can gain the cooperation needed to effectuate an intermeshing system. The chief justice holds this power in states such as New Jersey, Colorado, and Kansas. Though he may hold such power, it does not necessarily follow that the rank and file trial court judges appreciate this power or provide instant and comprehensive cooperation to either their chief judge or the chief justice.

The more common approach, as in California, Illinois, and Florida, is for trial court judges to select their own chief judge. Selecting their own chief judge is no guarantee, however, that his leadership will achieve greater court effectiveness. He may well have been selected as a representative of the status quo, as the least controversial, as one who will not rock the boat in which most judges are comfortable. Similarly, the relationship between the state court administrator and a trial court administrator is sometimes cooperative and other times antagonistic. When the former official determines to develop a statewide uniform case-reporting and statistical system for all courts, his intention to gain a useful data base for management and planning may be interpreted by the trial court administrator as a control device and not a service function. The state court system as well as the trial courts needs this information to better know where it is and to better determine where it should be going. But at the trial court level this may be seen as checking, looking over their shoulder, and the beginnings of unwelcomed control over how local administrators execute their tasks.

It is expected that state control of trial courts will increase, partly influenced by the trend to provide more of the costs of the local courts from the state legislative level. It is said that "power flows with the buck," and it is true that the chief justice and the state court administrator, as the primary liaison with the state funding body, must accept responsibility for how state funds are expended at the local court level. Accordingly they will utilize their positions to request, cajole, or order trial court compliance with standards of efficient functioning.

The judicial council or judicial conference structure offers an alternative to placing central administrative powers in a state chief justice. Georgia and Utah have more recently joined California and New York in this approach, though in the former two states a trial court judge, rather than a chief justice, serves as chairman.

The California Constitution authorizes its Judicial Council to "... survey judicial business and make recommendations to the courts, make recommendations annually to the Governor and Legislature, adopt rules for court administration, practice and procedure, not inconsistent with statute, and perform other functions prescribed by statute. The chairman shall seek to expedite judicial business and to equalize the work of judges; he may provide for the assignment of any judge to another court . . ."[22]

Chaired by the chief justice, the Judicial Council's membership includes judges from the strata of courts, as well as legislative and attorney members. It has developed a strong statistical system, conducts continuing studies aimed at improved administration, provides technical assistance, staffs committees which draft procedural and other rules, has influenced progressive legislation concerning the courts, and maintains a strong planning capacity, all within a consultative and participative process.

The fact that local funding provides nearly 90 percent of California court system costs has probably restrained any grant of strong administrative powers to the council. Consultation rather than directive is its primary operating method. The provision of state level assistance is seen there more as service than control. However, critics suggest that the absence of strong administrative powers vested directly in the chief justice hinder a more concerted direction.[23]

Regardless of administrative structure, effective consultation within the system is critical to the acceptance of centrally instigated change. Centralization of administrative powers in the chief justice does not lead, per se, to instant implementation of directives at other court levels. What is needed is a studied balancing of power between the chief justice and the state court administration, and the trial judges and their administration. Where authority is vested in a chief justice, much of this can be delegated, artfully, to chief trial court judges. Hostilities engendered by hierarchical management structures can be muted by individual consultation, representative committee processes, and a shared determination of court system goals and strategies.[24]

Questions for Discussion

1. Should the right to bail which applies prior to trial apply to a convicted defendant who chooses to appeal his conviction?
2. Should a convicted defendant who appeals only the length of his sentence be subject to a decreased or an increased sentence upon review?
3. What different skills are required of appellate court judges as compared with trial court judges?
4. Consider the implications of the suggestion that trial court judges should be paid a larger salary than appellate court judges.
5. Review the advantages and disadvantages of removing appellate court judges from the elective political process.

6. Should oral arguments by attorneys before an appellate court be eliminated in order to expedite appellate case processing?
7. What is a reasonable time frame to be used as a guideline for completing the decision of an appealed case?
8. Should a supreme court pass on the constitutionality of proposed legislation prior to enactment?
9. What are the advantages and disadvantages of centralizing responsibility for a state court system in a supreme court chief justice?
10. Should a chief justice testify before legislative committees on bills which have a substantial impact on the courts? On the court system's appropriation request?
11. Should a court system have an open account on the governmental treasury to expend funds it considers necessary to administer the courts effectively?

References

1. Pat Chapin, "Current Compensation Provisions," *Judicature* 58 (1974): 180. This article reviews the salaries, benefits, and retirement plans of all judges in all states for the year 1974.
2. Ibid.
3. Judicial Department of the State of New Mexico, *1974 Annual Report* (Santa Fe: Administrative Office of the Courts, 1975).
4. *1972 Annual Report to the Supreme Court of Illinois* (Springfield: Administrative Office of the Illinois Courts, 1973).
5. Charles W. Joiner, "The Function of the Appellate System," in William F. Swindler, ed., *Justice in the States, Addresses and Papers of the National Conference on the Judiciary* (St. Paul, Minn.: West Publishing Co., 1971), p. 102.
6. This presentation is concerned with appellate courts which are organized for the primary purpose of determining cases on review. This discussion omits the appeal remedy found in state lower trial courts where a dissatisfied litigant may appeal "de novo" to the upper trial court which is authorized by statute to hear such cases anew. This chapter, then, is concerned with courts which hear appeals following their final determination at the trial court level.
7. Daniel J. Meador, *Appellate Courts: Staff and Process in the Crisis of Volume* (St. Paul, Minn.: West Publishing Co., 1974), p. 10.
8. Ibid., p. 12.
9. Ibid., p. 14.
10. *1972 Report,* Illinois, p. 62.
11. *Annual Report of the Administrative Office of the California Courts* (Sacramento: Judicial Council of California, 1974).
12. Marlin O. Osthus and Robert A. Shapiro, *Congestion and Delay in State Appellate Courts* (Chicago: American Judicature Society, 1974), pp. 46–48.
13. Geoffrey C. Hazard, Jr., "After the Trial Court—the Realities of Appellate Review," The American Assembly, *The Courts, The Public and the Law Explosion,* ed. Harry W. Jones (Englewood Cliffs, N.J.: Prentice-Hall, 1965), p. 80.

14. Meador, *Appellate Courts,* p. 37.
15. Charles W. Joiner, "Limiting Publication of Judicial Opinions," *Judicature* 56 (1972): 198–99.
16. Marianne Stecich, "Speeding Criminal Appeals in the Second Circuit," *Judicature* 58 (1975): 289.
17. *New Mexico, 1974,* p. 16.
18. Ibid., p. 15.
19. Constitution of Illinois, Article VI, Section 16.
20. Edward E. Pringle, "The Role of the State Chief Justice," *Justice in the States,* p. 83.
21. Allan Ashman and James J. Alfini, *The Key to Judicial Merit Selection: The Nominating Process* (Chicago: The American Judicature Society, 1974), p. 179.
22. State Constitution of California, Article VI, Section 6.
23. See generally, *State Court Administrative Systems: Perspectives and Relationships* (Denver, Colo.: Institute for Court Management, 1975). This work breaks new ground in the study of state court administration in stressing the examination of the interrelationships between the chief justice and the state court administrator, the chief trial court judges, and local court administration, and state executive and legislative branches. This report goes beyond structure and organization to examine variables which influence these critical interrelationships.
24. Ibid.

7 The Prosecution Function and the Provision of Prosecution Services

The prosecutor, known in many jurisdictions as the district attorney or the state's attorney, is the chief law enforcement official of his community. "The responsibility of a public prosecutor differs from that of the usual advocate; his duty is to seek justice, not merely to convict."[1]

"The prosecutor has the responsibility of presenting the government's case in court, and his skill as a trial lawyer can be a crucial determinant of whether a defender is convicted."[2]

"Most prosecutors are young men with little trial experience because few experienced lawyers want the job. . . . The pay is so low most have a civil practice on the side, so the public isn't always properly represented. I was astounded to find that, except in the large cities, nearly every prosecutor in the United States is part time."[3]

While the courtroom is the setting in which the prosecutor executes his well understood trial role, it must be emphasized that the prosecutor is an official within the *executive* branch of government. It is vital to our system of checks and balances that the prosecutor be independent of judicial control. The independence of his role is also founded in the adversary system of American jurisprudence. The legal search for the truth and the mounting of legal proof is a contested rather than a collaborative effort. Prosecutorial independence is strengthened further by the political facts of the prosecutor's life: he was elected by the people. The elected status provides the public support for the wide discretion which attaches to this office. The prosecutor has the discretion to charge or not to charge, as well as what to charge. In 1974 the New York City District Attorney announced that, in the face of that state's harsh drug control laws, he would routinely reduce certain felony charges to misdemeanors to avoid apparent life sentences for lesser drug offenses. Almost simultaneously, the chief prosecutor in the nation's capital announced that police officers should stop sending his office cases of very limited marijuana possession.

Federal prosecutors and prosecutors in a few states are appointed rather than elected. The U.S. Attorney General disagreed with this prosecutor's directive on marijuana and obtained its withdrawal. In this case the federal prosecutor lacked the independent political base for maintaining his policy judgement. He was undoubtedly aware that public opinion had moved away from vigorous enforcement of marijuana possession violations, and that such prosecutions were among the less significant crimes processed through the court system. He was probably aware as well that drug prosecutions are often time-consuming, since defense counsel frequently move to suppress the admission of drugs as illegally seized, and that very frequently judges agree and the prosecutor's case is destroyed.[4]

The political election of the American prosecutor must be viewed with mixed emotions, although, on balance, the overall effect is a positive one. A prosecutor may present his candidacy for election on a strict law and order platform, oversimplifying the complexities of the crime problem and pandering to the lowest common denominator of public opinion. Not uncommonly, the challenger of an incumbent prosecutor argues the office holder has not been tough enough, that crime has risen during his tenure, and that he plea bargains too much.

Election is on a partisan basis, and elected officials tend to give employment priorities to loyal party workers when other more qualified applicants may be available. Conversely, many prosecutors have campaigned on an educational basis, interpreting the justice system to the public, with all its complexity, problems, and best directions. The political process has educational value to the public and to the candidate who interacts with a wide variety of people. This provides an important listening ground to hear what the public thinks and fears, and to test public reaction toward prosecutor ideas. Further, "The frequency of election, the turnover in the job, and the non-career attitude toward it all have affirmative values. A new man is likely to come to the office without a comfortable acceptance of the status quo; turnover reduces the dangers of stultification."[5]

The independent status of the prosecutor and his political power base provide him a wider latitude in his dealings with the police. The prosecutor is not the agent of the police department. Rather, the prosecutor utilizes police work to achieve his own goals of securing sanctions against law violators. It should not be assumed, however, that police agencies do not influence prosecutor practice, or that the police cannot subvert prosecutor interests. Police officers may represent a considerable political force, and their opposition to a prosecutor may be widely communicated to the public. Police noncooperation may also manifest itself in casual investigations and fragmented reports well below the standard required for effective prosecution. Generally, prosecutor-police relationships evolve into a reasonable balance where each recognizes the need for the other and extreme positions are avoided. Prosecutors hold the authority to modify or veto charges brought to them by the police, a reflection of the power inherent in this position. Certain prosecutors assign a staff member as legal adviser to a police department in recognition of the importance of police practice complying with legal requirements.

Prosecutors have additional roles. They are very active on the legislative front as advisers to legislators, and as vigorous proponents or opponents of legislation. They have a public opinion role, not only at election time but year round, to present an informed view of crime problems and crime prevention. In recent years they have expanded their activities in consumer fraud protection.

Infrequently, private attorneys are appointed as special prosecutors to act in place of the public prosecutor. This may be done on the request of a prosecutor who sees a possible conflict of interest in a particular case, as with the prosecution of a political, professional, or social acquaintance. A special prosecutor may be appointed by a judge in a case where the court considers that the public prosecutor has wrongly decided against proceeding with a case. This occurred in Chicago following the slaying by police of certain Black Panther leaders.

The prosecutor's relationship with the state attorney general is of interest. In a few states, trial prosecutors are staff members of the attorney general's office. In a number of states the attorney general may represent the state's interest in an appellate review of a trial court conviction. Some attorneys general provide a variety of technical assistance to local prosecutors. In some states the attorney general may be authorized by a governor to move into a district served by an apparently inadequate prosecutor, and on a temporary basis take over the management of that office.

Ethical Issues and Procedural Tactics

Serious ethical issues confront the prosecutor. At the forefront of these is the charging process. For example, two burglars are surprised by a homeowner in the course of a burglary. They throw a lamp against him as they escape with several stolen items. The prosecutor can charge burglary, larceny, assault and battery, willful destruction of property, and conspiracy to commit each of these, or a total of eight counts against each defendant. The proof of one offense, of course, provides a court with its jurisdiction to proceed to sentence a defendant. The existence of eight charges may well encourage plea bargaining; defense counsel may encourage his client to plead to one or two charges. Prosecution has facilitated the court's calendar problems by wiping a trial off its slate. But suppose the prosecutor has doubts whether the two arrested suspects are really the burglars. Charging them with all eight offenses would probably reach the same result, the defendants entering a plea on one or two counts to obtain dismissal of the others. But what if these defendants were really innocent?

The prosecutor who files the thin case, one where he may be trounced by defense counsel, risks judicial anger that the court's time was taken for such an obviously inadequate case. Yet to bury this case puts the prosecutor in the role of judge.

In another example, it is well known that gambling takes place at the local country club and this has been permitted for years. At the other end of town complaints are received of problems associated with low income persons gambling at a private club. There are reports of loud noises at all hours of the night, heavy drinking, fights, dishonest tabulations. The prosecutor will more likely move against the latter group of violators than the former group.

Another type of prosecutor practice received formal censure by a federal court. The case arose in the District of Columbia when a motor vehicle operator was stopped by two policemen for alleged traffic violations. He was neither charged nor ticketed at the time. Two days later the driver delivered a written complaint to the police department concerning the conduct of the officers who had stopped him. The prosecutor's office apparently entered into an agreement with the driver that he would not proceed further with his complaint and the government would not prosecute any traffic charges. Nearly three months later the driver, who was a retired police detective sergeant, filed a formal complaint with the city's Council on Human Relations. He was black; the two policemen were white. Following further conferences with the prosecutor, the driver refused to withdraw his complaint and he was then charged with and convicted of two traffic offenses. The prosecutor stated that originally, "everybody was happy to forget the whole thing. . . . But three months later he comes in and makes a formal complaint. So we said, 'If you are going to play ball like that, why shouldn't we proceed with our case?' . . . I had no reason to file until he changed back on his understanding of what we had all agreed on."

The appellate court determined that the prosecutor's motivation had been to protect police officers against a citizen's complaint in exchange for dropping the charges: "These agreements suppress complaints against police misconduct which should be thoroughly aired in a free society. And they tempt the prosecutor to trump up charges for use in bargaining for suppression of the complaint. . . . Courts may not become the 'enforcers' of these odious agreements. We must therefore bar prosecutions which are brought because a defendant refused to promise or reneged on a promise not to file a complaint against the police. Prosecutors will then have no incentive to offer or make such agreements."[6]

Another criticism of prosecutor ethics may be less valid. This view questions prosecution "where the primary motive for the prosecution relates to matters other than commission of the particular crime for which the defendant is being prosecuted."[7] This concern refers to the depression era prosecution of Al Capone for tax evasion when the government lacked sufficient evidence of more serious offenses for which he was suspect. It refers as well to the Jimmy Hoffa conviction for jury tampering initiated by the late U.S. Attorney General Robert Kennedy, who was concerned over Hoffa's administration of the Teamsters Union. The investigative and prosecutorial equipment of the federal government is rather enormous, and may well be able to find some violation, however small, by any public figure. While the criminal justice system assigns wide discretion to the prosecutor to charge or decline to charge, most of us believe this discretion is suitably used in refusing to charge a minor offense made by a first offender. Yet the assignment of discretion to this office grants the prosecutor the use of his social and political judgment in determining whether to proceed. Further, "The charges against Hoffa and Capone were not minor. They involved serious felonies for which many other individuals have been prosecuted."[8]

Further ethical questions arise under the title of conflicts of interest. American Bar Association Standards seek to clarify these issues:

> a. A prosecutor should avoid the appearance or reality of a conflict of interest with respect to his official duties.
> b. A conflict of interest may arise when, for example,
>   *i.* a law partner or other lawyer professionally associated with the prosecutor or a relative appears as, or of, counsel for a defendant;
>   *ii.* a business partner or associate or a relative has any interest in a criminal case, either as a complaining witness, a party or as counsel;
>   *iii.* a former client or associate is a defendant in a criminal case.[9]

Certain of these conflicts arise because prosecutors are frequently part-time officials who maintain private law practices and sometimes venture into business enterprises. The full-time status of a prosecutor alleviates but does not eliminate these problems; in urban offices where deputy prosecutors handle the bulk of cases, these conflicts are further reduced. The standards imply that the prosecutor should excuse himself from a given prosecution where there is a conflict or the appearance of a conflict, and that substitute counsel should be appointed in his place. An alternate view suggests the prosecutor should request an independent special prosecutor only with matters where he would be "unable to maintain proper professional detachment" or where the public is likely to believe conflicting interests "would impair his proper professional detachment."[10]

Pretrial Role

The contemporary trend is to increase prosecutor control over the charging process. The use of a mandatory grand jury to bring felony indictments is diminishing, and discretion in the prosecutor as to whether to initiate a criminal information is increasing. Prosecutor staffs have been augmented to interpose complaint deputies or screening staff between the police and the courts, evaluating the evidence and determining whether and what charges should be initiated. While this development has more generally been applied to felony charges, prosecutor screening is increasingly occurring with misdemeanor complaints, although not nearly as frequently. Prosecutor screening is sometimes cursory, other times rigorous. It is more careful with felonies than with misdemeanors, and more painstaking with the more serious felonies than the lesser felonies. Its object is to screen out legally insufficient cases and other cases where factors such as age, first offense status, heavy court docket problems, or unreliability of witnesses mitigate against formal filing. Its further purpose is to determine the charge or charges to be brought in the event of a filing decision.

The prosecutor decision whether or not to charge, what to charge, and who to charge involves a wide variety of considerations: the law, the evidence, public opinion, police opinion, court opinion, the complainant's opinion concerning enforcement, his own staff adequacy in terms of numbers and skills, sometimes the attitude of the defendant, whether a defendant will provide restitution to a complainant, the political influence of a complainant or defendant, recent press coverage about his office or about crime in the community, his own political career plans, the seriousness of the offense, and many other factors. This responsibility is a heavy one with which prosecutors must constantly struggle.

The decisions they make are criticized for responding to political pressures, for lack of uniformity, and for the low visibility of the decision-making processes. One writer asked, "Even if we assume that a prosecutor has to have a power of selective enforcement, why do we not require him to state publicly his general policies and require him to follow those policies in individual cases in order to protect evenhanded justice? Why not subject prosecutors' decisions to a simple and general requirement of open findings, open reasons, and open precedents, except when special reason for confidentiality exists? Why not strive to protect prosecutors' decisions from political or other ulterior influence in the same way we strive to protect judges' decisions?"[11]

A beginning step in this direction was taken in 1973 by the Cook County State's Attorney in issuing a report of his office's criminal division. The report noted "this is the first time the Cook County State's Attorney's Office has compiled such a report. This report begins a new system of accountability for the Office. The public has a right to know what has been done over the year. The report will be issued annually from now on." The report cited the expansion of the felony review unit providing around-the-clock staff attorneys to help police officials in the criminal charging process. The program provides legal assistance, review, and consultation. The office reviewed 5,570 felony charge referrals, approving 69 percent of these for formal filing.

The report also noted that "1973 was a year in which the Office was critically handicapped until the end of July by the abrupt removal of its investigative force by the Chicago Police Department, and the need to recruit and train eighty-one new investigators." This removal apparently related to differences between the Republican prosecutor and the Democratic administration of that city. In some communities, by agreement between police and prosecutor, a number of police officers are assigned full-time to assist in the investigations and trial preparation by the prosecutor. In other jurisdictions the prosecutor employs his own investigators, not infrequently retired police officers. While most referrals to the prosecutor's office arise from police agencies, citizens also come directly to the prosecutor with complaints of illegal activity. Beyond this, prosecutors need to initiate their own investigations into certain types of criminal activity, frequently utilizing grand juries to probe broad areas such as organized crime, illegal stock sales, fraudulent business practices, police corruption, and the like.

In recent years numerous prosecutors have asserted leadership in the development of rehabilitative programs in conjunction with the diversion of offenders from formal court processes. ABA Standards urge prosecutors to explore the availability of noncriminal disposition including rehabilitative programs and social agency resources in deciding whether to press criminal charges: "Especially in the case of a first offender, the nature of the offense may warrant noncriminal disposition."[12] Prosecutors have helped create pretrial intervention programs in many communities; these offer a variety of counseling, employment, educational, and medical assistance intervention efforts as alternatives to prosecution.

Prosecution staff also attend numerous bail hearings where judges determine the amount of bail which must be posted by a defendant to obtain release prior to trial. Pretrial release agencies in a growing number of communities facilitate defendant release from jail through alternatives to bail. While these programs are still insufficient, present projects have been useful, and prosecutor time taken up by bail hearings has been reduced. Defense counsel who represent persons retained in jail frequently bring motions to reduce the determined bail; prosecutors appear at these hearings and either agree to the requested reduction, suggest a more limited reduction, or urge retention of the original figure. Prosecutors increasingly support reform efforts to reduce pretrial jailing of less serious offenders.

A preliminary hearing is provided in many states for felony offenders, although the right to this hearing may be waived by a defendant. Different court systems may be said to have different "cultures" in this regard. In some systems this hearing is routine and essentially unchallenged. Dismissals occasionally occur where the evidence fails to show probable cause that a defendant had committed a particular crime. The hearing also may lead to a plea bargain agreement at this early stage of processing, the preliminary hearing having shown the strength or weakness of the prosecution's case.

Pretrial Discovery

The nature of the American criminal trial has changed sharply over the past decade or so as more and more states have broadened their pretrial discovery rules. Discovery requires that the prosecution turn over to defense counsel much of the information it has accumulated during the course of its investigation, together with copies of witness statements, scientific tests, physical or mental examinations, photographs, and other materials the prosecutor anticipates presenting at the trial. Such disclosure substantially reduces the surprise element of a trial. A trial is no longer the game of waiting to see the prosecutor's case as it unveils during the trial. The reasons for broadened discovery fall within the broad objective of the more efficient administration of justice. Courts can be better administered, pretrial attorney planning can be more complete, defendant's decision whether or not to go to trial can be more intelligently made, trials can be more evenly and more speedily conducted, fewer retrials will be needed since more latent issues are exposed and resolved prior to the original trial.[13] A further "balancing" rationale is that the resources available to the state—the variety of police agencies and investigative capabilities, scientific laboratories, funds for expert examination and testimony, the comparative size of the prosecution staff—have historically overwhelmed defense capability. Defense counsel, frequently appointed after the state has garnered its evidence, should have "at least the opportunity to do what the state does when the trail is fresh, namely, seek corroboration of the accused's story, or lack of it, from external facts, through avenues of inquiry opened by what the state has learned."[14]

What has developed, then, is an affirmative duty on the prosecutor's part to open up much of his case prior to trial. This information may well include the identity of the witnesses who will testify, together with their written statements in the prosecutor's file; statements made by the defendant to police officers or to grand juries; grand jury testimony of witnesses the prosecutor intends to call; copies of laboratory reports and scientific tests which have been conducted and which will be utilized; information as to prior criminal convictions of pending witnesses; information as to any electronic surveillance related to the accused. The defense is required to make certain disclosures as well, but nothing which would jeopardize the Fifth Amendment privilege against self-incrimination. The defense should disclose its physical, mental, and scientific examinations and tests, the witnesses it intends to call, and the nature of the defense it will offer.[15] Where respective counsel cannot agree on whether a particular matter is subject to disclosure, this is determined by the trial judge at trial hearing.

Plea Bargaining

Disclosure prior to trial not only facilitates the conduct of a trial, but is a powerful agent determining whether a trial will occur. Defense counsel may ascertain that the prosecution's case is so solid that his client would be wise to enter a plea of guilty. The prosecutor may gain information from the defense psychiatric examination which may suggest that a plea of not guilty by reason of insanity is more appropriate than an adversary trial of the crime. Disclosure invites communication between respective counsel; a dialogue may show certain questions as to the admissibility of evidence, and encourage the prosecutor to accept a guilty plea to a lesser offense than charged.

Somewhere between 80 and 90 percent of criminal convictions are the result of the entry of a plea rather than a guilty finding at the end of a trial. The prosecutor is the key to the plea bargaining system. While some bargaining may take place prior to charge, or at the preliminary hearing stage, far more occurs at the postdisclosure stage and in the few days prior to trial. There are typical situations which influence a plea bargain: pretrial jail status leads to acceptance by the defendant of a less generous plea bargain; representation by a highly skilled defense counsel leads to a more generous plea bargain; discovery which reveals the weakened prosecution case leads to a more generous bargain; a chronic criminal record leads to a less generous bargain; prosecution witnesses may testify unimpressively at the preliminary hearing, influencing a more generous bargain; a very crowded criminal court docket and judicial preference for plea entry leads to more generous bargains; understaffed prosecution offices lead to more generous bargains; negotiations which take place several months prior to the prosecutor's reelection bid reduces prosecutor generosity.

Juror Selection

"Since your purpose is to convince the jury to find the defendant guilty, your purpose in selecting the jury is to choose the twelve jurors most likely to return the verdict of 'guilty'."[16] Prosecutors tend to prefer as jurors persons of German or Scandinavian backgrounds; businessmen and bank employees; persons of more conservative dress; more stable individuals; persons who have a vested stake in maintaining a community's sense of propriety. Several years ago a number of leading prosecutors were asked to discuss their jury predilections: "Some prosecutors do not want a person on the jury who is an ego-maniac. . . . You will, of course, want to reject the loudmouth, the smart-aleck and the joker as jurors."[17] "From my own personal experience, I always avoid jurors who are somehow connected with the arts, such as musicians, painters or writers. . . . I never let an older woman sit on my jury who wears a hat."[18]

An advantage to the prosecutor's office is the practice of each deputy turning in a "box score." A box score is maintained on how individual jurors voted as to guilt or innocence. Where jury panels serve for two to four weeks, this information may be accumulated daily and circularized to all other trial deputies, so that when a juror appears on the panel for another trial he may be stricken from service within the number of peremptory challenges each counsel is allotted. One training program manual for prosecutors advises that when in doubt about whether a potential juror will be sympathetic to the prosecutor's position, the prosecutor should exercise a peremptory challenge and strike this juror from the panel.[19]

The voir dire examination during which respective counsel explore the attitudes and possible biases of potential jury members ends up with the selection of the jurors which each side, on balance, finds most appropriate to its objectives. Theoretically, its purpose is to select fair and impartial jurors. In reality it is an educational device where respective counsel seek to achieve a positive impression upon jurors, seek empathetic support for the approach they will take in the trial, clarify certain principal facts and law, and set a certain emotional tone for the trial. The prosecutor will seek to be friendly but not too friendly, to show a sense of humor without being condescending, to set a tone of seriousness but not overformality. By his questions the prosecutor will seek to challenge potential jurors to hold to a strong belief of guilt if, in deliberations, another juror raises a doubt which is not substantial. He will seek to neutralize possible sympathy for the underdog, clarify that a minor doubt does not nullify the "beyond-a-reasonable-doubt" standard of proof, and suggest that a police officer witness should be granted the same credibility as any other witness.

Trial Role

While law school training increasingly seeks to provide opportunities for students to work in prosecutor and defender offices, and to carry cases in nonfelony courts under supervision, the reality is that many young law school graduates join prosecutor offices and are only modestly prepared for their new roles. Larger prosecutor offices provide training opportunities for less experienced staff members to learn the more specialized law, procedures, and techniques they will need in their positions. Characteristically, prosecutor offices start novice staff members in the lower criminal court and in juvenile court. This practice is not particularly appreciated by the judges of those courts who prefer experienced and knowledgeable counsel. In time, and after he has gained respect for his preparation and trial skills, a deputy prosecutor is advanced to a felony court.

Chief prosecutors pride themselves on their conviction rate and take pleasure in publicizing that their overall conviction rate is 95 percent or 97 percent. Such figures are built up, however, by the large number of guilty pleas entered to felony charges. During 1973, in Cook County, Illinois, 6,136 felony cases were disposed of, 899 of these by trial. Of this number 531 were trials by judge, 368 were trials by jury. The conviction rate as to trials only was just 59 percent.

Careful pretrial preparation as well as effective trial execution are stressed in prosecutor offices. Good prosecutors consider it essential to personally interview all of their witnesses prior to trial so as to know their testimony before they are placed on the witness stand. Yet in the heavily trafficked lower courts, it is common occurrence for prosecutors to meet their witnesses for the first time shortly before trial. It is an axiom of trial practice not to ask your witness a question you do not already know the answer to. Where that rule is not observed, and witnesses respond with answers that surprise the prosecutor, the case may be severely weakened.

Following juror selection, a prosecutor makes his opening statement. This is a narrative, presented in logical and chronological form. It sets forth what the evidence will show, and concludes that all elements of the crime will be proven beyond a reasonable doubt. "It is unprofessional conduct to allude to any evidence unless there is a good faith and reasonable basis for believing that such evidence will be tendered and admitted in evidence."[20] It may also be disastrous; a wide hole has been opened for defense counsel to urge that the difference between the promise of evidence and the failure to produce evidence is proof the case has not been proven.

Witnesses are presented sequentially, and testify to what happened in a chronological order of time. In direct examination, the prosecutor cannot lead his witness. He cannot put words into witnesses' mouths such as "You saw John Smith robbing the bank, didn't you?" Rather, he must ask, "On the night in question, did you see the defendant John Smith? If so, tell us what you observed." Defense counsel uses cross-examination to weaken the thrust of direct examination testimony. Good prosecutors learn to stop their interrogation at the right time, to avoid duplicative questions, to build an orderly sequence of events, and to stop the testimony of a talkative or somewhat incoherent witness by speedily delivering the next question. They are dignified in dealing with their witnesses, are respectful of the jury, reach the high point of the testimony with their final witness, and then quickly sit down.

Prosecutors are urged to be professional and sincere in the conduct of the trial, and to reflect a confidence that their case is strong. "Prosecutor must project correct image, 'counsel for the people,' and not a prosecutor," and "must appear confident, tough, yet a gentleman."[21]

As defense counsel presents his case, the prosecutor cross-examines defense witnesses. Sometimes the prosecution can skillfully use such questioning to help prove the state's case. Where a defense witness has not damaged the prosecution case, prosecutors prefer to stand up and say "no questions," suggesting to the jury that the witness is not worth questioning, and avoiding possible answers which might strengthen his presently weak testimony. The prosecution's objective with a typical defense witness is to weaken credibility and raise doubts about the accuracy of the witness's memory. A favorite technique is to draw out a witness by reminding him of what he said earlier, asking him whether he is sure of this, and when he says he is, to present him with a significant inconsistency in regard to this testimony. Experienced prosecutors believe that cross-examination should be brief, should be limited to several major issues, and that only leading questions, permissible in cross-examination, should be used.

At the conclusion of a trial each counsel summarizes his argument from his point of view, the prosecutor speaking first. Defense counsel then criticizes the prosecution's case and advocates his own.

Finally, the prosecutor is given a second opportunity to speak, critiquing the defense case. That prosecution has the burden of proof is the justification for his having two closing arguments. The Denver district attorney's office gives the following advice to its prosecutors: "Closing argument is a speech and should be prepared and given like one. *Develop your own style* (what you do best will obviously most impress the jury), and most importantly *be organized.* Closing argument should be organized for emphasis—a composition. To assist you in making an organized and logical presentation you should develop a form outline which is usable in every case. Further, every trial lawyer should develop a method for recording facts during the trial so that he will have a ready reference sheet for closing argument."[22]

Depending upon the prosecutor's personal style, the closing argument may vary from completely factual to folksy to dramatic. In his initial argument the prosecutor seeks to challenge defense counsel to rebut his strong evidence, his strong witnesses. In his final argument he parries questions raised by defense counsel, and seeks to meet these head-on and confidently overcome any questions that defense counsel has raised. This final argument is usually the prosecutor's most forceful and emotional one. Some prosecutors test the bounds of propriety: "Turn this man loose if you wish and put your stamp of approval upon his lecherous conduct and let him go and rob the cradle and ruin other homes."[23]

Another prosecutor, urging the jury to vote the death penalty, charged the defendant as "the vilest type of character known to humanity. He has a warped brain, a degenerate mind. He should be killed just as a person would kill a rattlesnake."[24] On the appeal of the guilty verdict in this case the appellate court described this language as "very forceful," found that the record at the original trial completely supported the prosecutor's references, and refused to reverse the trial jury.

Other prosecutor references to a defendant as a human animal, as a mad dog, as not fit to be turned loose on society, have all been found on appeal to have been supported by the evidence, and not to have prohibited a fair and impartial trial. Such inflammatory characterizations, although not today's norm, still ring out in some contemporary trials.

Post-Trial Role

The prosecutor is present at the sentencing hearing. Certain sentencing scenarios are as follows: the judge announces he has read the probation department's presentence investigation report; defense counsel argues vigorously for probation, citing a variety of reasons why the offense or the defendant's prior record do not justify incarceration; the prosecutor argues that defendant cannot rehabilitate himself within the community and that the community is entitled to protection from the defendant for a period of time; the defendant comments briefly and the judge enters sentence. Another scenario is similar except that the prosecutor calmly informs the judge of certain factors which occurred at trial or are contained in the probation report which should be considered in determining sentence.

American Bar Association Standards opt for the latter approach. Consistent with the view of the prosecutor as an overall agent of justice, his larger function is to obtain a conviction rather than a severe sentence. ". . . He should seek to assure that a fair and informed judgment is made on the sentence and to avoid unfair sentence disparities. . . . The prosecutor ordinarily should not make any specific recommendation as to the appropriate sentence, unless his recommendation is requested by the court or he has agreed to make a recommendation as the result of plea discussions."[25] Further, he "should assist the court in basing its sentence on complete and accurate information," and "should disclose to the court any information in its files relevant to the sentence."[26]

Where a defendant has been found innocent at trial he may not be tried again. Even though the trial judge may have committed substantial error in his rulings, our legal system does not permit the prosecutor to appeal this judgment, obtain a reversal, and then try the defendant again. The Fifth Amendment of the U.S. Constitution states: "nor shall any person be subject for the same offence to be twice put in jeopardy of life or limb." State constitutions contain similar provisions. This is known as the prohibition against double jeopardy or former jeopardy. In some states, however, prosecutors are permitted to appeal such cases on matters of law. They may seek to obtain an appellate court holding that the trial judge erred on a matter of law. Where such a holding is pronounced, the law is clarified, but the defendant may not be retried.

When a defendant has been convicted at the original trial defense counsel may appeal this judgment, first through a motion for a new trial, asking that the trial judge reverse one or more trial rulings which may be significant enough to result in an order of a new trial. Such a reversal happens infrequently. Where reversals are ordered they are more typically determined by an appellate court. It is the prosecutor's duty to alertly defend against the motion for a new trial, substantiating for the record that there was no significant error.

A motion for new trial may be based upon "newly discovered evidence." Proof must be shown that such evidence could not be obtained prior to the trial despite diligent effort. The prosecutor seeks to counter such a motion by showing that the original failure to obtain this evidence was due to an absence of ordinary diligence. If this motion is based on an improperly constituted jury, the prosecutor would seek to show that defense counsel had failed to object to this at the time of the original jury selection, and if this is true, has lost his opportunity to make this challenge. Or if the motion is based on the trial judge's proceeding to trial despite a defense request for a continuance because of a missing witness, prosecution seeks to show that defense counsel failed to diligently search out this witness prior to the trial. Where defense counsel pursues a formal appeal of a conviction, the prosecutor has a duty of timely and vigorous participation. Larger prosecution offices have appellate divisions which spend all their time in the preparation and presentation of appellate cases.

The Provision of Prosecution Services

Just as reformers are urging the consolidation of nonurban law enforcement agencies into larger and more efficient units, and urging the consolidation of a variety of separate and often overlapping courts, so is there consensus that rural and less populous areas should join a number of counties into a larger district in order to afford at least one full-time prosecutor.[27] Adequate compensation for prosecutors is a parallel need. The extensive presence of part-time prosecutors—and this is not limited to rural areas—has diminished the administration of justice. There are further organizational problems, such as existed in Cleveland a few years ago, where felony screening was performed by the City Prosecutor's Office, but a separate office, the Prosecuting Attorney, tried the same felonies in the general trial court.

Another problem is the patronage employment of professional and nonprofessional staff members in many prosecutor offices. With the subsequent election of a district attorney from a different political party, the bulk of the staff is swept out and a new crew of patronage appointments receive positions. While there are positives in bringing in fresh personnel, full-scale replacement sets back operational efficiency. To counter such problems, the prosecutor's office in Los Angeles has placed all but its top personnel under civil service. The Denver district attorney has placed nonprofessional staff under a similar merit system. The National Advisory Commission of Criminal Justice Standards and Goals recommended against civil service protections for attorney staff members of a prosecutor's office as an infringement on the prosecutor's authority to select the personnel he needs to accomplish the task accorded him by the electorate. The commission also decided against recommending caseload standards of the number of cases each deputy prosecutor should be assigned annually. It did recommend assignment of at least two deputy attorneys for each trial judge conducting felony trials on a full-time basis.[28]

It is obvious that prosecutor offices require sufficient deputy prosecutors, investigators, secretarial and clerical assistance, an office manager for larger offices, appropriate quarters, and a suitable library. The award of U.S. Law Enforcement Assistance Administration funds to a large number of prosecutor offices has permitted the strengthening of staff and an expansion of activities which were not possible previously. For example, the district attorney in Brooklyn established a special unit responsible for the priority investigation and prosecution of more serious felony cases. Prosecutors in Houston, Detroit, Boston, and certain other cities initiated staff units for the investigation and prosecution of organized crime. Prosecutors in Baltimore and other cities have established units of specially trained prosecutors who function with police investigators to conduct a broad enforcement program against suppliers and distributors of narcotics. The district attorney in Denver established a consumer fraud unit which encourages consumer complaints, investigates fraudulent and deceptive trade activities, meets with various trade associations to advise them of illegal practices performed by certain of their members, and prosecutes violations of consumer law.

Prosecutor-police liaison projects have been authorized to locate prosecutors in police stations, available on a twenty-four-hour basis to advise police officers on legal technicalities incident to their practices: they review search warrant applications, advise on interrogation and line-up procedures, and suggest additional scientific tests useful in developing evidence. Such efforts initiate prosecutor participation at the earliest moment so as to speed such cases more quickly into and through the courts.

The assignment of prosecutor manpower to the juvenile court has increased substantially. The greater incidence of juvenile defense representation and the substantial increase in juvenile offenses have ovecome historic prosecutor reluctance to assign staff to this court and forced higher priority recognition for juvenile prosecution.[29]

Training opportunities have also increased. The National College of District Attorneys was formed at the University of Houston College of Law in 1970 (a related program for defense counsel was established at the same law school several years later). The National District Attorneys Association, based in Chicago, has facilitated educational programs nationally within states. Further, many states have established statewide prosecutor associations with a professional staff responsible for providing and coordinating training opportunities for local prosecutors, technical assistance to those offices, and a clearinghouse function to receive and transmit useful information.

They also serve as a catalytic force in organizing lobbying activities to achieve prosecutor objectives in the legislative arena.

Prosecutors are aware of the need to improve the internal management of their offices to achieve greater efficiency and staff productivity. Their record systems need to be modernized and appropriate records microfilmed, caseflow and paper flow procedures improved, filing systems reorganized, statistical reporting systems made more accurate and utilized more effectively, and, overall, greater attention given to management analysis.

Some prosecutors leave this office to enter private law practice and may demonstrate exceptional skill in the representation of criminal defendants. Conversely, some very good defense lawyers have been elected district attorneys, and have conducted this office with high standards. In Colorado, in 1974, the state deputy public defender was elected state attorney general. Some prosecutors have later become public defenders. While some lawyers, philosophically and temperamentally, are only comfortable serving as prosecutors and others are strictly committed to the defense, there are attorneys who prefer public to private practice and function equally well as either prosecutor or defender.

Questions for Discussion

1. What are the sources of friction between prosecution and police? Prosecution and judges? Prosecution and defense counsel?
2. What remedies are left to a victim when the prosecutor rejects filing a criminal complaint?
3. Assess the impact of broad pretrial discovery rules on criminal processing.
4. Should the district attorney who becomes a candidate for a different public office take a leave of absence or resign his position as soon as he announces his candidacy?
5. By what yardsticks should voters assess the performance of a prosecutor's conduct of his office?
6. Suppose that the most highly qualified candidate for a prosecution staff position is an attorney who is extremely active in the opposite political party to which the partisan elected chief prosecutor is a member. Should this candidate be employed?
7. Is it unprofessional conduct for a prosecutor to advise a witness to say nothing to defense counsel and to refuse defense counsel's request for an interview?
8. Should the prosecutor be authorized by statute to subpoena persons to appear for investigative interviews?

9. Assess prosecutor practice to go lightly with a defendant who has cooperated with the office and provided information which has resulted in the conviction of the major actors in a crime.
10. The mayor of a city has been slain in an armed robbery of his home, and the suspect is in custody. What is appropriate comment for the prosecutor to make to the media? Should the prosecutor oppose or acquiesce to defense counsel's motion for a change of venue?
11. Interview a member of the local prosecutor's office to learn staff assignments, staff training programs, and the extent of part-time attorney staff members.

References

1. American Bar Association Special Committee on Evaluation of Ethical Standards, *Code of Professional Responsibility,* Ethical Consideration 7–13 (Chicago: American Bar Association, Final Draft, 1969).
2. President's Commission on Law Enforcement and Administration of Justice, *Task Force Report: The Courts* (Washington, D.C.: Government Printing Office, 1967), p. 72.
3. Robert E. West, as quoted in Howard James, *Crisis in the Courts* (New York: David McKay, 1972), pp. 93–94.
4. "A survey of a six-day period in Cook County revealed, for example, that motions to suppress were made in 41 percent of all narcotics cases and were successful in 75 percent of those cases. Where the motions were sustained, the cases were usually dismissed for lack of evidence." Yale Kamisar, Wayne R. LaFave, and Jerold H. Israel, *Modern Criminal Procedure* (St. Paul, Minn.: West Publishing Co., 1974), p. 12.
5. *Task Force, Courts,* p. 73.
6. Dixon v. District of Columbia, 129 U.S. App. D.C. 341, 394 F.2d 966, (1968).
7. Monroe H. Freedman, "The Professional Responsibility of the Prosecuting Attorney," *Georgetown Law Journal* 55 (1967): 1034.
8. Richard L. Braun, "Ethics in a Criminal Case: A Response," *Georgetown Law Journal* 55 (1967): 1056.
9. American Bar Association Project on Standards for Criminal Justice, *Standards Relating to the Prosecution Function,* Standard 1.2 (Chicago: American Bar Association, Approved Draft, 1971).
10. H. Richard Uviller, "The Virtuous Prosecutor in Quest of an Ethical Standard: Guidance from the ABA," *Michigan Law Review* 71 (1973): 1164.
11. Kenneth Culp Davis, *Discretionary Justice* (Baton Rouge: Louisiana State University Press, 1969), pp. 189–90.
12. ABA, *Prosecution,* Standard 3.8.
13. See generally, American Bar Association Project on Standards for Criminal Justice, *Standards Relating to Discovery and Procedure Before Trial* (Chicago: American Bar Association, Approved Draft, 1970).
14. William J. Brennan, Jr., "The Criminal Prosecution: Sporting Event or Quest for Truth?" *Washington University Law Quarterly* 1963 (1963): 287.

15. ABA, *Discovery,* Standards 2.1, 2.3, 2.4, 3.1, 3.2, and 3.3.
16. James W. Bouska, "Selecting a Jury," in *The Prosecutor's Deskbook,* ed. Patrick F. Healy and James P. Manak (Chicago: National District Attorneys Association, 1971), p. 372.
17. Ibid., p. 374.
18. Evelle J. Younger, Lynn D. Compton, and Robert Fletcher, "Jury Selection," in *Prosecutor's Deskbook,* p. 369.
19. *Prosecutor Training Program* (Washington, D.C.: United States Attorney's Office for the District of Columbia and the Institute for Law and Social Research, 1974), p. 427.
20. ABA, *Prosecution,* Standard 5.5.
21. Daniel J. Bernstein and Thomas C. Green, "Direct and Redirect Examination of Witnesses," in *Advanced Prosecutor Training Program* (Washington, D.C.: United States Attorney's Office for the District of Columbia and the Institute for Law and Social Research, 1974), p. 247.
22. James H. Seckinger, *Trial Notebook* (Denver, Colo.: Denver District Attorney's Office, 1973).
23. Bouie v. State, 131 P. 953 (Oklahoma, 1913).
24. Williams v. State, 226 P.2d 989 (Oklahoma, 1951).
25. ABA, *Prosecution,* Standard 6.1 (a) and (b).
26. ABA, *Prosecution,* Standard 6.2 (a).
27. William F. Swindler, ed., *Justice in the States, Addresses and Papers of the National Conference on the Judiciary* (St. Paul, Minn.: West Publishing Co., 1971), p. 268; National Advisory Commission on Criminal Justice Standards and Goals, *Courts,* Standard 12.1 (Washington, D.C.: Government Printing Office, 1973).
28. National Advisory Commission, *Courts,* Standard 12.2.
29. See M. Marvin Finkelstein et al., *Prosecution in the Juvenile Courts: Guidelines for the Future,* U.S. Department of Justice, Law Enforcement Assistance Administration, National Institute of Law Enforcement and Criminal Justice (Washington, D.C.: Government Printing Office, 1974).

8 The Defense Function and the Provision of Defense Services

The basic requisites of fairness when one is accused of a crime are set forth in the Sixth Amendment to the United States Constitution: the right to a speedy and public trial; the right to an impartial jury trial in the state or district where the offense may have occurred; the right to be informed of the nature and cause of the accusation; the right to be confronted with the witness against you and to have compulsory process for obtaining witnesses in your favor; and, finally, the right to have the assistance of counsel for your defense.

The right to counsel is one matter; financial ability to secure counsel is another; effective performance by counsel is a third concern; trial preparation and trial strategy, including the resolution of certain ethical issues, is a fourth. These four factors also apply to the appeal of a case following the conviction of a defendant.

Our society has long proceeded on certain principles: that the people, in their pursuit of life, liberty, and happiness, have a right to be protected from injury by others, along with a right to the maintenance of public peace and order. Further, that certain regulation of behavior is necessary to safeguard the general health and welfare of the citizenry. Toward these ends legislators define illegal behavior or actions; law enforcement and prosecution officials, part of the executive branch, may bring allegations of law violations against individuals or organizations; the judicial branch superintends the trial procedures and fairly determines whether an offense has been committed by a particular person or persons, and if so, what sanctions shall be administered.

The need for a defense advocate, recognized as vital by James Madison and other constitutional drafters in the simpler legal climate of nearly 200 years ago, is yet more imperative with the technical law and procedure of today's criminal process. A citizen charged with a crime requires the assistance of a legally trained specialist to best protect his interest. But legal training per se is not a sufficient qualification for effective defense representation in other than the simpler cases. Despite the fact that the great percentage of criminal accusations are resolved by plea bargaining and negotiation rather than by trial, effective defense representation requires that the attorney possess effective trial skills. A lawyer who is awkward at trial and is known to strongly prefer a plea bargain may bargain away more of his client's freedom than necessary.

Partly to meet this concern, the State of California has developed a certification procedure for legal specialists in several fields of law, in much the same way that physicians may obtain certification in a particular branch of medicine. The initial California certification program has been directed at three legal specialties: criminal law, tax law, and workmen's compensation law. This development is being watched closely by the legal profession, and relates to the concerns of this chapter. Yet in a criminal defense, any lawyer is generally better than no lawyer.

In the groundbreaking 1932 United States Supreme Court decision known as the *Scottsboro* case, which mandated the right to free counsel for a capital offense, Justice Sutherland stated:

> The right to be heard would be, in many cases, of little avail if it did not comprehend the right to be heard by counsel. Even the intelligent and educated layman has small and sometimes no skill in the science of law. If charged with crime, he is incapable, generally, of determining for himself whether the indictment is good or bad. He is unfamiliar with the rules of evidence. Left without the aid of counsel, he may be put on trial without a proper charge, and convicted upon incompetent evidence, or evidence irrelevant to the issue or otherwise inadmissible. He lacks both the skill and knowledge adequately to prepare his defense, even though he have a perfect one. He requires the guiding hand of counsel at every step in the proceedings against him. Without it, though he be not guilty, he faces the danger of conviction because he does not know how to establish his innocence.[1]

Police officials, law-wise criminal defendants, judges, and attorneys know that a defense lawyer's effectiveness is related to how early in the criminal process he is employed or appointed. Police agents historically have aimed at obtaining a confession during their interrogating procedures. When a confession is obtained under legally satisfactory circumstances, the prosecution's case is largely won. Sophisticated defendants understand this along with their Fifth

Amendment rights, and respond to police questioning with basic silence. Defense oriented lawyers want to maintain the burden on the prosecution to prove the case at trial, and normally will advise their clients not to accept police requests to discuss a case with them.

Ethical Issues and Procedural Tactics

If a trial represents a search for the truth, why should attorneys not encourage their clients to be truthful with police investigators? This question relates to the next question: If one is guilty, should he not be required to admit his guilt and save everybody's time and expense, foregoing a trial? And the next question is, Why do lawyers frequently defend on technicalities?

The chain of answers to these questions begins with the canons of ethics for the legal profession, the historic precepts now generally called the Code of Professional Responsibility. The ethics provide that it is a lawyer's duty to zealously protect and defend his client's interests and rights, and to preserve his client's confidences. These ethics, together with certain hallmarks of our justice system—the presumption of innocence; the burden of proof on the prosecution (rather than the burden on the defendant of proving innocence); the defendant's right not to testify; the right to a jury trial; and the opportunity to request a change of venue where a community may be inflamed or a judge biased—all stem from the underpinning philosophy of protecting the rights of the individual against the great powers of the state. Such an approach reduces the probability that prosecutions will be brought on trumped-up charges or that false statements or manufactured evidence will be used against an innocent defendant. At stake is one's liberty. At stake is national honor. It would be far easier if we changed the rules, restricted defense attorney practices, and eased the proof of the prosecution's case. But we would also corrupt the system of justice, depart from our history as a nation of ordered liberties, and move a long way toward a police state.

Undoubtedly some guilty persons go innocent because of the obstacle course to conviction which is the American justice system. Undoubtedly also, some innocent persons are nonetheless convicted. Not all criminal cases are open and shut. Not all criminal laws can stand constitutional challenge. Not all laws are written with sufficient clarity that an individual knows when he is violating a statute. Witnesses are not always able to categorically identify the offender. The correct offender may be arrested, but the evidence utilized in seeking his conviction may have been illegally obtained. The goals of justice must be dignified by their means. Police searches, arrests, questioning, lineup procedures, laboratory procedures, and detention procedures must meet tests of constitutional and legal standards to be admitted into evidence at trial; the prosecutor must bring out into the open any information he possesses which may speak to the innocence of the accused, and he is not permitted to comment on a defendant's refusal to take the witness stand; judge and jury are also bound by procedures requiring fairness and impartiality.

There is another strong factor: virtually all defendants prefer their liberty to incarceration, and prefer to retain their liberty as long as possible before incarceration may be ordered. Incarceration interferes with what most people like to do, and our jails and prisons are not pleasant places. Defense lawyers prefer to keep their clients away from destructive prison environments. True, some defendants are extremely dangerous or sometimes continue to offend while their trial is pending, and lawyers recognize that the public may be better off if their clients were convicted and imprisoned. But this should not stop the zeal of their defense. It can go no other way. The lawyer's role is not to play judge. The lawyer is an advocate. He is the judge of trial strategy, but not of the trial or of society's concerns. There is a prosecutor, and the system would be out of balance if defense counsel also represented the interests of the state.

The traditions and responsibilities of the criminal defense lawyer have developed over hundreds of years. His role in the defense of juveniles is more recent, and he understands it less well. The public questions this advocacy. Judges, probation officers, parents, and even many children who are before the court feel uncertain about the role of the lawyer in juvenile court. Historically, children brought before the juvenile court were in reality presumed guilty rather than innocent; legal rights were unprotected; the basic issue was what actions should be taken to punish, to help, or both to punish and to help the child. Confession and the truth were seen as the starting points for rehabilitation. Lawyers were seen as inconsistent with and obstructive to this purpose. As the juvenile court was coerced into becoming a more legal forum in the late 1960s by United States Supreme Court decisions and updated state juvenile court acts, lawyers entering this court tried to discern their role and responsibility. Some became the vigorous advocate, transferring criminal court tactics to the juvenile court setting. Others overly encouraged their clients to admit to their offenses based on a parental belief that this would build character; they deferred to probation personnel and the judge, who seemingly had more knowledge of what would be helpful to the child. A further confusion pertained to the issue, conscious or not to the lawyer, of whom he represented. If the parents paid his fee, he might consider his loyalty to be to the parents rather than to the child whose liberty was in jeopardy. In principle, however, the attorney should represent the child.

A typical defense lawyer seeks to learn from his client the extent of his involvement in the alleged crime or delinquent act. He doesn't ask, usually, whether his client is guilty or innocent. While he may have doubts whether his client's account is a truthful one, he tends to accept this account and to utilize this to the best of his ability.

Trial tactics are the basic province of the lawyer. But the defendant should be the basic decision-maker on whether to plead guilty or to go to trial; whether the case should be tried before a judge or a jury; and whether the defendant will testify. An attorney may make suggestions on these questions, but the decisions should largely be those of the defendant. Conversely, the defendant may make suggestions to the attorney: which potential jurors might best be excused where there is a choice; whether or not a certain witness should be called in his defense; what persons should be interviewed in preparation of the defense.

Where a defendant wishes to testify, and even though the defense attorney believes his client will be untruthful under oath, the attorney should not act to bar his client's testimony. Even where a prosecution witness appears to be truthful, it is the defense attorney's duty to seek to weaken the credibility of this witness.[2] In short, the defense attorney is the advocate for his client who seeks to walk out of the courtroom innocent. Noted defense attorney F. Lee Bailey has commented that in a criminal case, the defendant does not want justice, he wants freedom. Persons who disagree with this approach not infrequently become converts when they are charged with crime. Former Vice-President Spiro Agnew, a major critic of courts and "soft-headed judges," was probably grateful that his judge sentenced him to probation without supervision, rather than incarceration, following the entry of his *nolo contendere* ("no contest") plea to a criminal charge.

Pretrial Role

A lawyer undertakes the preparation of a defense in a variety of ways. He talks with his client in a conference room at the local jail or in his office. The release of a client to the community pending trial may enable him to give his attorney greater assistance in trial preparation; the defendant can more easily find witnesses and bring them for interviews with his lawyer. It is often advisable for the lawyer to go to the scene of the alleged crime and to examine the location thoroughly. He may approach prosecution witnesses and request they answer his questions. Such witnesses have no duty to talk or not to talk, and may or may not accept an interview. Extensive legal research of state and federal appellate court decisions, and of the statute or statutes in question, is often critical.

Many public defender agencies employ trained investigators to perform certain of this work which does not require lawyer skills, much as the prosecution frequently relies on its investigators. It is equally important that private defense attorneys secure competent investigators. In certain cases defense counsel also needs to obtain the assistance of expert witnesses, such as fingerprint experts, psychiatrists, and chemical analysts.

It can be said that the nature of criminal trial preliminaries is changing from the prior model of "We don't tell the other side anything," to a more open search for the disputed issues and to a mandatory sharing by the prosecutor of certain evidence and information in his possession. The legal term for this is "discovery," and rules of criminal procedure, as well as certain statutes and case law, guideline what the prosecutor must turn over to defense counsel and under what conditions. Increasingly, the defendant, under certain safeguards, may be required to indicate the basis of his defense, but of course he cannot be compelled to divulge self-incriminating information.

Defense preparation should seek out before trial any written confession the defendant may have made to police agents, and during the trial, under the rules of a number of states, to obtain any written statement made by a witness to the police, once the witness has completed his trial testimony.

A rather wide variety of pretrial motions may be filed: that the statute alleged to have been violated is unconstitutional; that the jury panel is not representative; that the arrest was illegal; that the search was unreasonable; that the lineup was prejudicial; that a confession was illegal; that wiretap or electronic eavesdropping information was obtained improperly; that excessive publicity has rendered a fair trial difficult, and the offense should be heard in another district.

Prosecutor discretion largely determines whether a criminal charge becomes a criminal case. This discretion is wide, and is not generally subject to judicial review. A defense lawyer may occasionally seek to talk the prosecutor out of charging a defendant, and may suggest some other approach, such as restitution, in lieu of a formal case. Yet generally the prosecutor does not solicit such input to assist him in his decision. The decision of the prosecutor whether or not to proceed is largely outside the influence and strategy of the defense lawyer.

Grand juries, particularly used in eastern and southern states, determine whether or not to return a felony indictment. Defendants may be called before the grand jury, and their Fifth Amendment privilege against self-incrimination applies here—except where the prosecutor has offered them immunity from prosecution. Their attorney is not permitted to be present, but a witness may go outside the grand jury room to talk with his lawyer from time to time.

The bail decision is quite subject to defense intervention. The attorney may push to get bail set earlier or lower, or to obtain the defendant's release on recognizance. The attorney may file a motion to reduce bail, contending the bail asked is excessive.

In many states, by statute or rule, the preliminary hearing or probable cause hearing is the next phase in the processing system. Its purpose is to show to a judge that there is sufficient evidence against the defendant to go forward to the following stage. The right to counsel and free counsel has been held to apply to preliminary hearings.[3] Such hearings may be used unimaginatively and perfunctorily; the grand jury indictment may precede or follow such a hearing in certain states. By contrast, intensive preliminary hearing is useful to both prosecution and defense counsel in assessing the strength of witness testimony and demeanor in this dress rehearsal for the prospective trial.

The development of pretrial diversion/intervention programs, particularly in larger cities, augurs that defense counsel should consider routing their clients into such programs which offer rehabilitation services in conjunction with deferred pleas.

Pretrial plea bargaining is another hallmark of the justice system. Characteristically, prior to trial, lawyers confer to consider whether a case may be settled on the basis of an agreed upon proposal which the prosecutor would submit to the court. American Bar Association Standards set forth:

> When the lawyer concludes, on the basis of full investigation and study, that under controlling law and the evidence, a conviction is probable, he should so advise the accused and seek his consent to engage in plea discussions with the prosecutor, if such appears desirable. Ordinarily the lawyer should secure his client's consent before engaging in plea discussions with the prosecutor.[4]

Preparation for trial and possible plea bargaining requires that a defense attorney discover as much information from the prosecutor as is legally permitted. Usually prosecutors must turn over to defense counsel all statements made by the accused; grand jury minutes containing the accused's testimony; statements made by persons who will testify at the trial for the prosecution; any reports by experts, including physical and mental examinations and scientific tests; and other relevant testimony. Such information permits the defendant to better determine whether a plea or trial is more appropriate, and permits a trial to proceed in a more orderly fashion.

Juror Selection

Experienced criminal defense lawyers generally prefer to try a case before a jury rather than a judge. They feel the odds are a little bit better with a jury. Experienced judges, having carefully observed the testimony of substantial numbers of witnesses and defendants over a period of years, more quickly see through a thin defense, or may more incisively pierce through the testimony of a witness who is more believable to a jury. Such judicial insights are not always correct, however. In most states a unanimous jury is required to convict a defendant. One hold-out juror can create a "hung jury," and make it necessary to try the case again. Such a circumstance increases the defendant's bargaining power with a prosecutor the next time around. Sometimes the case is not retried. A criminal jury frequently takes its responsibilities very seriously, and may convert a limited doubt to a reasonable doubt.

Trial lawyers talk endlessly about the kinds of persons they like to have on juries. Their theories, however, do backfire. A juror they considered sympathetic or defense oriented may prove to be the leading advocate for conviction. The converse is sometimes true. In general defense lawyers prefer as jurors persons who are more emotional or empathetic, who have had certain troubles in their own life experiences, who derive from southern European rather than northern European backgrounds, members of minority groups, persons sensitive to society's social ills, people who listen well, who do not feel they know all the answers, who are thoughtful, and are either less or highly educated. Accountant-types are avoided, while bartenders would be selected. Engineers may be rejected in favor of auto mechanics. One who conforms to routinized work regimens would take lower priority to an upper middle class housewife.[5]

According to the rules of procedure each side is allowed a prescribed number of peremptory challenges: the attorneys can reject a prescribed number of persons as jurors without stating any reasons. Both sides are allowed an unlimited number of challenges for cause: when the judge agrees that a potential juror is not able to be fundamentally fair and impartial. Examples may include the wife of a police officer; one who has been a victim of a similar crime and carries emotional scars from that experience; one who admits to minority group prejudice when there is a minority group defendant; a person who reveals severe prejudice against police or courts; a person who cannot come back for the second day of trial because of a pressing personal problem.

Trial Role

The defense lawyer role has been described as:

> The primary role of counsel is to act as champion for his client. . . . A lawyer cannot be timorous in his representation. Courage and zeal in the defense of his client's interest are qualities without which one cannot fully perform as an advocate. . . . Against a "hostile world" the accused, called to the bar of justice by his government, finds in his counsel a single voice on which he must be able to rely with confidence that his interests will be protected to the fullest extent consistent with the rules of procedure and the standards of professional conduct.[6]

A criminal trial, of course, is much more than a "proving" contest to decide whether one has committed a particular crime. There may be substantial subtrials within the trial: the facts in comparison with the law regarding search and seizure, or the voluntariness of a confession, or the technical admissibility of certain evidence, or even a challenge as to whether the jury selection method in a community can provide a representative cross section of citizen jurors.

The selection of a jury, from the defense lawyer's viewpoint, includes an objective over and above the selection of persons who will be fair and impartial to the defendant. The selection process, called in the trade a "voir dire," is also an educational process. Counsel asks questions such as, "If you are convinced of a defendant's innocence, and if after discussion with fellow jurors who believe he is guilty you still believe the case against defendant has not been proven beyond a reasonable doubt, will you still stand on your belief as to his innocence?" And further, "Do you fully understand that the defendant is clothed with the presumption of innocence, that the burden is upon the prosecutor to prove guilt beyond any reasonable doubt, and the burden is not on the defendant to prove his innocence?" Or, "If you were to exchange places with the defendant, would you consider that someone such as yourself meets the high test of fairness and impartiality as a juror?" Through such questioning, and through treating each potential juror with dignity and interest, the lawyer seeks to neutralize the juror against any prejudices he may hold, including an assumption that since the defendant is on trial he must have done something wrong.

The prosecutor performs a similar questioning and neutralizing role. But in the federal courts the judges do all of this questioning, and at best the lawyers may only submit proposed questions for the judge to ask the jurors. This is done to expedite the trial, to eliminate the possibility of a mistrial at this stage through improper lawyer questioning, and perhaps because it is a more objective and a more controlled process. ABA Standards support the federal position, consider that questioning and statements aimed at influencing the jury toward counsel's view of the case are improper, and restrict the function of the voir dire to "reasonable inquiry to insure a fair and impartial jury."[7] Yet this view is anathema to criminal defense attorneys.

The next phase of a trial is the opening statement by respective counsel. The prosecution statement normally sets forth the evidence which will be introduced at the trial to prove the guilt of the defendant. Defense counsel may follow with a statement that prosecution will be unable to present sufficient evidence to convict, and that certain evidence will be presented by witnesses for the defendant which will disprove the prosecution's evidence. Defense counsel is not required to make such a statement at this time. He may reserve the right to present it once the prosecution's case has been completed.

The next step is for the prosecutor to examine his witnesses and to request the admission of his exhibits: weapons, stolen items found on or near the defendant, fingerprints found at the scene of the crime matching the defendant, handwriting testimony and other types of documents seeking to prove a chain of evidence that a crime was committed and that the defendant committed the crime.

Defense counsel enters objections to statements and proposed exhibits he considers legally inadmissible. A judge may sustain or overrule an objection, sometimes immediately, sometimes at a conference he will hold at the bench with the lawyers, and sometimes in his chambers where he may have retired with counsel to hear more prolonged argument. When an objection is sustained the judge normally asks the jury to cancel from their minds the statement or the proposed exhibit which had been ruled impermissible. Court observers recognize, however, that jurors do not always wipe out such statements or information from their consciousness. This is one of many reasons why there is interest in developing a new approach to trials, a videotape trial where the examination of witnesses is conducted by videotape prior to juror selection, where sustained objections result in the erasure of what was objected to, and where the trial consists of the selection of the jurors, opening statements by counsel, presentation and cross-examination of witnesses and exhibits on videotape, and then the final instructions to the jury and closing arguments by counsel. Further reasons for videotape trials include a substantially shortened time expenditure by jurors, and a greater convenience for witnesses whose testimony can be videotaped at any time.[8] Ohio has been the most noteworthy experimenter with such a system. Though there remain a number of unresolved legal issues which attach to the videotape trial, interest in and experimentation with this approach are increasing.

A trial may be brief, less than an hour, or it may require several months. In more serious trials the jurors are "locked up" each night once they have been empaneled and sworn, until the trial has been completed and they have concluded their deliberations. They generally eat together during this process under instructions from the judge prohibiting discussion of the case with anyone until the trial has been concluded and they have received their instructions. They are not to read the newspapers, watch news programs on television, or discuss the case with their family or friends by telephone; all this has the objective of isolating the jurors from outside comments on the case until they have completed their responsibility.

A trial is both a legal conflict and a psychological struggle. Each side, of course, seeks to win, and is under an ethical duty to utilize all trial artistry which is legally permissible. Defense counsel typically seeks to weaken the credibility of prosecution witnesses, to suggest that their memories are uncertain, to widen the spaces in the chain of evidence, to weaken witness identification of the defendant as the one who may have committed the offense, to oppose the admissibility of proffered evidence as illegally or unconstitutionally obtained. The seesaw continues: direct examination by the prosecutor, cross-examination by the defense counsel, redirect examination to strengthen prosecution testimony, recross-examination to further weaken the statements made in the redirect examination, the further narrowing by respective counsel of matters left unclear after the most recent examination, and so on, with witness after witness.

When all this testimony is in the prosecutor rests, and typically defense counsel moves for a directed verdict of acquittal, contending that the judge should remove the case from the jury and direct a verdict of acquittal based on a belief that insufficient evidence has been submitted which could convict the defendant. Occasionally this motion is granted and the trial is ended. More often the motion is denied and the defendant is offered his opportunity to present his case.

The defendant may or may not testify. The Fifth Amendment protects his silence. If he chooses to testify he is subject to cross-examination, which includes the question of whether he has earlier been convicted of a felony offense. The jury is permitted to know about prior felony convictions. For the defendant's testimony and that of his other witnesses, it is now the defense attorney who conducts the direct examination while the prosecutor cross-examines. When a defendant rests his case, prosecution may call rebuttal witnesses to offer testimony in response to matters placed into evidence for the first time in defendant's case. For example, if the defense has been based on alibi, that defendant was in another city at the time of the alleged offense, prosecution rebuttal witnesses may testify this is untrue, and that they saw him at the time and place stated by earlier prosecution witnesses. Defense counsel may submit surrebuttal testimony, witnesses to counter new information brought out in prosecutor's rebuttal testimony. And this can continue further.

When all evidence is in the defense lawyer will renew his motion for a directed verdict of acquittal, which may be, but is not typically, granted.

The jury is sent down for coffee while lawyers gather with the judge to develop and approve his written instructions to the jury. This may be a lengthy process with substantial argument as to which instructions should or should not be given; knowledgeable lawyers see this as an important stage for obtaining favorable instructions.

The jurors are reassembled. The judge then reads the instructions which constitute the basic legal framework for jury deliberations, and the lawyers make their closing statements, summing up the evidence which has been presented. The prosecutor leads off with his closing argument, reviewing the strength of his side of the case and clarifying the weak spots in the defense. Defense counsel reverses this approach, pointing out, based on what has occurred at the trial, that the prosecution's case is insufficient. The prosecutor is then furnished a final opportunity to comment on defense counsel's argument; he is given the last word because he has the burden to prove guilt.

The jurors are sworn anew, taken to their deliberation room where they choose a foreman and begin their own review of the trial, and initiate the process resulting, usually, in a decision, though at times in indecision.

Post-Trial Role

When a defendant has been convicted, whether by a jury or following trial before a judge, the next significant judicial process is the sentencing hearing. What should—but does not always—occur prior to this hearing is a probation study of the defendant, known in criminal courts as a presentence investigation and in juvenile courts as a social study or social history. In many court systems such a study is not always made, or it is frequently cursory. Also, in a minority of states the jury, regretfully, determines the sentence, not only in capital cases but in noncapital cases as well. Clearly the better practice is for the judge presiding at the trial to make the sentencing decision. This provides a greater opportunity for more consistent sentencing as between defendants since one person would make these decisions, and there is a greater opportunity for the preparation of a presentence investigation. In felony courts the sentencing hearing generally occurs two, three, or four weeks following trial, to afford the opportunity for the presentence study. The better practice is for the probation department to provide a copy of the study to both prosecution and defense counsel. There is merit for defense counsel to perform his own presentence investigation. He should be prepared to propose an imaginative rehabilitation program which might be more promising to the judge than what the probation department has recommended.

Defense counsel has the right to cross-examine the probation officer, although not enough defense counsel perceive this as their role and responsibility. More typically a probation officer presents his report, the defense lawyer may ask a question or two, may advocate his reasons why probation rather than incarceration should be ordered, and prosecution counsel offers a reverse argument: that incarceration is necessary for the protection of the community and for the rehabilitation of the defendant. The judge may ask questions, provide the defendant with an opportunity to make his own statement, and then enter the sentence.

Following this defense counsel has several options: he may prepare an appeal of the finding of guilt to a higher court after first going back to the trial judge to request reversal of the finding based on possible error in the proceedings. Or, in certain states, he may bring an appeal solely on the basis of the sentence: that it was harsh and unjustified, an abuse of discretion, or—rarely—beyond legally permissible statutory provisions.

The Provision of Defense Services

The right to counsel has evolved from a permission to be represented by a lawyer if you could employ one, to a judicial duty to advise each defendant of his right to free counsel if indigent, and the public duty to pay for lawyer representation of defendants unable to afford private counsel. In 1932 the United States Supreme Court interpreted the federal constitution to require that all states provide free counsel to indigents charged with capital offenses.[9] The court extended this protection to all felony cases in 1963.[10] Four years later the justices entered a similar mandate for juveniles charged with delinquency where they were subject to commitment to an institution.[11] The cycle was completed in the 1972 *Argersinger* ruling applying this right to persons charged with criminal misdemeanors or ordinance violations where their freedom was put in jeopardy.[12]

High court decisions are not self-executing. When the high court speaks, there is not instant and universal compliance with its mandates. A review of the implementation of the *Argersinger* opinion revealed that many court systems were ill prepared to fulfill its requirements.[13] The furnishing of more attorneys, free to defendants but costly to local and state government treasuries, is not embraced enthusiastically by a number of judges and funding bodies. The author has observed lower court judges ignore or slur over the advisement of the right to counsel and encourage waiver of this right. Felony courts, however, tend to require counsel in every case. The gravity of this right is less rigorously recognized in lower criminal and juvenile courts. Historically, lawyers were appointed to represent indigent defendants as a public responsibility of the legal profession. They did not receive payment for this service. In time, lawyers received limited payments for such representation. Today, compensation varies from token to reasonable to quite reasonable compensation. Some observers are concerned that token payment results in token justice.

There are now at least three approaches to the provision of defense services for the indigent: (1) The appointment of private attorneys (this is known as the assigned counsel system); (2) An organized defender service, organized as a public entity, the public defender, or under private charitable sponsorship such as a legal aid society, where a local or state governmental entity contracts with such a society to provide payment for defense services; or (3) A combination of the assigned counsel and an organized defense service, known as a "mixed system." The latter alternative, a combination or mixed system, was recommended by the National Advisory Commission on Criminal Justice Standards and Goals.

Assigned Counsel

Under this approach, judges may compile a list of attorneys who will accept appointment and assign cases to them either randomly or selectively. Upon completion of his representation the lawyer submits an itemized statement which sets forth the number of hours required by this task in interviewing, legal research, negotiations, court appearances, and trial. The judge sets the fee based upon a court schedule or the going rate for court appointments, and payment is made from a public treasury.

The primary advantage of this approach is the continuing involvement of the private bar in the criminal justice system. More lawyers develop or maintain criminal and juvenile defense skills, discern the problems in law and procedure, and participate in justice system improvement efforts. The lawyer may be a busy one, but his practice is varied and not routinized. Further, defendants consider they have their own lawyer, an independent private practitioner who is responsible to them and not to an organization. Experienced trial practitioners are accordingly made available to represent defendants. The same lawyer characteristically represents the defendant from the beginning to the end of the court experience. That counsel was appointed by the judge suggests the judge will not be hostile to him or his client.

There are negatives as well. A private counsel system is considered to be more costly. Judges here and there appoint their personal friends or political cronies. A small number of lawyers may be regularly appointed, and though they may be adequately qualified take in an excessive share of the appointed counsel budget. Reportedly, one California lawyer was compensated $60,000 in one year for appointments in a juvenile court. A Michigan lawyer reportedly received $56,000 in one year from one criminal court. In another court approximately twenty lawyers shared nearly $250,000 of payment for representing indigent clients.

In certain jurisdictions some of the least qualified lawyers stand nearby at daily arraignment hearings and are appointed on the spot because they are available. Young lawyers lacking in trial skills place their names on a judge's list and receive appointment because a judge wishes to help out a struggling attorney. Where counsel fees are low, the more successful attorneys reject appointment because it is not remunerative enough.

Appointed lawyers may prefer not to rock the boat and risk the alienation of the judge who is providing at least part of their bread and butter. Private counsel are not infrequently lacking in the skills and knowledge which accompany criminal law specialists.

A lawyer may defend his client well, but have little commitment to changing the system. He may be lacking in knowledge of the shortcomings of justice system practices, and fail to utilize certain meritorious defenses. He typically lacks investigative assistance that would substantially aid trial preparation and conduct of the trial. He is less interested in appealing a trial court ruling which if reversed might be advantageous to countless other defendants.

Appointive counsel are expected to make contributions to a judge's reelection campaign in those jurisdictions where judges are popularly elected.

Organized Defender Services

The *Gideon* v. *Wainwright* decision of 1963 sparked a rapid expansion in the provision of organized public defender services. This movement was further accelerated by the *Gault* and *Argersinger* decisions, as well as by other rulings which provided the right to counsel at additional stages in the criminal justice system.[14]

The National Defender Survey completed by the National Legal Aid and Defender Association in late 1973, examined the organization and delivery of defense services to indigent defendants.[15] While organized defender systems were common to only 3 percent of the more than 3,000 counties in the United States in 1961, this total had grown to 28 percent of counties in 1973. Even more significantly, organized defender systems provided defense services in jurisdictions totaling 25 percent of the American population in 1963, but a decade later this figure had grown to 64 percent.

In general, the more populous the county the more likely defense services were provided by an organized defender system rather than a private assigned counsel approach. Ninety-two percent of counties having populations in excess of 500,000 had organized defender systems; 53 percent of counties with population between 50,001 and 500,000 had organized defender systems; however, in rural counties with fewer than 50,001 persons only 20 percent had organized defender systems. That study's definition of organized defender system included public defender offices (governmental entities), legal aid societies (private, nonprofit agencies) compensated to represent indigent defendants, and programs where an attorney or group of attorneys represented defendants on a contractual basis with a governmental subdivision.[16]

A further clear trend was state rather than county assumption of primary responsibility to organize and fund defender services. As of 1973 sixteen states had taken this step. In 1974 New Jersey took a significant step in enhancing the status and broadening the role of an organized defender service. There the state public defender was retitled Director of the Office of Public Advocacy, became a member of the governor's cabinet, and was authorized to provide not only public defense services but also to insure representation in mental illness and retardation commitment procedures, to represent the public interest in public utilities rate hike proceedings, and to operate consumer protection services.

The National Advisory Commission on Criminal Justice Standards and Goals urged that each jurisdiction have both a full-time public defender organization and a coordinated assigned counsel system involving substantial participation of the private bar.[17] It noted that an assignment of private counsel should be coordinated between the bench and the defender service. The random or nonrandom assignment of lawyers from a judge's appointment list was opposed. There should be an assigned counsel system and not an assigned counsel patronage list. It was recommended that a public defender office compile and maintain a panel of attorneys from which a judge may appoint counsel. The trial court would have the right to add additional attorneys to the panel. Defender offices were urged to provide training to panel lawyers, support services such as investigators and expert witnesses, and to monitor the performance of appointed attorneys.[18]

Private counsel should be used both because a variety of benefits should result from the continued involvement of the private bar in criminal justice and because there were situations where the public defender was unsuitable for appointment. A defender should not represent codefendants when there is a conflict in joint representation: the interest of one might suggest a legal strategy injurious to the other. Both defendants should have different lawyers, and the two attorneys should not come from the same law office. Further examples for the need for private counsel occur when a defendant lacks confidence in the defender office and categorically refuses representation from that office. Also, workload pressures may suggest that prolonged trials or cases involving extensive preparation be assigned to private counsel when the defender office simply lacks the manpower to accept such appointments. This survey found that perhaps eight million persons were referred to courts annually for nontraffic offenses, and that half of these cases might qualify through financial indigency for publicly-paid counsel. The burden in providing effective defense services for so many persons represents an enormous challenge to our public responsibility to fulfill the rights of the accused.

What can happen where there is inadequate funding of defense services combined with judicial sensitivity for effective legal defense is illustrated by a 1974 District of Columbia case. There, the Public Defender Service accepted appointment to an agreed-upon percentage of indigent defendant cases; the remaining appointments were assigned to a number of private attorneys who appeared frequently in the criminal and juvenile divisions of that court. Congress then ceased appropriating funds to pay for private counsel. Two defendants asked to be relieved of private counsel appointed for them prior to the congressional cut-off period. The judge agreed that "neither counsel has demonstrated any particular degree of diligence, legal acumen, or perseverance in a host of prior appearances before this Court." The judge was urged by prosecution counsel to appoint lawyers at no pay from the general noncriminal bar, or to continue the two cases indefinitely until funds became available. Instead the court dismissed these cases and freed the defendants, pointing out (1) that the public defender caseload was already above its thirty felony cases per attorney standard and that a further burdening of the defender's office would threaten defendants' right to effective counsel; (2) that coercing private attorneys who lacked criminal trial skills into volunteered service would not provide the quality of defense service a defendant must receive; and (3) that at least one of the defendants was incarcerated, and to indefinitely postpone the trial would unfairly continue him in jail.

Judge Halleck concluded his opinion noting that on the day in question twenty-three victimless crime cases "were set for trial on the misdemeanor calendar, resulting in the unavailability to the Court of the services of the lawyers assigned to defend those cases, lawyers who could well have been employed in representing defendants charged with serious crimes. In a criminal justice system plagued by scarce resources, it is sheer folly to squander what little is available on wholesale prosecution of victimless crime. . . . "[19]

Strengths of Organized Defender Services

It is believed that organized defender services are cheaper to operate per case than the assigned counsel system. As an example, a defender may travel ten miles to the county jail, interview four clients, and then return to his office or the court. The private attorney travels the same distance and more typically visits a single client. Economies of scale occur with defender representation of a number of clients at arraignments and trial proceedings in a given court. The Defender Survey cited an average case cost of $122 reported by 100 defender systems, an amount which appears especially reasonable.[20]

Specialists better comprehend court procedures than generalists, and have more knowledge of case decisions, judicial practices, and useful trial bargaining techniques. A number of defender organizations have staff counsel, paraprofessional aides, or law students visiting the jails daily and attending all arraignments, thereby enabling staff to provide earlier counsel; typically private counsel is assigned by a court to represent a defendant when he first appears before a judge at arraignment hearing. Defenders, in daily communication with other defenders, share experience, knowledge, and assistance which is valuable to their job performance. Periodic in-service training seminars are more easily programmed for defender organizations. They more readily take advantage of defense bar seminars provided in their state. They increase their skills through participation at the National College of Criminal Defense Lawyers and Public Defenders, located at the College of Law, University of Houston. This college provides training opportunities at basic and advanced levels for attorneys specializing in the defense of criminal offenders. They more typically have the assistance of other useful adjuncts: investigators, medical and other specialist witnesses, and social workers to assist in designing alternate sentencing recommendations or in providing direct helping services to clientele. They challenge existing shortcomings in the criminal justice system through legal attack, testimony before legislative bodies, meetings with criminal justice agency personnel, and through other formal or informal means. They seek to go beyond their first duty to represent their client well, to the further goal of seeking to ensure that all criminal justice system personnel treat all clients well.

Weaknesses of Organized Defense Services

The caseload crunch often overwhelms a defender, reducing his case-by-case effectiveness and burning him out more quickly. The National Advisory Commission has suggested defender caseload standards: "Felonies per attorney per year: not more than 150; misdemeanors (excluding traffic) per attorney per year: not more than 400; juvenile court cases per attorney per year: not more than 200; Mental Health Act cases per attorney per year: not more than 200; and appeals per attorney per year: not more than 25."[21] The National Defender Survey found, however, that full-time attorneys averaged 173 felony defendants per year. Further, full-time defenders in misdemeanor courts averaged 483 defendants per year.[22]

One disgruntled defendant or substandard performance by a defender, rubs off on the credibility and respect clients have for other defenders. A jail grapevine quickly passes the word, and jailed defendants may stereotype all defenders as substandard. Defender services may be functionally fragmented: one defender represents a client at arraignment and bail hearings; there is a different defender at preliminary hearings; a third attorney is the defendant's attorney for plea bargaining or trial. Clients appropriately become dissatisfied having to adjust to multiple attorneys. Private attorneys, resentful that the advent of a public defense service has reduced their income from criminal practice, are unsupportive of organized defender service funding requests.

When a single defender and a single prosecutor are assigned to a single courtroom for a period of time, the relationship between defender and prosecutor may become or appear to become too casual and insufficiently adversary, and a defender may hesitate to risk alienating the judge whom he has to appear before day in and day out.

There are problems in the methods for selecting chief defenders in certain states and districts. In Colorado the chief state defender and his top deputy are selected by the justices of the Supreme Court, a process which brings into theoretical question the fundamental independence of this office. In Illinois a chief circuit defender is selected by the circuit court judges "to serve at their pleasure"; the same prospect for restricted independence applies there. An Illinois defender told this author the problem would be minimized if he were appointed for a defined term of three or four years, but when he can be terminated any day upon alienation of a sufficient number of judges there is an overly restrictive burden on his independent role. In Florida public defenders are elected in each circuit, a prospect which adds the questionable dimension of having to sell a certain brand of justice to a somewhat unenthused electorate. The National Advisory Commission suggests that "the most appropriate selection method is nomination by a selection board and appointment by the Governor. If a jurisdiction has a Judicial Nominating Commission . . . that commission also should choose public defenders. If no such commission exists, a similar body should be created for the selection of public defenders."[23]

Questions for Discussion

1. Why should defense lawyers seek to get their clients off on technicalities? Represent defendants who are obviously guilty?
2. What can an indigent defendant do if he believes his public defender is ineffective? What can a judge do if during trial he recognizes a defense lawyer is incompetent?
3. Should a police officer be allowed to question a defendant outside the presence of an attorney? Why? Why not?
4. Should the existence of a really good prison system in a state affect a lawyer's defense of his client?
5. What are the advantages and the problems involved in the videotaping of criminal trials?
6. Why is the burden of proof on the prosecution, and is this a fair rule?

7. Why do courts increasingly require probation departments provide a copy of the presentence investigation to defense and prosecution counsel? Could this practice affect what probation officers enter into such reports?
8. How should defense counsel prepare for a sentencing hearing?
9. Discover the cost of providing defense services to all courts in your jurisdiction last year. Three years ago. Compare these costs with prosecution costs.
10. Talk with a criminal court judge and a public defender or private attorney who practices in the criminal courts about how defense services are provided, and the strengths and weaknesses in this program.

References

1. Powell v. Alabama, 287 U.S. 45, 68–69, 53 S.Ct. 55, 64 (1932).
2. Monroe H. Freedman, "Professional Responsibility of the Criminal Defense Lawyer: The Three Hardest Questions," *Michigan Law Review* 64 (1966): 1469.
3. Coleman v. Alabama, 399 U.S. 1, 90 S.Ct. 1999 (1970).
4. American Bar Association Project on Minimum Standards for Criminal Justice, *Standards Relating to the Prosecution Function and the Defense Function,* Standard 6.1(b) and (c) (Chicago: American Bar Association, Approved Draft, 1971).
5. Henry B. Rothblatt, *Successful Techniques in the Trial of Criminal Cases* (Englewood Cliffs, N.J.: Prentice-Hall, 1961); F. Lee Bailey and Henry B. Rothblatt, *Successful Techniques for Criminal Trials* (San Francisco: Bancroft-Whitney Company, 1971); Ann Fagan Ginger, *Jury Selection in Criminal Trials: New Techniques and Concepts* (Tiburon, Calif.: Law Press Corp., 1975).
6. American Bar Association Project on Standards, *Prosecution Function and Defense Function,* pp. 145–46.
7. American Bar Association Project on Minimum Standards for Criminal Justice, *Standards Relating to Trial by Jury,* Standard 2.4 (Chicago: American Bar Association, Approved Draft, 1968); ABA Standards, *Prosecution and Defense,* p. 263.
8. *Videotaping of Court Procedures* (Denver, Colo.: National Center for State Courts, 1973).
9. Powell v. Alabama, note 1 above.
10. Gideon v. Wainwright, 372 U.S. 335, 83 S.Ct. 792 (1963). Also see Anthony Lewis, *Gideon's Trumpet* (New York: Vintage Books, 1964).
11. In re Gault, 387 U.S. 1, 87 S.Ct. 1428 (1967).
12. Argersinger v. Hamlin, 407 U.S. 25, 92 S.Ct. 2006 (1972).
13. *Implementation of Argersinger v. Hamlin: A Prescriptive Program Package* (Denver, Colo.: National Center for State Courts, 1973).
14. The right to counsel: when police officials seek to interrogate an accused in police custody (Escobedo v. Illinois 378 U.S. 478, 84 S.Ct. 1758 [1964]); at identification lineups after charging a defendant (United States v. Wade, 388 U.S. 218, 87 S.Ct. 1926 [1967]); at pretrial arraignment hearings (Hamilton v. Alabama 368 U.S. 52, 82 S.Ct. 157 [1961]); at preliminary hearings in states providing such hearings (Cole-

man v. Alabama, note 3 above; at probation revocation hearings (Mempa v. Rhay, 389 U.S. 128, 88 S.Ct. 254 [1967]); upon appeal of an adverse trial court decision (Douglas v. California, 372 U.S. 353, 83 S.Ct. 814 [1963]); at parole revocation hearings (Morrissey v. Brewer, 408 U.S. 471, 92 S.Ct. 2593 [1972]). An increasing number of states also provide right to counsel for those against whom involuntary mental health or retardation commitment procedures have been initiated, and for dependent or neglected children who may be removed temporarily or permanently from their parent's custody, as well as for the parents themselves who are subject to the temporary or permanent loss of their children's custody.

15. See *The Other Face of Justice* (Chicago: National Legal Aid and Defender Association, 1973).
16. Ibid., p. 13.
17. National Advisory Commission on Criminal Justice Standards and Goals, *Courts,* Standard 13.5 (Washington, D.C.: Government Printing Office, 1973).
18. Ibid., Standard 13.15.
19. U.S. v. Chatman, D.C. Sup. Ct., May 7, 1974, 15 Crim. L. Rep. 2157–59.
20. National Legal Aid, *Justice,* p. 32.
21. National Advisory Commission, *Courts,* Standard 13.12.
22. National Legal Aid, *Justice,* p. 29.
23. National Advisory Commission, *Courts,* Standard 13.8.

9 Court Administration

Few American courts today are seen as models of efficient management. Far too many courts operate essentially in the same fashion as fifty years ago. Cases crawl through the system under the control of lawyers who manipulate the court to enhance their clients' legal position. Too many judges have failed to effectively administer control of their own court calendar. Clerk records and files are laboriously prepared[1] and stored in crowded file cabinets, and later in warehouses. Prospective jurors are summoned from real estate tax lists or other sources which do not encompass a representative cross section of citizens. They often wait in barren rooms, and may never actually sit on a jury during two weeks of jury service. An indigent defendant cannot pay the bail bondsman's fee and his family goes further into debt as he remains in jail awaiting trial. Some courts reduce their trial calendars during the summer months although their local jails might be bulging with poor defendants unable to post bail. New court budgets simply add one or two positions and provide for minor salary raises and slightly increased equipment costs. The annual report is a simple recitation of statistics. Court employees are deferential to the judges or to a political party organization, and are provided no access to training programs which could heighten their skills and advance the court's efficiency. While court reformers have over the years worked to revise laws, develop more uniform rules, depoliticize judges, and do away with justices of the peace, reformist energies have only more recently addressed the disarray of court management.

A new and important professional is now rapidly joining the court team. He is known by different titles, but most typically he is called the court administrator. In different state or local court systems he may also be referred to as a judicial administrator, a court executive officer, a court coordinator, administrative director, or executive secretary to the courts. He may be a state court administrator, with either administrative responsibility or a coordinating responsibility for all courts in a state. He may be a trial court administrator, with management responsibility for his local court. He may be a criminal court coordinator, managing the criminal division of a general trial court under the supervision of the trial court administrator. He may be a juvenile court administrator.

Efficiency, by itself, must not be the only goal of court administration. The primary purpose of a court system is to do justice. Justice should be done efficiently and effectively; since courts do serve people, the means as well as the end product must be just. Our constitution throws substantial obstacles into any practice of assembly line justice. Yet our constitution is not self-executing. The guarantees of due process of law compel fair hearings and procedures to maximize a party's opportunity to be heard. But a court system may be so overloaded and/or mismanaged that citizens' exercise of their rights is discouraged or frustrated.

While we can apply to the courts a wide array of technologies borrowed from industry and other governmental agencies, the courts are a unique organization. They operate in a unique climate, and ultimately must adapt their own management machinery.[2] For too many years, judges administered court systems much like physicians administered hospitals. But the judicial forte has been knowledge of the law and legal procedure, much as a physician's skill, hopefully, was in the operating room or in improving the health of bedridden patients. Neither professional had undertaken specific training in organizational management. Perhaps two or three decades ago the medical field began training nonphysician hospital administrators to take over the day-to-day responsibility for running hospitals, generally working under the supervision of a citizen board and in consultation with a hospital physicians' committee. Particularly in the past five years, judges have turned over similar responsibilities for the management of their courts to court administrators.

It must be emphasized that all of the judges of a court, and more particularly the presiding judge, retain the legal responsibility for the administration of the court. Court administrators manage the nonjudicial activities of the court, but remain ultimately responsible to all of the judges. In effect, the judges represent a board of directors, the presiding judge their chairman of the board, and the court administrator their executive secretary. The judges determine policy; the court administrator implements policy. The judges, whether appointed or elected, select their court administrator and are responsible for his conduct of the office. His performance, including his supervision of other judicial system employees, must facilitate the achievement of the court system's goal of justice.

While this line of authority is quite clear, we shouldn't see the court administrator as in a servile position. Perceptive, respected administrators define issues, suggest alternative courses of action, and have very strong influence over what their judges ultimately agree upon as court policy. Still, judges expand or constrain an administrator's ability to execute his functions, depending on such factors as judicial willingness to permit strong administration, and the capabilities of that administration.

Generally the chief justice of a supreme court works in close concert with a state court administrator, while the chief judge of a trial court maintains a close working relationship with the trial court administrator. The influential American Bar Association Standards relating to Court Organization recognize this development:

> The importance of capable and efficient administrative assistance for an effective court system is second only to the importance of having competent judges. A modern court system is especially dependent on auxiliary staff, because its large volume of business requires that judges delegate as many nonjudicial responsibilities as possible. At the same time, the complexity of modern court operations requires that the persons to whom these responsibilities are delegated be able to discharge them efficiently and intelligently. The administrative office is the organization through which this assistance is provided.[3]

And yet perhaps no field of administration has received less research emphasis. There is little information gathered to suggest that current practices are good or bad. When it comes to measuring the ultimate objectives of the criminal justice system—justice and reformed behavior—we permit ourselves to remain in the dark.

Trial Court Administrators

The National Advisory Commission on Criminal Justice Standards and Goals has urged that each trial court with five or more judges should have a trial court administrator.[4] Let us now examine certain of the functions of a trial court administrator, together with the more prominent principles which guide him.

Caseflow Management

Guidelining the function of caseflow management is the principle that the court should control its calendar and determine the pace of litigation "from the cradle to the grave."[5] In criminal cases it should not be the prosecutor who decides which cases shall be heard and when and before which judges. In civil cases it should not be the lawyers who tell the court when they are finally ready to hold a trial. Rather, the judges and their administrative staff must develop and promulgate rules on case processing, preferably in consultation with attorneys and related justice system agencies, and create the structure, assign the personnel, and direct the personnel in the management of court calendars.

Effective calendar management involves the coordinated scheduling of judges, their clerks, certified shorthand reporters, bailiffs, jurors, prosecutors and defense counsel, victims, witnesses and expert witnesses and police witnesses, the defendant, and a courtroom.* While coordinating civil cases may be less complex, effective civil case management is also critical.

Although speedy trial rules, promulgated in an increasing number of jurisdictions, have forced greater speed in criminal case processing, and may well involve the assignment of more judicial manpower to criminal cases, the civil courts cannot be slighted. The slow resolution of personal injury claims may create severe economic hardship for injured plaintiffs. Substantial delays in resolving contract disputes, real estate ownership contests, the distribution of the assets of a deceased person, the litigation of a child custody dispute growing out of a divorce action, are important matters to these litigants. Good calendar management measures caseflow of all court cases, searches out the bottlenecks, studies the reasons for destructive delays, searches for more effective scheduling of judge time, and maintains an information system providing continuous and comprehensive data on caseflow. Figures 15 and 16 illustrate criminal felony and civil litigation caseflow processes and decision points which are evaluated by court administrative staff to facilitate more effective case management.

Judges of a multijudge court organize themselves in different ways for calendaring considerations. The two major methods are: 1) the individual calendar system: cases are randomly assigned to each judge, who is then responsible for that case from the beginning to the end of its life in the court system; 2) the master calendar system: one or more judges are assigned to hear the preliminary motions and pretrial issues of cases, while other judges are the trial judges. Cases ready for trial are assigned from a central scheduling office, or by an assignment judge, to a trial judge, who, upon completion of the trial, notifies the scheduling office, and then receives another case from among the parties awaiting trial and available in the central office.

*For a graphic statement of a juvenile court's chaotic caseflow coordination problems, see the end of this chapter. This frustrated employee's narrative followed the redesign of the calendar system to a master calendar.

Figure 15. Typical Progression of Criminal Felony Litigation

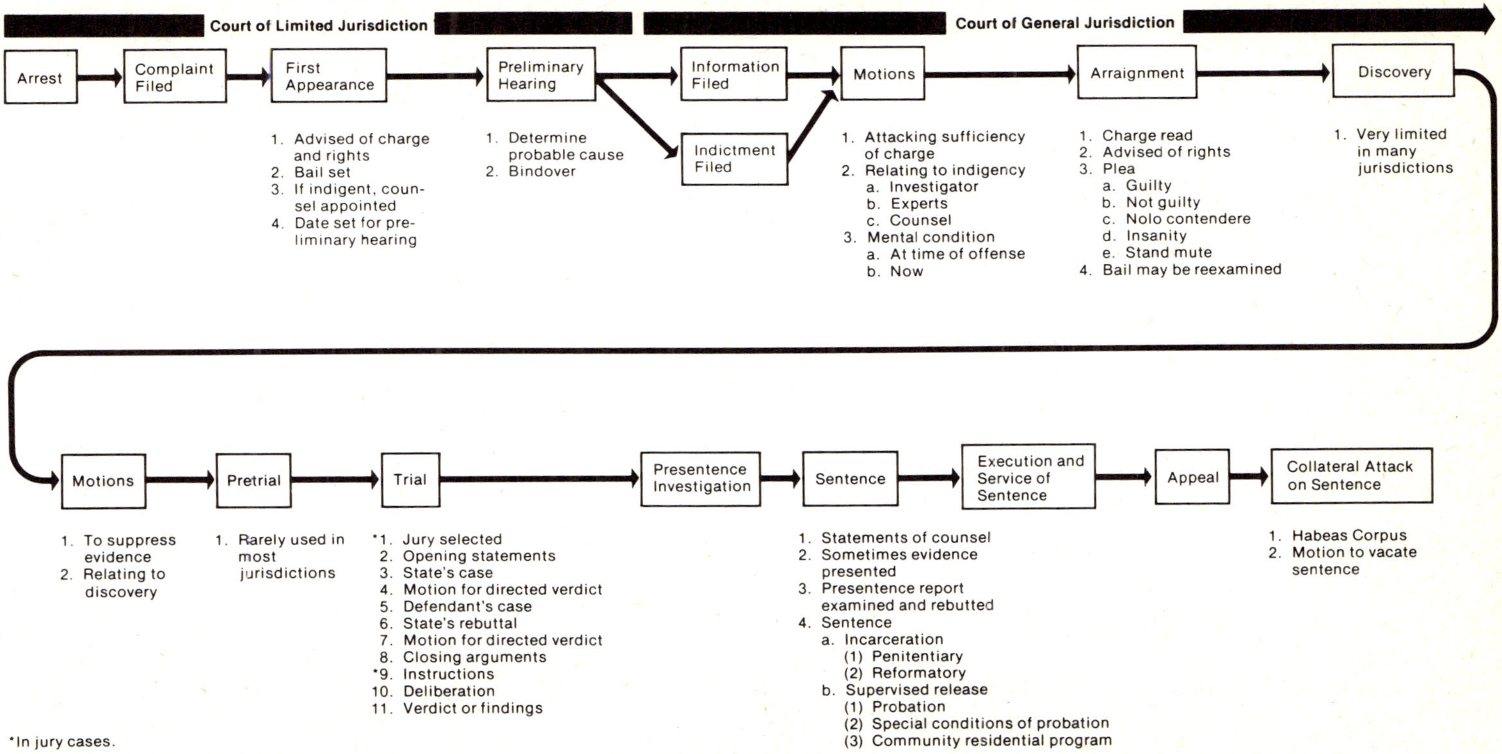

*In jury cases.

Figure 16. Typical Progression of Civil Litigation

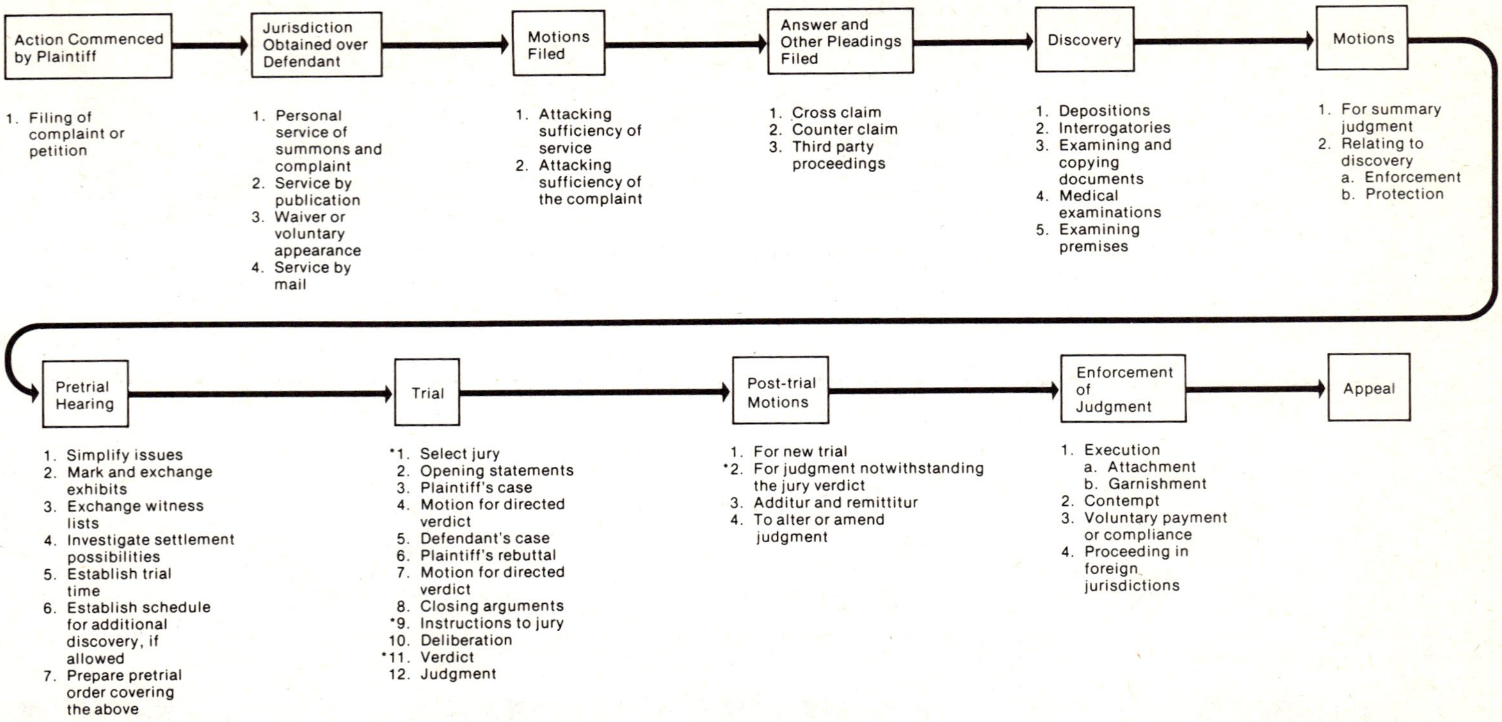

*In jury cases.

There are variations and modifications of these major assignment methods. One hybrid form which has gained some favor has been centralized arraignment, followed by individual case responsibility thereafter. These three forms of judicial calendar assignments are illustrated in Figures 17, 18, and 19.

Budget Preparation and Fiscal Management

A court's budget should be a well planned and well documented effort. It should include an annual incremental phase of long-term planning objectives, as well as normal extensions and short-term planning goals. The preparation phase should provide the opportunity for input and comment from judges and other administrative personnel. Some courts administer probation departments and juvenile detention facilities, and these court budgets must carefully provide for these programs. Legal developments—new statutes, rules, or appellate court decisions—impact upon the courts and their budgets and must be considered. Consultation with prosecutors, public defenders, and pretrial release programs should be included. It is the presiding judge, however, who must present and defend the budget when court funds are derived from local government.

Monitoring budget expenditures throughout the year is necessary to maintain expenditures within funding limits. A major problem for the court administrator, given his budgetary constraints, is his struggle to achieve greater efficiencies in the face of mounting case filings. Court administrators must engineer an efficient and accountable money collection system. Courts collect large sums of money from case filing fees, court and juror costs, traffic fines, fees in connection with the probating of estates, child support and alimony payments, and other moneys. The financial system must guard against employee embezzlement, and accounts should be audited regularly.

Personnel System

The courts have not fully phased out of their long-term role of serving as a center for political patronage. And many courts which have moved away from patronage have failed to establish a professional personnel system.[6] Another problem is that many courts depend largely upon county or state executive branch merit systems in obtaining their employees. The point is that the courts are a separate and independent branch of government, and should administer their own well-planned personnel system.

A personnel system requires extensive written rules and procedures. Merit hiring and promotion are critical ingredients of such a program. Written procedures must guide the recruitment, screening, selection, placement, promotion, downgrading, and termination of judicial system employees. Programs for in-service training and arrangements for out-service educational opportunities are necessary to improve personnel efficiency. Provision must be made for vacation and sick leave, overtime pay, pay schedules, job descriptions, and classifications. A fair grievance procedure must replace the dominant practice of employees serving "at the pleasure of the court" (that is, of the judges).

Courts, like other employers, must face developing personnel issues. The unionization of court employees is a growing trend, along with the requirement of affirmative-action hiring and promotion procedures for minorities.[7] Further, there is increasing question whether the concept of merit can be operationalized. Examinations used in qualifying applicants for positions may not measure the particular skills needed for the successful performance of a particular job.[8] From a different viewpoint, we may "overhire" more than we "underhire." Certain provisions do not require the highest ranking applicant: the most apt person in a less demanding job may experience limited satisfaction and depress the morale of coworkers.

Court administrators, working under judicial supervision, can find directions, if not solutions, to these challenging concerns. Judges should not be involved in the selection of rank and file

Figure 17. Individual Calendar

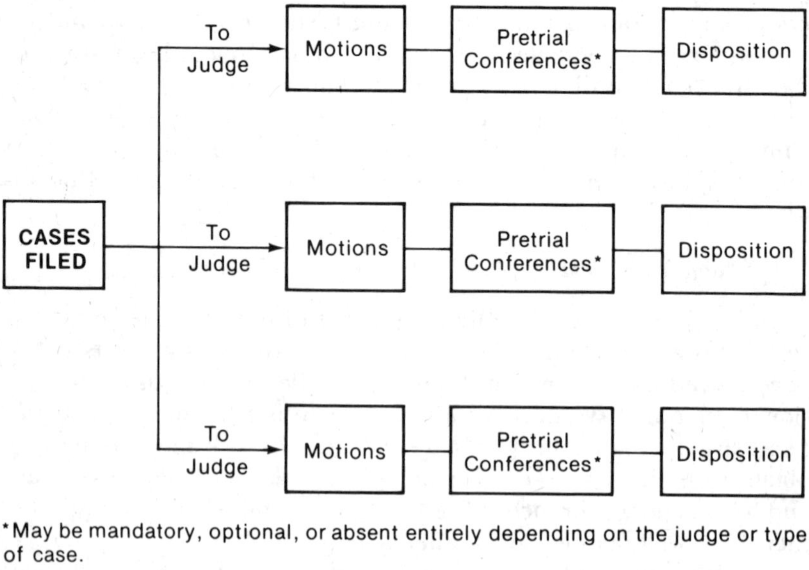

*May be mandatory, optional, or absent entirely depending on the judge or type of case.

SOURCE (figs. 17–19): Adapted from Maureen Solomon, *Caseflow Management in the Trial Court*, Supporting Studies 2, American Bar Association Commission on Standards of Judicial Administration (Chicago: American Bar Association, 1973).

Figure 18. Master Calendar

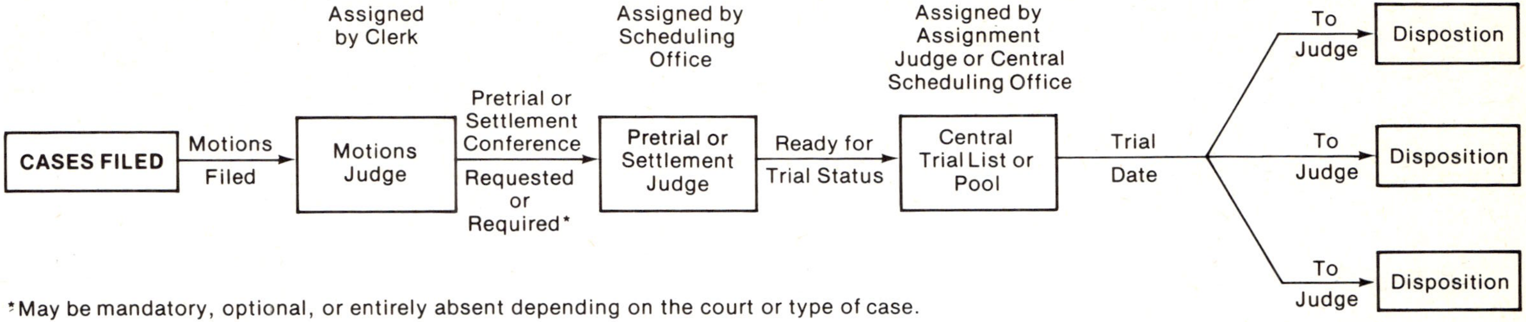

*May be mandatory, optional, or entirely absent depending on the court or type of case.

Figure 19. Hybrid Calendar: Central Arraignment Followed by Individual Case Responsibility

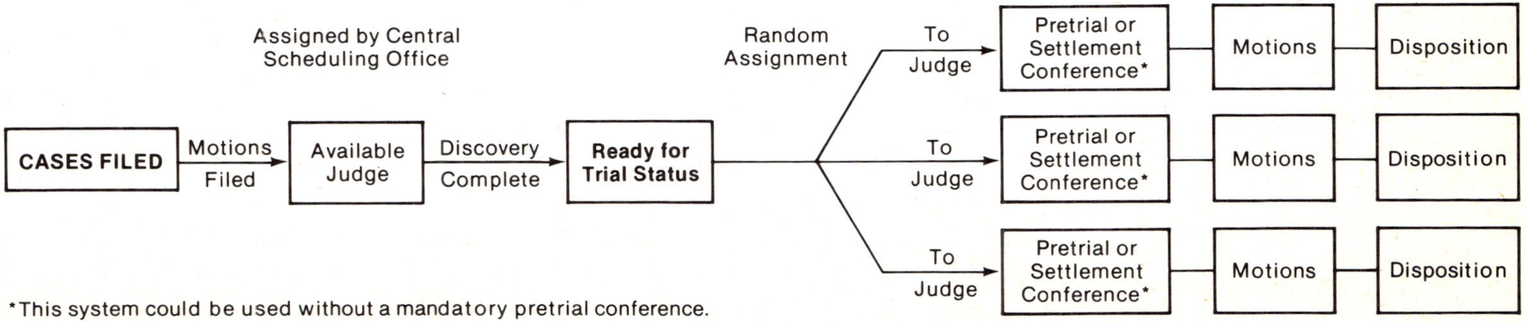

*This system could be used without a mandatory pretrial conference.

personnel for the system. They should select the administrator and other key employees and participate in the formulation and approval of personnel rules and procedures.

Records Management

Courts must maintain a vast amount of individual case records. A court must gain control of all the records its different divisions maintain, and centralize responsibility in the trial court administrator for the design and implementation of a good records system. Court legal forms are prepared in many civil and criminal actions in initiating cases. These forms need to be evaluated periodically to make sure that neither too little, nor too much, nor outdated information is obtained. Case control cards, filled out by court staff with the filing of a case and following each subsequent action, can assist caseflow management. The card shown in Figure 20 automatically duplicates the initial entry onto an attached second card, the respective cards are placed in (1) a numerically ordered file, and (2) a chronological file according to the next action date, and both cards receive separate entries with each action taken.

Courts need to implement printing and storage economies. Modern mechanical filing systems achieve economies of manpower and space. Enlightened court administrators develop schedules for the retention and destruction of records. A microfilming plan can save extensive warehousing costs. Care must be also given to the security system for records.

Management Information System

The term "management information system" refers to the collection of statistical information, by hand or automated means, and the planned use of this data to enable a court to know what is happening and what is or is not working. Caseflow management is a dimension of this. In sophisticated, computerized form, an on-line terminal screen can immediately tell what a judge's calendar looks like on a given date in the future; or it can show all the dates on which a given lawyer is scheduled to appear in the different divisions of a court; or when a defendant was arrested, jailed, bailed, tried, convicted, and sentenced. It can show patterns and bottlenecks, print out deficiencies in child support payments, and tell us how many days criminal or civil cases take from filing to disposition in one judicial district as against other judicial districts in a state. Not all courts need such a sophisticated information system, and the principles of computer information can be achieved manually in smaller jurisdictions. But most courts need more information than they now obtain. And few courts use the information they do obtain in the most effective fashion.

Figure 20. Case Control Card

Next Action			Est. Time
D/T	Action	Judge	

Filing-Pretrial Lapse	Pretrial Trial Lapse

Remarks:

Case No.	Date Filed		Nature of Case
Date at Issue	Jury	Court	

Plaintiff, Name & Address

Plaintiff's Attorney & Address

Defendant, Name & Address

Defendant's Attorney & Address

Civil

Juror Management

In some courts the jury commissioner is independent of the court administrator, although this is now generally seen as undesirable. In most courts vast improvements can be made in the ways jurors are obtained and utilized. We select from citizen lists which are discriminatory as to economic circumstance. We often recruit more jurors than we need. Juror subpoenas do not always get served, and juror notices are not always delivered. We have often too readily excused too many from jury service because of stated inconvenience, although the jury is an important link between the court and the community. We usually pay jurors too little, and this is a reason many seek to be excused. We do not schedule them efficiently. Typically, they all arrive at the same time each day, although characteristically they are called to different courtrooms at different times, often predictably. They are often held waiting in rather dingy quarters, and spend much of the day waiting to serve. In some jurisdictions, jurors serve for one month. In others, they serve for two weeks, and in the District Courts in Houston, Texas, they serve on one case only.

Computers are increasingly used in juror management to select potential jurors randomly, address their letters for juror service, and handle juror payment. Computer or manual information systems should monitor the age, race, and sex of jurors, how many jurors are actually used, how long trials require, and other information which can then be used to redesign a more representative juror pool to accomplish savings, use jurors more efficiently, and accordingly improve juror attitudes toward their service.

The juror utilization worksheet (Table 5), illustrative of new forms of court managerial methods, shows that substantially more jurors were available than were needed (column 3). The daily use of this worksheet enables a jury pool commissioner to reduce the number of underutilized jurors.

Space Utilization and Facilities Planning

The trial court administrator is the best person to be given the responsibility for the care and control of court facilities and the management of courthouse space. Obviously, overseeing courthouse security, maintenance, janitorial services, and repairs and remodeling, is better handled by an administrator than a judge, although judicial consultation is essential. While city or county governments frequently maintain the courthouse buildings, the administrator must maintain an active liaison with these governmental agencies. Courts not infrequently must rent space in private buildings for temporary courtrooms or branch probation offices or other purposes. Long-term planning of new facilities, or remodeled or refur-

Table 5. Juror Utilization Worksheet

Total Jurors at Court Today 131 | Date: 9/20/74

(1) *Time Jurors Leave or Return to Waiting Room**	(2) *Number of Jurors Leaving or Returning*	(3) *Total Jurors in Waiting Room After This Activity*	(4) *Judge's Name*	(5) *Type of Case*	(6) *Activity*
60 jurors carried over in trial from 9/19 leaves: 71 at 9:00 A.M. in waiting room					
9:00 F	+ 12	83	Smith	Criminal	Jurors return—trial ends
9:13 T	– 24	59	Jones	Civil	Panel sent to voir dire
10:00 F	+ 12	71	Brown	Civil	Jurors return—trial ends
10:00 F	+ 12	83	Green	Criminal	Jurors return—trial ends
10:20 F	+ 12	95	Wilson	Civil	Jurors return—trial ends
10:22 T	– 28	67	Levy	Civil	Panel sent to voir dire
10:35 F	+ 12	79	Jones	Civil	Challenged jurors return
11:12 T	– 26	53	Johnson	Civil	Panel sent to voir dire
11:25 F	+ 16	69	Levy	Civil	Challenged jurors return
11:45 T	– 30	39	Brown	Civil	Panel sent to voir dire
11:59 F	+ 14	53	Johnson	Civil	Challenged jurors return
1:30 F	+ 12	65	Craig	Civil	Jurors return—trial ends
1:52 T	– 27	38	Green	Criminal	Panel sent to voir dire
2:00 F	+ 18	56	Brown	Civil	Challenged jurors return
3:30 F	+ 15	71	Green	Criminal	Challenged jurors return
4:00 F	+ 12	83	Jones	Civil	Jurors return—trial ends
4:00 F	+ 12	95	Johnson	Civil	Jurors return—trial ends
4:00 F	+ 12	107	Brown	Civil	Jurors return—trial ends
Carried Over In Trial = 24					

*Use "T" after time (*e.g.*, 10:00 T) to show jurors going to courtroom; Use "F" to show jurors returning from courtroom.

SOURCE: Maureen Solomon, *Management of the Jury System,* American Bar Association Commission on Standards of Judicial Administration (Chicago: American Bar Association, Supporting Studies 3, 1975).

nished facilities, is another important dimension. Administrators may need to invoke architectural consultants who are interested in integrating their design skills with careful study of a court and its processes. The design or redesign of a court facility needs to consider workflow, traffic flow, security, future needs, costs, flexibility of use, and other factors, and requires a careful planning process as shown in Figure 21.

Other Court Administrator Functions

Court administrators in many jurisdictions fulfill such additional functions as serving as executive secretary to meetings of judges and their committees, preparation of an annual report and providing the release of public information to the community, administration of a court library, arranging centralized purchasing for the trial court, playing a coordinating role with the state court administration, acting as liaison with local executive and legislative branches of government, or as liaison with the bar association and related criminal justice agencies such as law enforcement, prosecutor, public defender, pretrial release programs, jails, and correctional facilities. Court administrators are increasingly involved in research and planning, often coordinating court research studies conducted by independent organizations.

To effectuate his duties, a trial court administrator requires more assistance than the usual array of clerks and stenographers. He also requires the assistance of management personnel.[9]

State Court Administrators

All but a few states now have state court administrators, although their authority, functions, and staffing patterns are very different. Those state court systems which are essentially state funded, as opposed to locally funded, normally vest greater authority and functions in the state court administrator. Alaska, Colorado, Hawaii, North Carolina, and South Dakota illustrate these states. These administrators largely prepare, present, and monitor the budget for the overall state court system. They seek to monitor caseflow in all the courts, study where additional judges may be needed, assist trial court administrators in redesigning caseflow systems, and serve a major liaison responsibility with the state legislature and state government.

They may require that all federal funding requests flow through their office for approval, and that any local court management information system dovetail with a statewide management information system plan. They may develop and implement a statewide personnel merit system to which local courts must conform. They may prepare guidelines for local juror selection

Figure 21. Court Space Management Research, Programming, and Planning Process

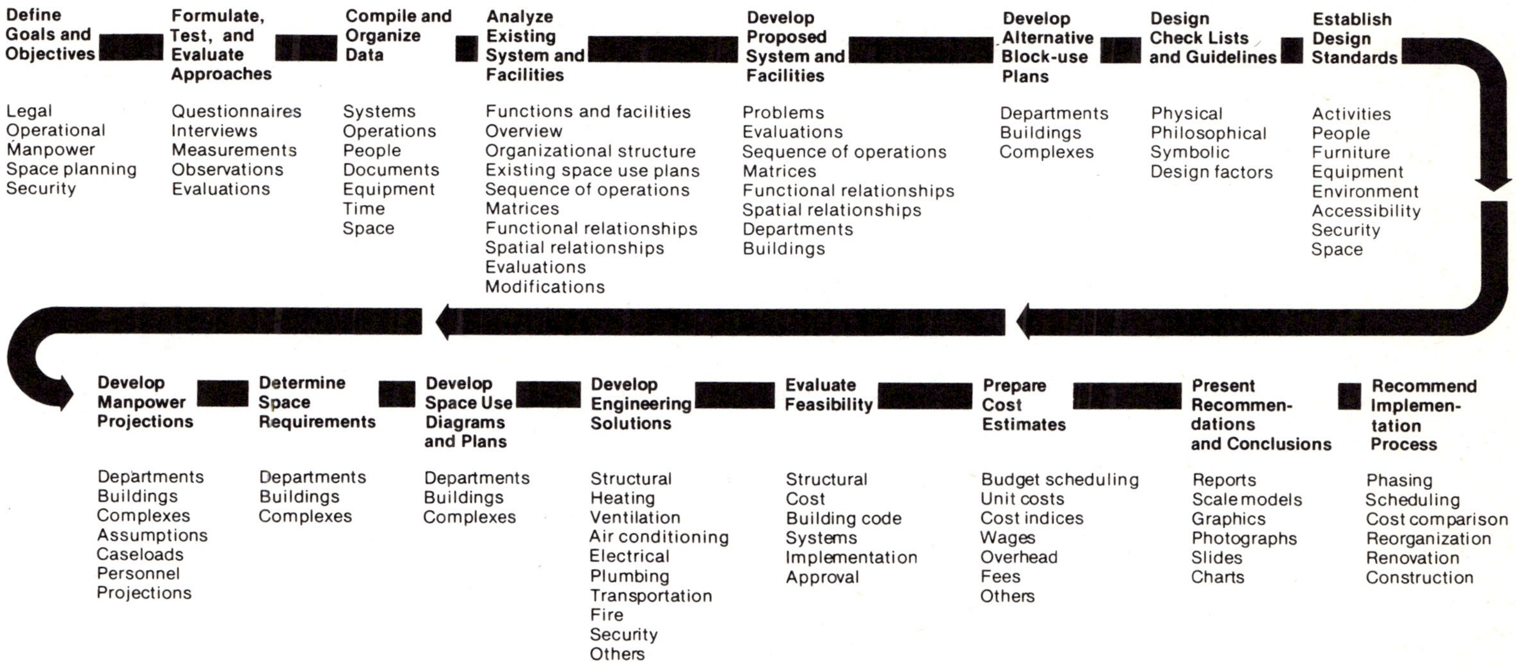

SOURCE: F. Michael Wong, *Space Management and the Courts*, National Institute of Law Enforcement and Criminal Justice (Washington, D.C.: U.S. Department of Justice, 1973), p. 22.

methods, or even computerize juror selection and management for an entire state. They may promulgate court forms to be used uniformly throughout the state, and promulgate records systems to be used in each jurisdiction. They may coordinate judicial education programs for the entire system and develop and coordinate training programs for nonjudicial personnel.[10]

The implementation of these and other functions is largely done under the supervision of the chief justice of the supreme court, or a judicial council. States such as California and New York have long had a judicial council or conference, an official organization, dominated by the judiciary in California and composed exclusively of the judiciary in New York, which works continuously to improve the court system.

In states where local government provides the more substantial part of the costs of the court, state court administrators maintain a less powerful responsibility for the administration of courts within the state. This is a far more common pattern at this time, and these systems are illustrated by California, Illinois, and most southern and midwestern states. Here, the state court administrator is more of a facilitator, a coordinator, and a consultant to trial court administrators and their courts. None of our largest states have yet gone to basic state funding of the court system, although the trend to fundamental state funding is increasing.

Issues of interrelationships between the appellate courts and the trial courts, and between the state court administrator and trial court administrator, require careful balancing. Relationships can become severely strained when authority is basically centered in the supreme court and the state court administrator. On the other hand, when each trial court can go its own merry way justice is less uniformly administered throughout a state, and there is no clear lever with which to push a slower and less efficient court into the general mainstream of judicial administration.

The Training and Employment of Court Administrators

It is clear that an increased use of court administrators will accompany the future direction of court reform in this nation. This is a relatively young profession. Its educational prerequisites have not yet become standardized, but the complexities of its functions are immense.

The first state court administrator began his duties in New Jersey in 1948. Until 1970, there were few trial court administrators. Since then there has been a rapid expansion of these positions in many states as courts and legislatures have begun to recognize the need to strengthen the management of courts, and as federal funding has become more available for the improvement of local and state court systems.

The role of court administrator is a difficult one, with huge tasks to perform. But these tasks must be implemented in concert with judicial acceptance and support. Judges tend to be independent persons. They are not always eager to delegate the power they have historically exercised in the management of the courts. They do not always embrace change, and they may be haunted by the specter of an administrator looking at how they manage their calendar or courtroom. An administrator cannot effectuate change as rapidly as he may prefer because his judges may not be prepared to push for the funds to accomplish these changes. The courts, dependent upon the legislative branch of government for funding, have often passively taken what legislators provide rather than carefully documenting their problems and needs, aggressively developing public support, and actively advocating more expansive financing. A community's critical view of a court also affects timing and methods, and influences administrator priorities and approaches.

Legal training is not a requirement for a court administrator, although a number of judicial systems prefer this training for their administrators. Probably more court administrators are not law school graduates than are. Many have risen from an earlier position as an administrative clerk of a court to take on the far broader responsibilities of a court administrator. Others have come out of fields of public administration or business administration, or even prior military service. Some have been law clerks to judges, and others were political acquaintances of key judges. Few universities offer training in this field, although small graduate programs train court administrators at the University of Southern California, the University of Denver, the University of Indiana, and possibly at several other universities.

The major training ground for court administrators is the Institute for Court Management, Denver, Colorado. Initiated in 1970 and sponsored by three national legal organizations, the Institute designed crash programs to train persons earlier trained in related fields such as law, public administration, and business administration, and to upgrade promising court employees into court administrators. The Institute's basic training program is a six-month course which can be completed over a two- or three-year period. It begins with a guided Research Immersion in a local court where, according to an instructional outline, the new trainee observes a variety of court procedures, tracks certain cases, and interviews certain court officials and attorneys.

This is typically followed by a five-week Colorado Residential Seminar where the curriculum focuses on calendar management, personnel management, records management, budget management, and information systems. The basic technologies of court administration are the focus of this instruction presented by Institute staff members and visiting court administrators, jurists, and university professors from related disciplines. A four-week seminar either follows this experience or may be undertaken a year later. This seminar emphasizes the internal and external environment in which the court administrator operates, and draws heavily on a faculty with rich prior or present experience in the justice system. An internship in a court system is then required, the trainee designing his court research project in concert with Institute staff, and then completing it prior to a final two-week seminar.

Variations of this schedule now occur where the first seminar series may be taken in one-week modules, five times during a year, in a regional training site closer to one's residence. University credit is not provided by the Institute, but a graduate is certified as a Fellow of the Institute. Institute graduates now manage trial courts in countless jurisdictions, have become state court administrators, perform auxiliary management roles in these types of settings, have become the executive officers of federal circuit courts, serve as court specialists for state or federal criminal justice planning agencies, teach court administration, conduct court research, and fill other positions in related agencies. The Institute also conducts extensive court research, and research into related justice system agencies, feeding back this experience in its instructional training programs for court administrators.

The following statement was written by one employee of a metropolitan juvenile court, describing staff frustrations with a "nonsystem" of case calendaring:

> The greatest void is administrative leadership. There is no central authority or leader, and the court suffers drastically as a result. This lack leads to a complete lack of coordination within the court. There is no communication or cooperation between the divisions. There is no communication between the court administrator and his staff. There is no communication between the ancillary services, or between these services and the court, nor is there any coordination of these services. The docket clerk is lacking in authority and has no backup. Judges call and insist on priority settings. Attorneys do not personally set the cases with the docket clerk, so as to avoid conflicts. Probation officers and attorneys can still judge-shop. Attorneys, probation officers, etc., do not inform the docket clerk when cases are not going to go on. These same people switch cases around without telling the docket clerk. Welfare attorneys handle cases informally, and don't tell the docket clerk what has happened. Minute clerks have trouble getting through to the docket clerk when the division can take another case. Probation officers and others complain that the dockets are inaccurate when distributed, and that hearing times are changed

> without notification. Welfare sets cases where service has not been made. Obviously, the cases fold. Minute clerks do not know their procedures, nor do they help each other out. There is confusion about the role of the minute clerk. If a division calls to take a case, there is no one to round up the parties involved. Docket clerk should decide how much time to set for a particular type of case, but doesn't have authority to do so. Case jackets are floating all over the court with no central control. Probation officers complain they do not get enough notice of settings to contact the children and make physical arrangements to get them to court. Everyone is late for everything in this court. Public defenders, district attorneys, private attorneys, probation officers, judges, referees, welfare, etc., are late to work and to hearings. Nothing starts on time. Jury trials must be handled better. No one knows if they will go until they haven't. Continuances are granted willy-nilly in this court. Public defenders, district attorneys, welfare attorneys are not prepared for hearings and trials. There is no coordination of persons involved in hearings and trials. There is no schedule of which judge or referee will be where, when. They all come and go as they will. Judges do not control their confidential employees, who fail to keep order in their offices. The law clerks don't have anything to do. Welfare attorneys are using court personnel to do their paperwork for them. Welfare attorneys are using improper service, and negotiating with those served when they arrive in court. Judges and referees sit around and wait for welfare cases that never are heard, because welfare doesn't organize its own docket, or inform the court when cases go off. Probation officer nonappearance reports waste referee time, and should be submitted on paper. Adoptions, marriages, etc., are still interspersed among hearings and trials, instead of being heard at their allotted time, or performed off court time.

Modern court administration seeks to alleviate problems such as these.

Questions for Discussion

1. Should legislative bodies which fund the courts monitor how the courts administer justice?
2. Is there a correlation between the courts developing their own administrative capability, and the courts achieving greater independence as a coequal branch of government?
3. Should trial court administrators be appointed by the state court administrator or by the judges of the trial court?
4. Should individual judges appoint their own bailiffs and court reporters, or should these employees be collectively assigned to a staff pool where, under the supervision of court administrative staff, they are assigned to different judges?
5. What are the advantages and disadvantages of the individual case calendaring system? The master calendar system?

6. What might a trial court administrator do about a judge who handles only about 50 percent of the caseload of the average judge in the court?
7. Where there is court administered probation, should the chief probation officer be administratively responsible to the trial court administrator or to the chief judge?
8. To what extent can a supreme court chief justice tell a trial court chief judge how to run his court?
9. How might a court administrator proceed when he wishes to discharge a grossly inefficient employee who has the strong backing of an influential judge?
10. At least one urban trial court has passed a rule that no attorney may represent more than a certain number of criminal defendants. Is this curb on a citizen's right to select his own lawyer outbalanced by the court's duty to reach the constitutional requirement of speedy trial?

References

1. "Finally, criminal justice documents more often than not are one-ply forms. Carbon paper seems to be viewed with suspicion for judicial transactions, perhaps as something alien to recordkeeping concepts rooted in colonial traditions. As a consequence, court and county clerks' offices are bogged down in repetitive writing of the same information. The need to rewrite and to copy invites transcription error, costs more, and throttles the movement of information." Norbert A. Halloran, *Modernized Court Administration,* President's Commission on Law Enforcement and Administration of Justice, *Task Force Report: The Courts* (Washington, D.C.: Government Printing Office, 1967), p. 168.
2. See Ernest C. Friesen, Jr., Edward C. Gallas, and Nesta M. Gallas, *Managing the Courts* (Indianapolis, Ind.: Bobbs-Merrill Co., 1971).
3. American Bar Association Commission on Standards of Judicial Administration, *Standards Relating to Court Organization* (Chicago: American Bar Association, Approved Draft, 1974), pp. 86–87.
4. National Advisory Commission on Criminal Justice Standards and Goals, *Courts,* Standard 9.3 (Washington, D.C.: Government Printing Office, 1973).
5. The Committee on the Administration of Justice, *Court Management Study: Report for the Use of the Committee on the District of Columbia, United States Senate* (Washington, D.C.: Government Printing Office, 1970), p. 56.
6. "Our research revealed that, of 117 courts surveyed, approximately 80 percent of the employees serve at the pleasure of the court." *Courts and Personnel Systems* (Denver, Colo.: Institute for Court Management, 1975), p. 7.
7. Carter v. Gallagher, 452 F.2d 315 (8th Cir. 1971), 452 F.2d 327 (8th Cir. 1972).
8. Griggs v. Duke Power Co., 401 U.S. 424 (1971); Arrington v. Massachusetts Bay Transportation Authority, 306 F.Supp. 1355 (D. Mass.

1969); Carter v. Gallagher 452 F.2d 315 (8th Cir. 1971), 452 F.2d 327 (8th Cir. 1972).

9. David J. Saari, *Modern Court Management: Trends in the Role of the Court Executive,* National Institute of Law Enforcement and Criminal Justice (Washington, D.C.: Government Printing Office, 1970).

10. National Advisory Commission, *Courts,* Standard 9.1.

10 Reform of the Courts

Evaluating the Judicial System

This chapter, pointing toward the future of the courts, seeks to assess the directions for reform and the obstacles to reform, presents reviews of the more significant national commissions which have elaborated pathways to court reform, and anticipates accelerated progress in achieving effective state and local court systems. The emphasis will be on criminal and juvenile justice reform and overall court organization and modernization. In the preceding chapters presentation of the shortcomings of the courts has perhaps outweighed the description of the positive achievements of the American court system. But this is as it should be. The reality is that we have major problems along with certain progress. Few observers, interested or disinterested, are satisfied with our administration of justice.

A strong and independent court system is critical to a free society. It has been suggested that a major reason for our rebellion against King George III was the concern of the early patriots over the king's control of the colonial courts. The Declaration of Independence charged, "He has obstructed the Administration of Justice, by refusing his Assent to Laws for establishing Judiciary powers. He has made Judges dependent on his Will alone, for the tenure of their offices, and the amount and payment of their salaries."

Today we seek to overthrow political party domination of the still common approach of electing judges, since we want judges responsive to the rule of law rather than to the influence of political organizations. It would be naive, however, to suggest that the gubernatorial appointment of judges will be exercised without certain political considerations, or that appointive judges will not be responsive to the broadly political concerns of the public or segments of the public.

The Watergate trauma has been an object lesson not only in revealing the necessary roles of the legislative branch and the judicial branch as checks on the executive branch, but also in the critical complement of the sanctioning role of the courts over the other branches. While we may argue appropriately that the Watergate burglars and high-up White House criminals received lesser sentences than many courts assign to "common criminals" who commit lesser crimes, the point is that the courts exist as a vehicle for bringing to public task persons guilty of political corruption. We have learned from Watergate: (1) the vital role of a free press, and the critical importance of the First Amendment to a democratic society; (2) that "freedom of information," the citizen's access to governmental documents and records, should be facilitated; (3) that our intricate system of checks and balance serves us well; (4) that the Congress must provide greater supervision over the administration of laws and funds by the executive; (5) that the law and the Constitution are supreme; (6) that an independent judiciary is necessary to measure the legality of the governmental process.[1]

Those guilty of federal crimes are dealt with by the federal court system. Far more numerous crimes are dealt with by prosecuting systems within the states. Our forefathers decided long ago that burglary, assault, murder, and rank-and-file crimes are the province of the states. The United States was formed by the several states which were fearful of granting pervasive powers to a federal government. Those who designed and accepted the United States Constitution and the Bill of Rights preferred to see criminal justice fundamentally administered by the states.

The thirteen original colonies had courts which ruled on whether crimes had been committed, and punished guilty offenders. This basic approach to jurisdiction was not altered upon ratification of the Constitution and the Bill of Rights, the Ninth and Tenth Amendments reserving to the people and the states those powers not delegated by the Constitution to the United States. So we have fifty different state court systems, and a far greater number of local court systems, each with some commonality and some differences. We register some shock at these dissimilarities. Legislatively determined penalties in some states are more severe than in others. Further, within a given state, and even within a multijudge court in a given city, disparate sentences are ordered. One of our goals is to achieve a greater uniformity between the states and within a state, and yet we want to leave considerable room for flexibility, for experimentation, for some reflection of the concerns of local residents as they may influence a criminal justice system.

The federal constitution is one way we get at local practices which may be abusive. The Bill of Rights, as applied through the great Fourteenth Amendment to state practices, requires at least minimum standards of universal fairness. The national commissions which increasingly promulgate critiques, guidelines, and directions, reflect our search for medium to maximum standards of justice. For many years, model laws have been drafted by national bodies, and many state legislatures have accepted and enacted certain of these acts, so that a more common thread has been woven voluntarily into the substance and procedures of justice throughout the land.

In his historic 1906 address to the American Bar Association, Roscoe Pound, for years dean of the Harvard Law School, suggested there is an inherent popular dissatisfaction with *any* legal system, and that the causes for this are: "(1) The necessarily mechanical operation of rules, and hence of laws; (2) the inevitable difference in rate of progress between law and public opinion; (3) the general popular assumption that the administration of justice is an easy task, to which anyone is competent, and (4) popular impatience of restraint."[2] Pound cited additional reasons for dissatisfaction with the *American* legal system, concerns which haunt our courts seventy years later: the multiplicity of courts, overlapping jurisdiction, and the inefficient use of judicial manpower.[3]

In 1906, as today, state constitutions and state and local legislation structure the nonfederal courts. A more efficient court structure requires constitutional or legislative amendment. A more efficient court administration requires technical skills and judicial support. Judicial concern which is limited to today's case fails to resolve yesterday's structural or caseflow deficiencies, and inhibits directing the changes to prepare for tomorrow.

The Assumptions of Reform Recommendations

A reform movement is in process to modernize court structure and administration and to achieve additional court-related objectives around which some consensus has developed. It is important to examine the assumptions of the major recommendations for reform.

The State Court Unification Package

One observer of the judicial process has noted that proposals for unified state court systems generally include the following four components:

1. The elimination of overlapping and conflicting jurisdictional

boundaries (both as regards subject matter and geography), i.e. the unified trial court.
2. Hierarchical and centralized state court structure with administrative responsibility vested with the Chief Justice and state supreme court. Authority often includes assignment of judges, promulgation of rules, designation of presiding judges of local trial courts, and general administrative procedures relating to jury selection, case processing time standards, monitoring techniques, statistical collection, etc.
3. Unitary statewide financing of the courts at the state level.
4. A separate personnel system centrally run by the state court administrator covering a range of personnel functions (recruitment, selection, promotion, etc.) and encompassing all personnel including clerks of court.[4]

To this prescription should be added the merit selection of judges, with appointment by a governor from among nominations submitted by judicial nominating commissions. One other component would be a procedure for disciplining and removing judges who fail to adhere to norms of competency and stability.[5]

The assumption that all nonfederal courts should be subject to some form of state level administrative guidance has received wide acceptance.[6] Whether the chief justice should be designated as the executive head of the state court system is not universally accepted. The strength of this approach is to centralize overall responsibility in a single, authoritative person. Where such authority is combined with strong state financing of the courts, the chief justice is the analog of the governor who is accountable for all executive branch administration and expenditures. This approach seems modeled after the judicial system decision-making process: decisions made at the top (supreme court) govern all courts within the state.

Important variables include the capacity of the chief justice to deal with administrative matters, the skills of the state court system administrative staff, the chief justice's ability to secure implementation of his directives and requests, whether trial court judges are appointed (more cooperation) or elected (less cooperation),[7] whether the chief justice is authorized to appoint the presiding judges of the trial courts (more cooperation, at least from presiding judges) or whether presiding judges are elected by their peers (less cooperation, generally, from presiding judges), the extent of local financing of local courts (with more local financing, less cooperation), and other factors.

The central, hierarchical approach suggests greater efficiency, more flexibility in manpower assignment, greater uniformity in the administration of justice throughout a state, a central spokesman for improving the court system (increasingly chief justices deliver a biennial "state of the courts" address to state legislative bodies, though this useful approach can be taken by chief justices who are not the administrative heads of their judicial systems), and certain benefits through central oversight (the Colorado Chief Justice advises chief trial court judges each month of lagging criminal and civil cases, requesting explanation), central service assistance (New Jersey provides a repair service for electronic recording equipment in the trial courts), central training programs (many state court administrators employ an educational coordinator to develop in-state, in-service programs for a spectrum of judicial system personnel, and to facilitate their participation in regional and national training opportunities), and central research and development functions.

Critical evaluation of the hierarchical state court system is largely absent from the literature. Concerns about its tenets and implementation, however, take several forms:

The real-life world is in the trial courts, and central regulation of trial court administration causes credibility, practicality, and resentment problems.

Centralization leads to conformity; courts have different personalities, they serve different communities, and their problems suggest heterogeneous experimentation and peculiarly local solutions.

Major collaborative groups — prosecutors, defense agencies, private attorneys, sheriffs, police, and others—are more typically local organizations and need to be negotiated with at the local level, and with a flexibility that encourages individualized rather than standardized bargaining.

Central management leads to central control, particularly in state-funded court systems. Services offered centrally may be perceived as control at the local level.[8]

Well-managed, well-staffed, and well-funded local courts will lose certain funds and staff upon entry into a state-funded system where resources are more evenly spread.

It is easier for employees to maintain job commitment in a local organization than as part of a somewhat faceless bureaucracy.

Centralization leads to the issuance of orders and directives; local management tends to be more consultive and participatory.

There are significant problems associated with too little state administration and a too heavy state administration. The courts in states such as Texas and Louisiana are so individualized, overlapping, and disparate, and those in Colorado and New Jersey so dependent on central management, that greater centralization is needed in the former jurisdictions and increased decentralization in the latter. A wise balance suggests, in general, a higher share of state funding of local courts, but the retention of a sufficient local funding provision to afford a legitimacy to local court management; a judicial council structure representative of all courts so as to provide trial judge input into state court system administrative rules and policies, and a stronger interest in implementing such rules and policies; state court system powers and functions agreed to as needed by the representative judicial council; probably, trial judge appointment of their own presiding judge, in accordance with a state rule that this position should be filled by judges with the keenest administrative skills rather than by seniority; appointment of trial court administrators by the trial judges rather than by the state court administrator.

The unified trial court, as contrasted with a centrally directed and unified state court system, has fewer conceptual or organizational problems associated with it. All trial courts within a district would become a single court, utilizing specialized divisions as indicated. Its assumptions include greater efficiencies in the deployment of judicial and court system support staff; elimination of duplicative and overlapping jurisdiction; centralized management and direction as being advantageous as compared with separate court administration; development of judicial generalists, capable of effective performance in any judicial function; a single-tier and equalized judiciary which draws the previously inferior lower court judges and specialized juvenile-family, probate, and other judges into the judicial mainstream.

However, trial court unification may involve larger geographical districts than were previously common, separating the citizen further from the courts. Judicial rotation to different court divisions may further fragment familiarity between court clientele and judges. Present specialist judges would become more generalist judges. Or balance, the advantages of unification sharply outweigh the disadvantages, though 200- and 300-judge courts in our largest metropolitan counties will require strong organizational and management capabilities.

There are problems associated with the appointive approach to selecting judges: the public is effectively disenfranchised, since experience has shown that few incumbents are dislodged when no opponent challenges them and the public simply votes yes or no on retention; further, upward mobility into judgeships by nonestablishment lawyers is discouraged since the political election route has been eliminated;[9] governors may name partisan commissions and appoint political partisans or friends to the judiciary,[10] and nominating commissions may not be representative of the community.

Yet the advantages are strong. Judicial elections have been contests of political party popularity and name identification more than rigorous measures of judicial qualifications; political patronage in the courthouse disappears, replaced by personnel approaches oriented more toward merit; nominating commissions may buffer political factors and carefully assess applicant capabilities; judges spend more time on the bench and less time campaigning.

Any system of obtaining judges will have some trade-offs. Probably, selection rather than election offers promise of a more qualified, more professional judiciary. Selection anticipates relatively secure tenure in office, and is tied to the reform recommendation of a judicial discipline procedure. Attorneys and the public need a body to turn to when they have a grievance against a judge. There must be a process to ease a senile, alcoholic, corrupt, or incompetent judge out of office. A disciplinary body is an acceptable American practice with most professions, so long as its procedures are both clear and fair. Concerns to date have suggested that such bodies have been too protective of alleged judicial misconduct, too conservative in bringing formal removal proceedings. The privacy of these proceedings in certain states has drawn criticism as well.

Caseflow Process

Conventional wisdom in the area of caseflow subsumes (1) speedy processing; (2) reduced pretrial jailing through bail reforms and pretrial release services; (3) court control of caseflow; (4) reduction or elimination of plea bargaining; (5) comprehensive defense counsel services and due process provisions.

The Constitution mandates a speedy trial, and this is our wisest authority. Crime control spokesmen urge that deterrence is based on certainty of apprehension, celerity of conviction, and severity of punishment. Data in support of this theory are difficult to find. Recent victimization studies report that many crimes are not reported to the police, and of those reported identification information or available evidence frequently fails to lead to apprehension.[11] Speed of conviction has been the hallmark of only the lower criminal courts, criticized because their assembly line functions without rigorous check or balance and is woefully lacking in carefully individualized justice. While we provide for severe sentences, these are ameliorated by common grants of probation at one end, and by parole release at the other.

Our complex, heterogeneous society needs major reordering for the old deterrence truism to be realistic. Besides its support in the Constitution, the requirement of speedy trial helps a court be more efficient, is extremely useful to defendants who remain in oppressive jails pending trial, and makes sense in terms of witness memories and the overall value of early conflict resolution. It may be that speedier probation–social service delivery reduces the likelihood of recidivism.[12]

More limited pretrial detention supports the legal presumption of innocence and helps equalize the opportunities for pretrial freedom of the poor and the rich. It curbs the explosive problems of overpopulated jails and of general jail management. It reduces welfare rolls. While 6.4 percent of defendants released without bail were rearrested for additional crimes in one seventy-two-city survey, this figure was higher, 8.2 percent, for defendants released after paying money bail.[13] Data do show a very high appearance rate at trial for persons released without money bond.[14]

Court calendar control flows from the thesis of the independence of the judicial branch and its responsibility, therefore, to administer its own processes. Some judges have historically run a tight ship. More often, judicial calendar administration has been casual. Objection to court control will come from attorneys who will resist relinquishing their opportunity to judge-shop, to exploit systemic deficiencies, and to defer trials until their clients have paid their fees. Court reports show advances in moving cases more quickly.[15] The utilization of court administrators and the developing literature on caseflow have been basic prerequisites to this progress.

Plea bargaining is a controversial issue. It has a strong element of public interest: citizens believe justice should be clear and simple—if you have a case why bargain? Well, we bargain because prosecutors sometimes overload criminal charges, or do not have an ironclad case, or the court backlog is severe and the judge would strongly prefer the case be settled, or the jail is bulging, or if we deal with this defendant he will give us information useful to convicting a more serious offender, and other reasons. Regretfully, the simple question begets a complex answer. Experienced prosecutors and defenders believe plea bargaining cannot and should not be eliminated. We cannot easily eliminate prosecutor discretion in the charging process, and judicial sentencing discretion may, in time, be harnessed but not eliminated. Along with the uncertainties of trial, and in the absence of a full complement of judges, prosecutors, and defense counsel, these complicating factors suggest a more practical direction to regulating the bargaining process.

Due process of law, or fundamental fairness, underpins and permeates court procedures. It protects against arbitrary actions in the name of justice and assumes that just procedures obtain acceptance by defendants or court clientele because they are fairly arrived at, and court orders and sentences will therefore theoretically receive adherence and implementation. Courts are given enforcement powers, however, and not just by chance.

Traffic fines are paid, divorce property settlement orders receive general compliance, insurance companies pay off court ordered awards. But offenders recidivate, schools do not desegregate, and fathers, with or without good reason, fail to comply with child support orders. Due process receives varying interpretation. The Constitution requires due process, but wisely does not specify the particular minimums of due process which must be met at each of the many types of court hearings which occur.

The ready availability of defense counsel, from the earliest stage of the criminal justice process, including appointed counsel for the indigent, meets constitutional concerns regarding the assistance of counsel and equal protection. The touchstone of requiring counsel is the awesome threat of deprivation of freedom, merged with the complexity of contemporary law and procedure. The further assumption is that government has a legitimate interest in seeing that justice is done. Unilaterally providing for prosecution is insufficient; balancing and fairness require equally available and skilled defense counsel.

The cost burdens of fully providing defense counsel are rather immense. Prosecution staff must necessarily be increased, along with more trial and appellate judges, and various support staffs. Police and lay witnesses must be present at more motion hearings and trials, and police investigative practices become more time consuming. Philosophically stated, justice is of inherent value in a free society, and its cost is irrelevant. Practically stated, extensive crime and pervasive due process force price-tagging and compromise with the ideal.

Internal-External Issues

There are a multitude of internal-external court issues, but this examination will consider four of the more important: (1) judicial activism, and the courts' relationship with the public; (2) the court as a component agency in a criminal justice system; (3) reduction of the volume of the criminal caseload; and (4) community corrections.

The reform assumption is that judges should more aggressively take their case to the community, to the funding bodies, and, by implication, to the political corridors.[16] This direction meshes with the concept of the courts' functional independence. At one pole the courts would order legislatures to fund what the courts consider desirable, or at least necessary. But exercise of the inherent powers doctrine is politically treacherous. On the other extreme, courts would passively await whatever responsibilities and funds are provided them. The contemporary consensus supports judicial activism, cautions against exercise of inherent powers except following intergovernmental cooperation and rebuff of well-planned voluntary strategies,[17] and urges solicitation of citizen advice on court operations.

Severe limitations on the garnering of LEAA funds by the courts[18] mirrors judicial passivity and weak administrative capacity. The accelerating call by the judiciary for its fair share of these monies, and for a largely exclusive judicial determination of the expenditure of these funds,[19] reflects the growing vitality of judiciary spokesmen. To assist with their operational and political deficiencies, courts would seek citizen advice and support. While the courts' constituencies require expansion, it is vital that citizen involvement be well-planned and utilized, otherwise it will be token.

The assumption of systems planning invokes all component organizations into a cohesive and deliberative body, where shared knowledge and opinion facilitates individual agency effectiveness, improves coordination at the interface where an organization integrates its services with another, and establishes a more unified approach to a multiagency process. This is attractive, but for the courts, largely unrealized. Judges and court officials are members of criminal justice councils which approve the award of federal funds. There are scattered examples of local coordinating vehicles through which courts join in overall efforts to improve the system. The recommendation to collaboratively draw guidelines and criteria to aid police, pretrial detention-diversion, prosecution, probation, and judicial decision-making, is a partial approach to the systems direction, and is at an early stage of development. Political advantages accrue from collaboration; component agency criticism may be at least partially avoided through a legitimated co-optation process.

Victimless crimes should be eliminated from criminal and juvenile court caseloads. This assumption rejects the moral basis of these laws and the belief that courts can deter behavior injurious essentially only to the misbehaver. Implementation of this assumption arises primarily through the law's catching up with public opinion and practice. Legislative repeal (public drunkenness) or judicial declaration of unconstitutionality (Alaska's invalidation of limited, private marijuana use) is influenced further by recognition of severe judicial workloads, a determination that judicial priorities must be recast, and relative judicial ineffectiveness in regulating and deterring such conduct. A judicial activist view would urge that this is not the law's business but the community's responsibility, and also that the public needs to be more tolerant of behavior which is noninjurious though offensive to others. The problems, of course, are society's preference for a sanctioning authority and the reluctance to implement widespread alternatives to court jurisdiction.

Community corrections is both an old and a new concept. Probation is a longstanding alternative to incarceration. However, the provision of an array of alternative rehabilitative programs, filling the space between limited probation offerings and secure institutionalization, is relatively new to the criminal justice system though time tested in juvenile justice.

The assumption is that prisons are counterproductive except in severe and recalcitrant cases. The further assumption is that correction in the community is more natural, more real, less costly, and more effective. Despite numerous research demonstrations of community corrections which show positive results,[20] minor and major reoffenses occur, program administration may be ineffective, staffing patterns and program offerings may be lacking. Severe political problems arise. "Halfway houses may be a good idea, but not in our neighborhood!";[21] "He's back home already!"; "It's okay for first offenders, but look who's there!"; "They should have consulted us first!"; "Doesn't anyone believe in punishment anymore?" There *is* increased short-term risk to the community, but not to advance in this direction increases our long-term risk with incarcerated offenders who return to the community unprepared and possibly less well adjusted than upon institutionalization. Community corrections can be justified as less costly and more humane.[22]

Obstacles to Reform

Certainly judges themselves are frequent obstacles to reform. As a group they are still too isolated from the crosscurrents of change, still too concerned with managing the cases assigned to them without a strong investment in improving the overall system, too involved in their status and the preservation of their narrow turf, too unaware of their enormous powers to impel improvements not only in the courts but in related criminal justice agencies. Yet nationally, in many states and communities, judges are also the spearheads for reform.

Legislative indifference to the needs of the courts is another prominent obstacle to court reform. State legislators are frequently strident opponents of one vital reform—the assumption of greater court financing costs by state government. Contrary to public belief state legislators are more frequently than not nonattorneys. Neither state nor local legislators march to the beat of the court drummer, and other constituencies far exceed the importance of the court system in the eyes and ears of elected lawmakers. Court systems have contributed to legislative apathy. State legislators, for example, are usually more interested in executive branch prosperity than in the effectiveness of the judicial system. For it is the executive branch which implements most legislation, and lawmakers have a more vested interest in the effective implementation of the laws they produce.

The executive branch—the governors, mayors, and county commissioners—will provide more support to the agencies they govern than to a court system independent of their supervision. This is understandable, but narrow. It should be more than rhetoric to suggest that the true strength of any one branch of government is symbiotically related to the strength of each branch.

The pervasive scope of the criminal law is a further obstacle to court reform. While there is gathering interest in decriminalizing a variety of victimless crimes, legislative repeal has been limited largely to those states which have stricken public drunkenness per se as a criminal activity. Legislators approach such repeal timidly for fear they will alienate voters. Governors and mayors see other priorities. The courts passively await these "offenders" reaching their system.

Media personnel limitations and competitive priorities hamper a broader interpretation to the public of the larger issues in the courts.[23] And public attitudes and apathy, part of which reflects the apathy of the courts in informing the public, remain in the end as a major obstacle to court reform.

Spearheads for Reform

There are substantial numbers of progressive persons and forces —judges and court personnel, legislators at various levels, executive branch representatives, attorneys, media personnel, and members of the public—who through organizations or individually have contributed to reforms in our courts. The organizational list is huge, but let us name some of the most valuable groups: the American Judicature Society, the American Bar Association and state and local bar associations, the National Council on Crime and Delinquency, the League of Women Voters, the Institute of Judicial Administration, the many national courts organizations, of Supreme Court Chief Justices, state court administrators, judges of metropolitan courts and specialized courts, the National Council of Juvenile Court Judges, the National College of the State Judiciary, the Institute for Court Management, the National Center for State Courts, the National District Attorneys Association, the National Legal Aid and Defender Association, the national commissions which have addressed criminal justice issues, and on and on. With such an array of impressive professional and citizen involvement in improving the justice system, one pauses to ask whether the courts really are in critical shape.

But if you ask the average citizen and if you search the studies of criminal and juvenile justice issues, you will know that we have serious problems. The public often shakes its head negatively when asked about the state of the courts; the average employee of the system, when speaking candidly, will admit to myriad shortcomings; and no commission has closed its books saying all is well and there are no recommendations to make. Let us see how some of these commissions view the courts.

The President's Commission on Law Enforcement and Administration of Justice

This Commission, appointed in 1965 by President Lyndon B. Johnson, promulgated its major volume, *The Challenge of Crime in a Free Society,* in February, 1967.[24] It also published a number of task force reports, and its findings and recommendations influenced congressional enactment a year later of the Safe Streets and Crime Control Omnibus Act, which established the Law Enforcement Assistance Administration (LEAA) in the U.S. Department of Justice.

The Commission scored the lower criminal courts as probably the weakest link in our criminal justice system. It noted there: the frequent presence of lesser qualified judges, prosecutors, defense attorneys, and court officials; the absence or undernourishment of probation services; the common rural practice of compensating justices of the peace, generally nonlawyers, by fees based on the numbers of persons they found guilty. The physical facilities of the lower courts were seen as "likely to be old, dirty, and extremely overcrowded."[25] The Commission recommended the unification of the lower criminal courts and the felony courts. It urged sharply improved physical facilities, and an increased number of and increased capability of judges, prosecutors, defense counsel, and probation personnel.

Concerned with crowded and degrading jail facilities, the Commission recommended comprehensive bail reform legislation, a systematic approach to furnishing judicial officers with sufficient information to permit pretrial release without financial condition for the bulk of defendants, and further, that police agents should cite lesser offenders into court instead of taking them to local jails. The prosecutor should become the charging agent, screening out from the system those cases where evidence is lacking to convict a defendant. The Commission recommended a more controlled release of criminal case information by agents or officers of criminal justice agencies, urged legislative penal code reform to provide a simplified grading of offenses, and called for a more rational structure for sentencing discretion by judges. It urged strengthened probation services, the abolition of jury sentencing in noncapital cases, and procedures for correcting disparate sentencing of offenders by judges.

The Commission recommended measures for judicial selection and retention in several forms: removal of partisan judicial election and the substitution of an appointive system for judges, coupled with a board or commission in each state empowered to remove judges from their benches for reasons of incompetency or misconduct. Strengthened educational programs for judges, prosecutors, and defense counsel were advocated. Public financing of criminal and juvenile defense services was a further priority, and the slow movement of criminal cases was first criticized and then followed by recommendations for moving cases more quickly through the system. For example, processing time for felony cases from arrest to trial was set at no more than four months, and from trial through appellate decisions within five additional months. Professional court administrators were urged upon the courts, along with improved consideration for witnesses and jurors. Court restructuring, involving state more than local organization, together with strengthened state high court administration over the entire court, were stressed.

Other facets of criminal justice were offered directions for improvement: the police, the correctional agencies, the juvenile justice system.

National Advisory Commission on Criminal Justice Standards and Goals

Building upon the earlier work of the President's Commission on Law Enforcement and the Administration of Justice, as well as the experience of the intervening years, the National Advisory Commission on Criminal Justice Standards and Goals promulgated, in late 1973, three primary volumes and three additional works of great importance to the future administration of justice.[26] The three major volumes deal with *Police, Courts,* and *Corrections.*

The Commission was funded by LEAA, and we should detour to take a look at that organization. LEAA, the Law Enforcement Assistance Administration, was created by the Congress in 1968 to focus and guide national crime control funds to state and local criminal justice planning councils. Primary responsibility for the allocation of these funds was vested at the state level. Strong criticism was directed at this agency in its early years for an alleged overfunding of police hardware. Correctional programs subsequently received increased financial attention, and in turn court improvement was accorded greater attention.

Recent attacks have challenged the overall effectiveness of LEAA activities in the light of spiraling crime rates. Further, executive branch intrusion into the administration of the courts has now been called into question. Court organizations are asking for the direct allocation of federal funds to state court systems so they can plan and develop their own priorities for improvement.[27] Nonetheless, on balance the creation of state planning agencies under this act, for the first time in our fifty states, instituted some form of necessary criminal justice planning and priorities. The process of official representatives of police, courts, and corrections sitting down to plan together has improved communication between these forces and has begun the difficult chore of advancing from a nonsystem to a system. LEAA restrictions were placed on large-scale applications of funds for capital construction purposes. Large sums were expended in nontraditional ways to innovate new, different, and better administered approaches within police, courts, and corrections. Evaluation requirements were built into many of these programs. For the first time significant federal monies were made available to the states to expand undernourished budgets, to modernize many practices, and to strengthen undermanned staff in critical areas. Education and training programs for a wide array of personnel were subsidized. There is still stumbling and fumbling, but there has been movement and change.

Returning to the National Advisory Commission reports, their format, specifying standards for a panoply of criminal justice organizations, personnel, and procedures, is an advance and a refinement in how commission reports are written. Each state was subsequently asked to compare its practices with each of the standards set forth in these volumes. Where a state or community was deficient by such comparison, the carrot of LEAA funds was available, at least in part, to uplift local practice to the defined standards. Not all standards will be adopted by all states. But implementation of these standards is a propelling force for criminal justice planning agencies. These standards should receive greater implementation than have many other national reports.

Let us look at how the standards guide the courts. Prominent in the *Courts* volume is recognition of the informal discretionary decisions made by police, prosecutors, and judges in case processing. It is urged that decision-making criteria be made more visible, that they be harnessed to written guidelines and involve different criminal justice agencies in the development of the other's guidelines, to make justice more uniform and equal. Prosecutors, for example, should be consulted by police officers in developing guidelines for taking persons into custody (1.2).[28]

The abolition of the routine grand jury indictment on felony charges, as used in nearly half our states, was recommended, retaining its use only for the exceptional case (4.4). The prosecutor, then, is the major charging agent, and no case should be filed without his formal approval. This volume's initial standard calls on the prosecutor to screen out from the system all accused persons "if there is not a reasonable likelihood that the evidence admissible against him would be sufficient to obtain a conviction and sustain it on appeal" (1.1). Ten guides to prosecutor screening are detailed.

Perhaps this volume's most controversial standard, to prohibit plea negotiation and plea bargaining "as soon as possible but in no event later than 1978" (3.1), clearly expresses the Commission's scorn toward the bargained plea as demeaning justice. Yet the National District Attorneys Association disapproved this standard, taking the view that plea bargaining is a necessity because of our overloaded criminal court system, and that plea bargaining is inherently a valid and useful method of settling cases.

The standards moved up the criminal processing timeframe, and would require that a felony be tried generally no later than sixty days from the date of arrest, and misdemeanors generally no later than thirty days from arrest (4.1). Police were further encouraged to issue citations and summons in lieu of arresting alleged misdemeanants and certain lesser felony cases (4.2), and those arrested should be brought before a judicial officer within six hours for advisement of rights, determination of pretrial release, and provision of counsel (4.5). The use of bail bondsmen to obtain releases following arrest would be eliminated (4.6), replaced by a series of alternative approaches—release on recognizance, a 10 percent deposit of the bail amount with the court to be refunded upon appearance at trial, required supervision of defendants' activities prior to trial—all largely patterned after the earlier work of the American Bar Association's Project on Minimum Standards for Criminal Justice.

Criminal juries of less than twelve persons and no less than six persons were urged (4.14), as was experimentation in the use of videotape trials where the examination and cross-examination of witnesses would be conducted by attorneys prior to trial and then presented to the jury by videotape along with the opening statements and closing arguments of counsel (4.2).

The Commission called for the merit selection of judges (7.1), a commission in each state empowered to discipline and remove disabled or incompetent judges (7.4), increased judicial compensation, expanded judicial education, and substantial court reorganization. All courts should be fully state funded, all judges should be attorneys, the lower and upper trial courts should become a single unified trial court (8.1). Basic traffic violations would be handled by administrative rather than judicial agencies (8.2).

The Commission would establish an office of state court administrator in each state (9.1) who, subject to his supreme court, would establish policies, implement guidelines, and monitor the administration of all courts within the state. He would be assisted by local trial court administrators. Court administrators would among other responsibilities monitor the movement of cases to insure that speedy trial rules were met, and that only reasonable delays occurred. The provision of stronger public and private legal defense services was underscored (13.5).

In the juvenile area the standards recommended a family court division in the highest general trial court, with a breadth of jurisdiction encompassing the range of juvenile and divorce matters, together with adoption, paternity and support, and assaults within a family. Further, only juveniles who violated criminal laws could be committed to delinquency institutions (14.1).

American Bar Association Project on Minimum Standards for Criminal Justice

The American Bar Association, by far the largest national legal organization, earned well its conservative image over many decades, but more recently it has gotten more in step with the times. Attention must be given to the ABA Standards for Criminal Justice, one of the major achievements of that organization. At the instance of the Institute of Judicial Administration at New York University, the American Bar Association, starting in 1963 and continuing for more than a decade organized, developed, and then promulgated a series of seventeen volumes of standards relating to criminal justice. "The objectives of the Standards are to promote effective law enforcement and the adequate protection of the public and to safeguard and amplify the constitutional rights of those accused of the commission of crimes."[29] Drafted by law professors, screened through committees of distinguished judges and attorneys, and approved finally by the ABA House of Delegates, the seventeen volumes have received serious consideration in virtually all of our states, and have formed the backbone for those standards and goals of the National Advisory Commission which encompass similar areas.[30] These ABA volumes include: *Providing Defense Services, Pretrial Release, Fair Trial and Free Press, Electronic Surveillance, Discovery and Procedure Before Trial, Pleas of Guilty, Joinder and Severance, Speedy Trial, Trial by Jury, Sentencing Alternatives and Procedures, Probation, Criminal Appeals, Appellate Review of Sentences, Post-Conviction Remedies, The Prosecution Function and the Defense Function, The Function of the Trial Judge,* and *The Urban Police Function.*

Significantly, this project has been concerned substantially with the implementation as well as the content of the standards. Funds were obtained to permit comparison of ABA standards with the statutes and criminal rules of each state, so that lawmakers and rulemakers would have an organized rundown as to what was needed to bring each state into line with the standards. The modernization of criminal statutes and procedures in many states has accompanied the implementation work. Further, appellate court decisions have regularly cited ABA standards in support of more progressive, more modernized holdings.

The volume *Providing Defense Services* skirts the issue as to whether a public defender system is a preferred model to an organized system for assigning private counsel to defendants unable to retain their own attorney. Substantial hardship to the family, rather than indigency, is the eligibility standard for appointment, and defense counsel should be furnished funds for case investigators, expert witnesses, and other supporting services. The *Pretrial Release* volume recognizes the discriminatory patterns and ineffective results of our present bail system and urges the use of money bail only as a last resort. These standards clearly and unequivocally seek to do away with commercial bail bondsmen. A network of pretrial release programs, including release conditioned on reporting to a probation or other agency staff member, is within the prescription of alternatives.

The ABA volume on *Fair Trial and Free Press* provides for court restrictions on the widespread dissemination of pretrial publicity concerning alleged criminals, but does not bar media exercise of First Amendment rights to publish information it is otherwise able to obtain. The volume calls for official sources to promptly release basic facts concerning crimes and the circumstances surrounding them, and encourages agreements between the media, the bench, and the bar so that publicity does not impinge on the right to a fair trial.

The *Standards Relating to Electronic Surveillance* would prohibit private electronic surveillance, and subject surveillance by public law enforcement personnel to strict limitation, and, in the absence of consent by one of the parties, would require judicial approval. Such judicial approval should only be granted following the submission of an application containing facts similar to the request for the issuance of a search warrant. The volume dealing with *Discovery and Procedure Before Trial* opens up much of the prosecution's case prior to trial, so there would be fewer surprises, shorter trials, and an opportunity for defense counsel to comprehend the strength of the prosecution's case prior to trial. Defense counsel is also required to make certain disclosures, though none which would abridge the Fifth Amendment privilege to remain silent.

The volume *Pleas of Guilty* makes plea bargaining visible, and approves it when in compliance with suggested procedures. These standards are in direct opposition to the abolition of plea bargaining urged by the National Advisory Commission. Careful consideration of whether a proffered plea of guilty is truly voluntary, and whether a defendant fully understands the consequences of this plea, are rigorously required. The volume on *Joinder and Severance* governs difficult legal issues where there is more than one defendant, where one defendant has entered statements which may implicate another defendant, whether a defendant might be tried for more than one offense when these several offenses are not part of a single plan or event. The *Speedy Trial* standards embrace the view that criminal trials should take priority over civil trials, and that jailed defendants should take priority over those released pending trial. It also seeks to regulate speedy trial concerns when a defendant incarcerated in one state also has a charge pending against him in another state.

Trial by Jury anticipated subsequent controversial decisions of the United States Supreme Court and accepted less than unanimous criminal juries, as well as criminal juries of fewer than twelve persons. These standards would clarify that jurors be permitted to take notes during the course of the trial. *Sentencing Alternatives and Procedures* urges shorter sentences for run-of-the-mill offenders and a discriminating use of long sentences for exceptionally dangerous offenders. In general, presentence investigations would be required prior to sentencing. An array of alternative sentences in lieu of prison is urged, and measures to reduce unequal sentences are recommended. *Probation* takes the advanced position that probation should be the sentence unless (a) confinement is necessary to protect the public from further criminal activity by the defendant, (b) the offender is in need of residential correctional treatment, or (c) a grant of probation would unduly depreciate the seriousness of the offense.

Other volumes suggest approaches to speedier appeals, encourage states to permit limited appeals on the issue of the length and type of sentence (sentences could be lowered as well as increased upon review), and provide enlightened guidelines for the functions of prosecution and defense counsel and for the trial judge. Finally, in the volume on *Urban Police Function,* the standards seek to reduce the irregular administration of discretion by police officials, and suggest improved organization of police resources and review of police decisions.

The Institute of Judicial Administration–American Bar Association Joint Commission on Juvenile Justice Standards

In searching through the reports of the National Advisory Commission on Criminal Justice Standards and Goals, one finds only limited reference to juvenile justice. Instead, this Commission expressly yielded more detailed consideration of juvenile justice standards to the pending reports of the juvenile justice standards project.

The same two organizations which formed the secretariat and the approving authority for the criminal justice standards project, the IJA and the ABA, launched a several-year effort in late 1971 to recommend detailed practices for juvenile justice. More than twenty volumes are envisioned, and their scope is even broader than that of the adult counterpart project. Reports are underway covering precourt, court, and postcourt dimensions of the handling of juveniles, together with a variety of other volumes which will relate to areas such as the rights of minors, the neglected child, the monitoring of juvenile justice, planning for juvenile justice, and special issues of the minority community and juvenile justice.

American Bar Association Commission on Standards of Judicial Administration

A separate commission of the American Bar Association promulgated in 1974 an influential volume, *Standards Relating to Court Organization.*[31] This publication focused on the structure and organization of courts, the selection and retirement of judges, the rule-making authority, internal administration for the courts, the financing of courts, and court personnel and record systems. Certain of these standards should be cited verbatim:

> 1.10. The structure of the court system should be simple, consisting of a trial court and an appellate court, each having divisions and departments as needed.
>
> All judges should be selected on the basis of professional competence and experience through a merit system of appointment. They should have substantially secure tenure in office, subject to removal for cause and to a requirement of compulsory retirement at a designated age.
>
> 1.11(d). Responsibility for making policy, including regulations concerning court administration and participation in making procedural rules, should be vested in the state's highest court or in a council composed of judges.
>
> 1.11(e). Administrative supervision of the court system as a whole should be exercised by a chief justice.

Envisioned by these standards is a unified trial court structure, covering the trial stages of all criminal and civil cases regardless of amount or severity. This court would be presided over by a single class of judges, and these judges would be assisted by legally trained "judicial officers" performing judicial and quasi-judicial functions under the authority of the judges. Election of judges would be abolished, and judges would be appointed by a governor from three or more nominations made by an independent commission.

The chief justice of each supreme court would preside over a judicial council, representative of a cross section of the judges of each state or composed of all justices of the supreme court, which would determine policy and procedures for administration of all courts in the state. The chief justice, however, would exercise powers of general supervision over all court personnel, the assignment of judges, financial matters, and relationships with other branches of government and with the public. These standards urge that each state court system maintain a strong central staff which, under the authority of the judicial council and pursuant to the supervision of the chief justice, would perform central guidance and administration of the day-to-day business of the courts, and establish certain administrative policies as for calendar rules and practice, court records and forms, and statistical reporting procedures for the entire court system.

These standards urge upon the courts the administration of their own personnel system. Courts should not depend upon executive branch merit personnel systems to regulate employees of the independent judicial branch. Further:

> 1.50. Responsibility for the financial support of state court systems should be assumed by state government. Where this is not practicable at once, a program should be adopted for gradual assumption of this responsibility in the course of time. . . . The financial operations of the court system should be administered through a unified budget in which all revenues and expenditures for all activities of all courts in the system are presented and supervised.

During 1975 this commission published a tentative draft of *Standards Relating to Trial Courts.*[32] This volume takes its basic direction from the first work, elaborates the desired organization and administration of a unified trial court, and contains a few surprises. It goes beyond U.S. Supreme Court holdings to urge a jury trial right whenever jail or imprisonment may be imposed, and calls for a unanimous jury verdict (2.10 [a]). It recommends that a party be permitted one peremptory (automatic) challenge of the judge assigned to hear this case. This would be similar to jury selection procedures where parties are allowed to remove without citation of cause a certain number of prospective jurors. It is grounded on the proposition that parties should be entitled to an additional measure of assurance that their case will be justly determined. The subsequently assigned judge may then be challenged, but only for cause (2.32).

Lawyers who persistently request continuances should be warned, and where such measures fail the court should limit the number of cases in which this attorney may participate at any one time (2.56 [2] [3]). The presiding judge should take "appropriate corrective action" with judges who are persistently and unreasonably indulgent in granting continuances (2.56 [3]). The standards also urge that court reporters (responsible for the verbatim recording of court proceedings) should be responsible to and supervised by the court administration rather than individual judges, and that their private contract activity should be regulated in order to give priority to speedy transcription of trials for appeal purposes (2.42).

The responsibilities of the trial court presiding judge are extensively set forth (2.32), principles of caseflow management are explicated (2.50, 2.51), time frame standards are detailed (2.50), and a rotation system for judges assigned to special divisions, such as juvenile or family, is recommended for one year and not more than three years (2.35 [a]). Other standards would narrow the duration of juror service (2.63) and provide juror pay of not less than $20 per day plus transportation expenses (2.64 [6]), organize probation services within the judicial branch (2.71 [e]), encourage simplified small claims procedures up to $500 or $1,000 (2.75), and retain court jurisdiction over traffic violations (2.76).

The Future of the Courts

The basic direction of future court systems has been sketched, and succeeding years will see substantial implementation of what these reports have emphasized. The time between conceiving a reformist idea, the development of a consensus in support of the idea, and the state-by-state implementation of the idea, seems to take from ten to twenty years. Sometimes it requires a longer span; rarely shorter.

There are certain known and unknown variables which may substantially impinge upon the future of the courts: the make-up of the United States Supreme Court may change significantly, with a resultant redirection in rulings on important cases; the severity and extent of criminal offenses—in the face of other critical shortcomings in our society—is prompting mandatory sentence legislation, resulting in greater crowding/overcrowding of prisons, and could spark radical efforts to take private action against offenders rather than permit normal public procedures to operate; other elements include the extent of political corruption by elected and appointed public officials, the exposure of police corruption, the grave implications of the organized crime conglomerates, a relatively unchecked inflation, militant action resulting from the decay of our cities or a backlash to such action, the hot fuse of school integration tempers, and the police state methods of military organizations. These and other present or future problems could change our society in major ways, and with it the form and function of our court system. Yet this nation has surmounted the countless crises of the past, and we should expect that political and social trends and changes should speed rather than retard, should strengthen rather than weaken, the fundamental role of the courts in a democratic society.

We should feel optimistic about the courts of the future. The rate of their change, the speed of their modernization, the pace of their improved delivery of justice, will vary between the states and within a given state. But largely we know where we are going, and we are creating the vehicles for centering the responsibility for change.[33]

Judges will remain the fulcrum of the criminal justice system. They are ultimately responsible for the performance of the courts. We are providing them with professionally trained administrators to carry out day-to-day administration of the courts under judicial supervision. The power of the courts to enact administrative and procedural rules has increased, so that they have greater control over what happens in their own workplace.

While an amazing system was developed years ago whereby state and federal appellate court decisions could speedily be retrieved for immediate reference, we are only now speeding up the development of a system where other forms of information vital to court administration are easily stored and retrieved. We now have the technology to tell us at a glance the caseload of a court system, or of a given judge or of a probation officer, the length of time cases require to move from one processing point to another, where the logjams exist, to utilize computerized or noncomputerized information systems to aid us in the improved deployment of existing staff or in planning for additional staff, and to improve ways of budget planning and management. The courts are gaining better control of their own case calendars, and the tripod of justice is now better understood: that effective criminal justice requires well-trained judges assisted by well-trained prosecutors and well-trained defense counsel. Each leg of the tripod, and the assistance required to hold each leg strong, requires support systems which understand their goals and priorities and see the whole of the criminal justice picture. Prosecutors must manage their offices well, must screen out the legally insufficient case, should divert defendants to alternative community resources where the formal adjudication of a case is not critical to a community's sense of well-being. The way a community or state organizes its criminal defense services for the indigent requires ongoing assessment to provide that quality of defense which reduces appeals based on the contention that a defendant had been represented at trial by ineffective counsel. Probation services must also be constantly evaluated, and their policy interface with the court system clarified, whether probation is part of the judicial or executive branch in a particular state.

Far more public money will be critical to the forward march of the courts in the future. Yet, wholesale spending is ill-advised. The improvisation of pretrial release and pretrial intervention programs diminishes the need for the construction of new local jails. An array of community-based correction alternatives shortstops the need to construct additional prison facilities. Decriminalization of victimless crimes reduces the need for additional judges, prosecutors, defenders, and probation personnel, and permits the wiser use of present functionaries.

The movement to depoliticize judges is accelerating. Higher job performance standards will be required for court clerks and ancillary court personnel. Political protection is being replaced by professional merit systems. Cumbersome recordkeeping is yielding to mechanical methods that are speedier and simpler to store or to retrieve. Law school training is broadening the perception of future lawyers of the whole of the justice system, and is providing wider student trial practice.

Closer links between the courts and legislative and executive bodies are on the horizon. More supreme court chief justices are presenting state-of-the-court messages to assembled legislatures. Close liaison between legislative committees and state court administrators holds hope for improved coordination between these branches. Greater state funding of state court systems has developed and should increase. Citizens are learning more about the courts, and the courts are more solicitous of citizen convenience and interest.

The judiciary is recognizing that it must do far more than simply process cases; it is striving to put its own house in order. It now more fully supports the directive that "[the] positive aspect of separation of powers imposes on courts affirmative obligations to assert and fully exercise their powers, to operate efficiently by modern standards, to protect their independent status, and to fend off legislative or executive attempts to encroach upon judicial prerogatives."[34]

As future professionals who may directly or tangentially aid in this movement, as citizens who may be future jurors or witnesses to court proceedings, as electors who will vote on the selection or deselection of judges, as taxpayers who will assist in the financing of the courts, and as members of the public who understand the serious and independent role of the courts in the democratic scheme of America, we should join in advancing changes and improvements in our courts. These are our courts. Let us make them good courts.

Questions for Discussion

1. What may have been the implications had the United States Constitution granted basic criminal law jurisdiction to the federal courts rather than to state and local courts?
2. What are the major citizen critiques of the courts? Your concerns?
3. How can the judiciary increase its use of citizen assistance to help attain its objectives?
4. Consider the impact on society if victimless crimes such as drug use, gambling, and prostitution were decriminalized.
5. Should state and local judges, like federal judges, be appointed for life?
6. Should potential political ramifications influence judges in reaching their decisions?
7. Is it wise policy that the judicial system must obtain its funds from legislative bodies?
8. Is the independent role of the judiciary threatened by a state

LEAA planning agency board's determination of how federal funds should be allocated for state and local court improvement?

9. Why is greater state funding of court systems more strongly recommended than increased local funding of the courts? What are the implications of such a direction?
10. Is it better policy for chief trial court judges to be appointed by the state supreme court chief justice or elected by their colleagues on the trial bench?
11. How can courts improve their efficiency without impairing their goal of individualized justice?

References

1. *United States v. Nixon: The President Before the Supreme Court,* ed. Leon Friedman (New York: Chelsea House Publishers, 1974); Carl Bernstein and Bob Woodward, *All the President's Men* (New York: Simon and Schuster, 1974); Mary McCartney, *The Mask of State* (New York: Harcourt, Brace, Jovanovich, 1974); The Staff of the New York Times, *The End of a Presidency* (New York: Holt, Rinehart, and Winston, 1974).
2. Roscoe Pound, "The Causes of Popular Dissatisfaction with the Administration of Justice," *Journal of the American Judicature Society* 46 (1962): 55. The 1906 address is reprinted in this journal issue.
3. Ibid.
4. Geoffrey Gallas, "The Conventional Wisdom of State Court Administration: A Critical Assessment and an Alternative Approach," mimeographed. Manhattan Beach, Calif., 1975, p. 1.
5. See for example, *A Unified Court System for Vermont* (Denver, Colo.: National Center for State Courts, 1974). The comprehensive recommendations of this study advocate the conventional wisdom of state court unification, trial court unification, and judicial merit selection and discipline.
6. Allan Ashman and Jeffrey A. Parness, "The Concept of a Unified Court System," *DePaul Law Review* 24 (1974): 1.
7. Edwart E. Pringle, "The Role of the State Chief Justice," *Justice in the States,* p. 82.
8. *State Court Administrative Systems: Perspectives and Relationships* (Denver, Colo.: Institute for Court Management, 1975).
9. George F. Cole, *Politics and the Administration of Justice* (Beverly Hills, Calif.: Sage Publications, 1973), p. 188.
10. Allan Ashman and James J. Alfini, *The Key to Judicial Merit Selection: The Nominating Process* (Chicago: American Judicature Society, 1974), pp. 70–85; Richard A. Watson and Ronald G. Downing, *The Politics of the Bench and the Bar: Judicial Selection Under the Missouri Non-Partisan Court Plan* (New York: John Wiley & Sons, 1969).
11. National Institute of Law Enforcement and Administration of Justice, *Criminal Victimization in the United States, A National Crime Panel Survey Report,* Washington, D.C.: U.S. Department of Justice, 1974).
12. See Roger Barron and Floyd Feeney, "Preventing Delinquency Through Diversion," *Federal Probation* 37 (1973): 13.

13. Paul B. Wice, *Freedom for Sale* (Lexington, Mass.: D. C. Heath & Co., 1974), p. 75.
14. Ibid., p. 67.
15. *Annual Report of the Administrative Office of the California Courts* (San Francisco: Administrative Office of the California Courts, 1975), pp. 94–109.
16. Carl Baar, "Will Urban Trial Courts Survive the War on Crime?" in Herbert Jacobs, ed., *The Potential for Reform of Criminal Justice* (Beverly Hills, Calif.: Sage Publications, 1974).
17. John M. Connors, "Inherent Power of the Courts—Management Tool or Rhetorical Weapon?" *Justice System Journal* (1974): 63.
18. See *Report of the Special Study Team on LEAA Support of the State Courts* (Washington, D.C.: Criminal Courts Technical Assistance Project, The American University, 1975).
19. See Resolution, Conference of Chief Justices, August 16, 1974; Resolution, Conference of the State Court Administrators, August 15, 1974, and 1973, in *Report of the Special Study Team* (The American University, 1975), pp. 191–94.
20. See reports on Probation Subsidy, California Youth Authority, Sacramento; Ellsworth House, San Mateo County Probation Department, Belmont, Calif.; Court Counselor Program, Inc., Peoria, Ill.; Probationed Offenders Rehabilitation and Treatment (PORT), Rochester, Minn.; Citizenship Training Group, Boston Juvenile Court; Community Treatment Project for Recidivist Offenders, Circuit Court Probation Department, Pontiac, Mich.
21. *A Time to Act* (Washington, D.C.: Joint Commission on Correctional Manpower and Training, 1969), p. 65.
22. James Robinson and Gerald Smith, "The Effectiveness of Correctional Programs," *Crime and Delinquency* 17 (1971).
23. Donald R. Fretz, *Courts and the Community* (Reno, Nev.: National College of the State Judiciary, 1973).
24. See generally, President's Commission on Law Enforcement and Administration of Justice, *The Challenge of Crime in a Free Society,* and *Task Force Reports: The Police; The Courts; Corrections; Juvenile Delinquency and Youth Crime; Organized Crime; Science and Technology; Assessment of Crime; Narcotics and Drugs; Drunkenness* (Washington, D.C.: Government Printing Office, 1967).
25. President's Commission, *Challenge,* p. 129.
26. See generally, National Advisory Commission on Criminal Justice Standards and Goals, 6 vols.: *Police/Courts/Corrections/A National Strategy to Reduce Crime/Criminal Justice System/Community Crime Prevention* (Washington, D.C.: Government Printing Office, 1973).
27. *Report of the Special Study Team* (The American University, 1975), pp. 191–94.
28. Numbers in parentheses refer to the enumerated standards in Report of the National Advisory Commission on Criminal Justice Standards and Goals, *Courts,* 1973.
29. See generally, William H. Erickson, *ABA Standards for Criminal Justice,* reprinted from Robert M. Cipes, ed., *Criminal Defense Techniques* (New York: Matthew Bender, 1972), Appendix A.
30. An eighteenth volume, a 640-page composite of all the standards, together with the introduction from each report, was published by the American Bar Association in 1974.

31. American Bar Association, Commission on Standards of Judicial Administration, *Standards Relating to Court Organization* (Chicago: American Bar Association, Approved Draft, 1974).
32. American Bar Association, Commission on Standards of Judicial Administration, *Standards Relating to Trial Courts* (Chicago: American Bar Association, Tentative Draft, 1975).
33. Ernest C. Friesen, Jr., Edward C. Gallas, and Nesta M. Gallas, *Managing the Courts* (Indianapolis, Ind.: Bobbs-Merrill Co., 1971), p. 6.
34. Jim R. Carrigan, *Inherent Powers of the Courts* (Reno, Nev.: National College of the State Judiciary, 1973), p. 2.

Appendix A: Organizational Charts of State Court Systems

Figure A-1. California

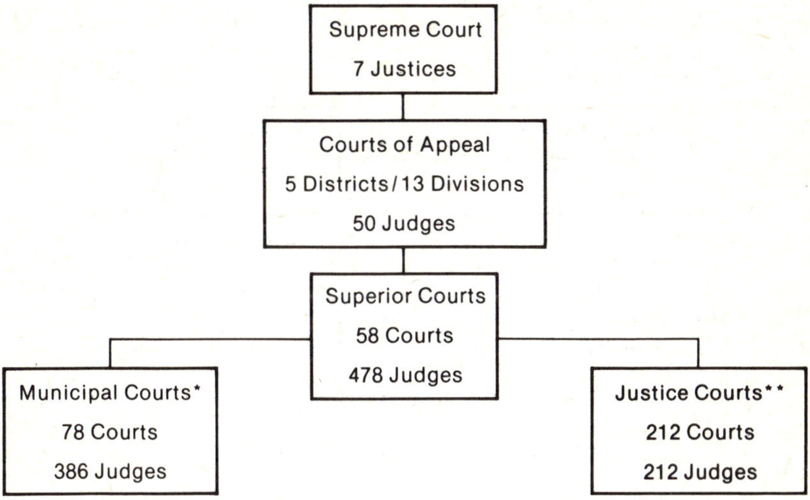

* Districts of more than 40,000 residents.
**Districts of 40,000 or fewer residents.

Figure A-2. Colorado

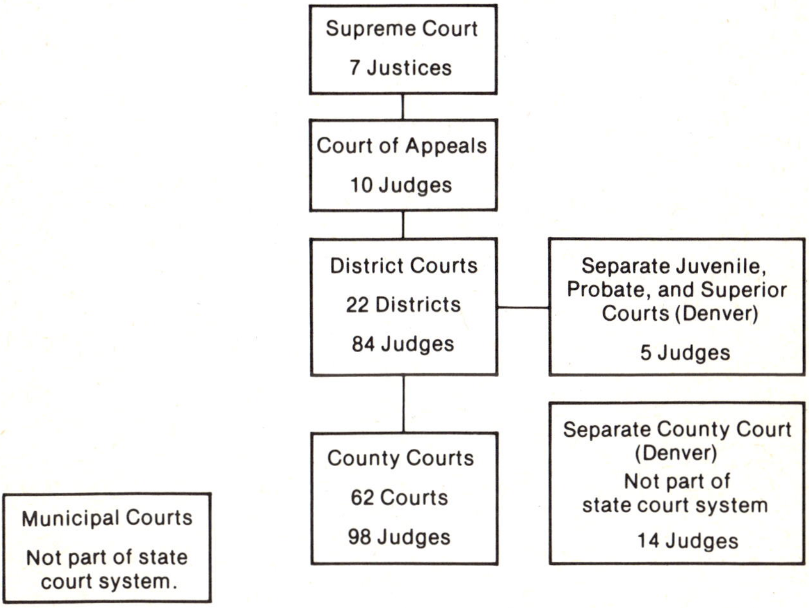

Figure A-3. Delaware

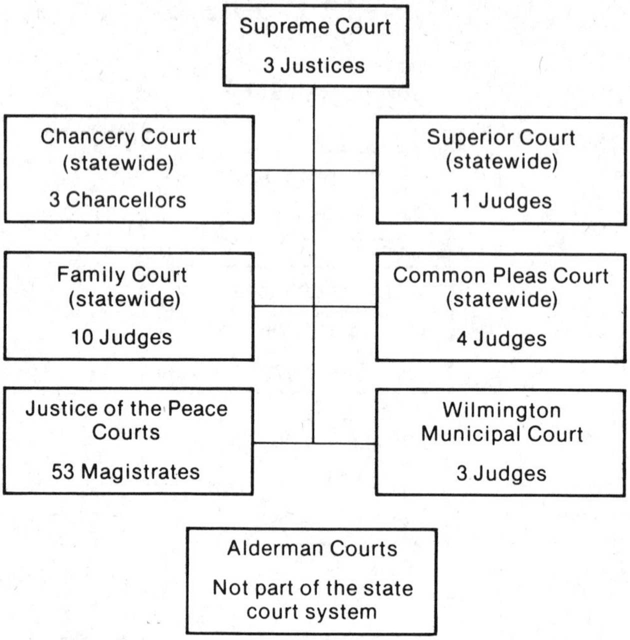

Figure A-4. Florida

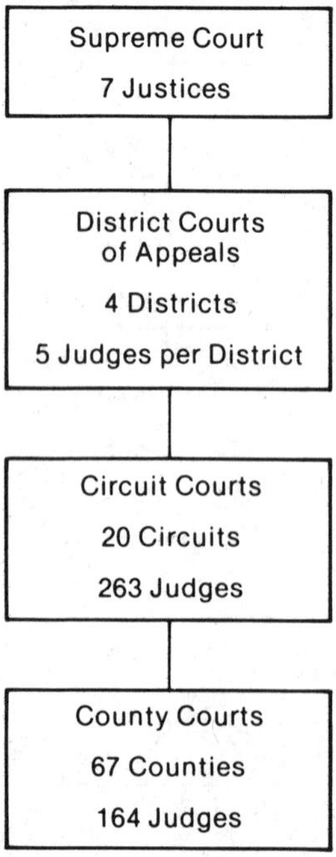

Figure A-5. Illinois

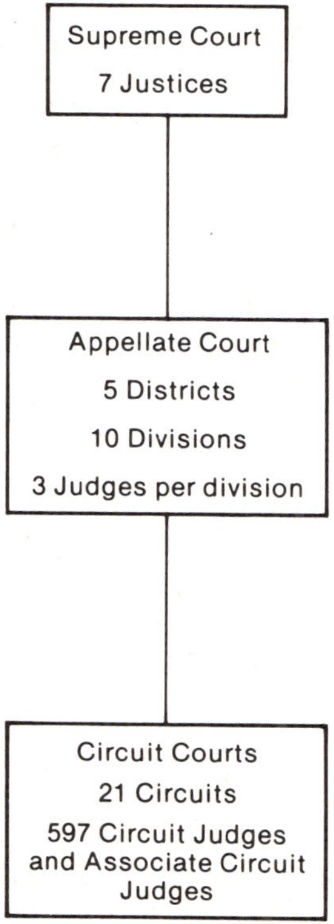

Figure A-6. New York State

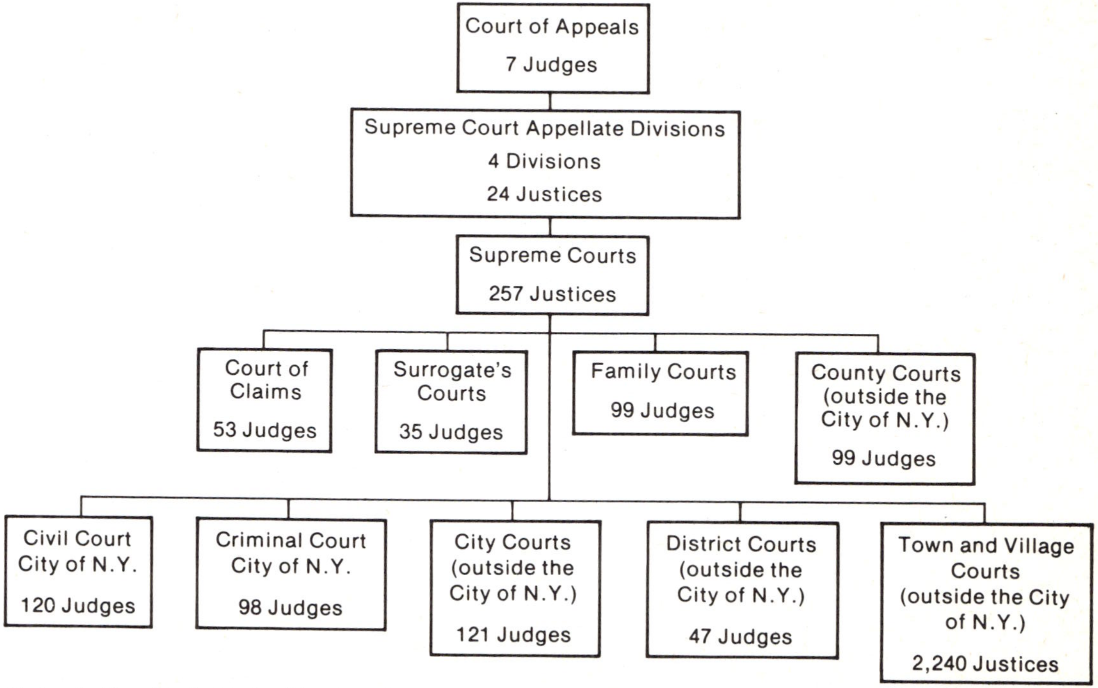

Note: In New York, "judge" is the official title for jurists of the highest court of appeals, and "justice" is the official title for jurists of the general trial court (supreme court) and its appellate divisions.

Appendix B: Selected Amendments to the United States Constitution

Article I

Congress shall make no law respecting an establishment of religion, or prohibiting the free exercise thereof; or abridging the freedom of speech, or of the press; or the right of the people peaceably to assemble, and to petition the government for a redress of grievances.

Article IV

The right of the people to be secure in their persons, houses, papers, and effects, against unreasonable searches and seizures, shall not be violated, and no Warrants shall issue, but upon probable cause, supported by Oath or affirmation, and particularly describing the place to be searched, and the persons or things to be seized.

Article V

No person shall be held to answer for a capital, or otherwise infamous crime, unless on a presentment or indictment of a Grand Jury, except in cases arising in the land or naval forces, or in the Militia, when in actual service in time of War or public danger; nor shall any person be subject for the same offence to be twice put in jeopardy of life or limb; nor shall be compelled in any criminal case to be a witness against himself, nor be deprived of life, liberty, or property, without due process of law; nor shall private property be taken for public use, without just compensation.

Article VI

In all criminal prosecutions, the accused shall enjoy the right to a speedy and public trial, by an impartial jury of the State and district wherein the crime shall have been committed, which district shall have been previously ascertained by law, and to be informed of the nature and cause of the accusation; to be confronted with the witnesses against him; to have compulsory process for obtaining witnesses in his favor, and to have the Assistance of Counsel for his defense.

Article VIII

Excessive bail shall not be required, nor excessive fines imposed, nor cruel and unusual punishments inflicted.

Article XIV

Sec. 1. All persons born or naturalized in the United States, and subject to the jurisdiction thereof, are citizens of the United States and of the State wherein they reside. No State shall make or enforce any law which shall abridge the privileges or immunities of citizens of the United States; nor shall any State deprive any person of life, liberty, or property, without due process of law; nor deny to any person within its jurisdiction the equal protection of the laws.

Index